THE PRICE OF RIGHTS

THE PRICE OF RIGHTS

REGULATING INTERNATIONAL LABOR MIGRATION

MARTIN RUHS

Princeton University Press
Princeton and Oxford

Copyright © 2013 by Princeton University Press
Published by Princeton University Press,
41 William Street, Princeton, New Jersey 08540
In the United Kingdom: Princeton University Press,
6 Oxford Street, Woodstock, Oxfordshire OX20 1TW

press.princeton.edu

Third printing, and first paperback printing, 2015

Paperback ISBN 978-0-691-16600-1

The Library of Congress has cataloged the cloth edition of this book as follows

Ruhs, Martin.
    The price of rights : regulating international labor migration / Martin Ruhs.
      pages cm
    Includes bibliographical references and index.
    ISBN 978-0-691-13291-4 (hardcover : alk. paper)   1. Foreign workers—
Civil rights.   2. Foreign workers—Legal status, laws, etc.   3. Labor laws and
legislation.   4. Human rights.   5. Emigration and immigration—Economic
aspects.   6. Emigration and immigration—Government policy.   7. Emigration
and immigration law.   I. Title.

    HD6300.R84 2013
    331.6′2—dc23   2013006552

British Library Cataloging-in-Publication Data is available

This book has been composed in Trade Gothic LT STD and Sabon LT STD

Printed on acid-free paper. ∞

Printed in the United States of America

10 9 8 7 6 5 4 3

Contents

Chapter 6

Chapter 7

Chapter 8

Appendix 1 Tables A.1–10

Appendix 2 Overview of Openness Indicators

Appendix 3 Overview of Migrant Rights Indicators

References

Index

Acknowledgments

Writing this book turned out to be a much more ambitious and demanding project than I initially anticipated. Straddling economics, politics, and law, the book aims to be "global" in its reach, and hopes to engage academic researchers as well as a policy audience with an interest in international labor migration and the rights of migrant workers. One of my main arguments—that there can be a tension between promoting more international labor migration and more rights for migrant workers—has proven controversial, especially outside academia, but I think it is a key issue that needs to be better analyzed and more openly debated than has been the case so far. The book should be read as a contribution to analysis and debate about an underresearched and underdebated topic of critical importance. I hope it will lead to more research and discussions.

I owe a huge debt of gratitude to a large number of people who, in many different ways, have helped me develop my analysis and arguments over the past few years. It is impossible to thank them all, and I apologize in advance if I have accidentally forgotten anybody.

My interest in the tension between openness and rights in labor immigration policy began in the early 2000s, when I spent a year working for MIGRANT, the migration unit of the International Labour Organization (ILO) in Geneva. I am grateful to Manolo Abella, the head of MIGRANT at the time, for introducing me to the many dilemmas and trade-offs in international labor migration, and encouraging my interest in developing a more systematic analysis of the relationships between states, migrants, and rights. Manolo provided useful comments on my discussion of the drivers of labor immigration and labor emigration policies in chapters 5 and 6.

Philip Martin has been a key influence on my work on international labor migration. The analysis in this book builds on joint work with Phil, especially our paper "Numbers vs. Rights: Trade-offs and Guest Worker Programs," published in the journal *International Migration Review* in 2008. I am grateful to Phil for the many discussions about the issues in this book, for his comments on most of the draft chapters, and his encouragement and support.

Bridget Anderson, my coauthor for many years, has had a huge influence on my work and this book, although she may not immediately recognize it. Bridget and I continue to argue over definitions and the role of the state in regulating labor immigration and labor markets—and I have a feeling we won't agree anytime soon!

A big thank you also to David Keen, who has encouraged and supported me in writing this book. I have greatly benefited from his comments, and all our discussions of my half-baked ideas and contentions. A big reason why this book ever got completed was that I finally accepted David's argument that books generally get "abandoned," not "finished."

I have had the good fortune of working with a team of truly outstanding research assistants. The empirical analysis in chapter 4 would not have been possible without the help of (in alphabetical order) Ana Aliverti, Lucie Cerna, Agnieszka Kubal, Sophia Lee, and Pablo Marquez. Ruchi Hajela played a crucial role in the analysis of the case studies in chapters 5 and 6, and helped me complete the manuscript during the last six months of the process.

I would also like to thank the many friends and colleagues who have provided comments and critiques of my developing arguments and draft chapters. Robin Cohen, Cathryn Costello, Matthew Gibney, Sarah Spencer, and Mimi Zou have helped me better understand some of the key legal and normative issues discussed in this book. Scott Blinder, Alan Gamlen, Michael Keith, Lindsay Lowell, Cinzia Rienzo, Alisdair Rogers, Nick van Hear, Carlos Vargas-Silva, and Jonathan Wadsworth have all provided useful comments on my empirical analysis. Ryszard Cholewinski and Pia Oberoi offered critical and extremely helpful comments on my discussion of the human rights of migrants along with the roles of the ILO and the Office for the High Commissioner for Human Rights (OHCHR). Samuel Engblom aided me in better understanding Sweden's recently emerged "exceptionalism" in labor immigration policy.

Oxford University's Centre on Migration, Policy, and Society has provided a highly stimulating research environment for writing this book. I am grateful to all my colleagues there for their feedback, critical conversations, and support over the years.

At Princeton University Press, I would like to thank Richard Baggaley, who was my editor during the first few years of this book project, for his encouragement and comments on early draft chapters. I am also grateful to Seth Ditchik, my editor when I completed the book, for his patience and continuing support despite my delivery "behind schedule." Thank you also to Cindy Milstein, my copy editor, and Natalie Baan, my production editor, for helping bring the project to a conclusion.

There were many points over the past few years when I was not sure whether I would ever be able to complete this book. I could not have done it without the constant support and encouragement of my family and friends. Thank you for keeping the faith in what must have appeared as an endless, somewhat-mysterious book project. I am especially grateful to my father, Sepp; Rose, Joe, and all the "foxes"; and Emma, Pauline, and Vivian.

My biggest thanks go to my wife, Clare, for her love, support, and endurance of all the ups and (many more) downs of writing this book. In addition to tolerating my (occasional!) absentmindedness, she has patiently and critically discussed all the ideas and arguments in this book, many times over. I could not have written this book without Clare. Thank you for everything.

When I was halfway through writing this book, my daughter, Emily, bounced into our lives. She is still too young to understand why exactly I had to spend all those evenings and nights staring at books and computer screens. But she was a constant source of happiness that kept me going.

This book is dedicated to Clare and Emily.

Abbreviations

CMW	International Convention on the Protection of the Rights of All Migrant Workers and Members of Their Families
ECHR	European Court of Human Rights
EEA	European Economic Area
GATS	General Agreement on Trade in Services
GCC	Gulf Cooperation Council
GFMD	Global Forum on Migration and Development
GNI	Gross National Income
ILO	International Labour Organization
IOM	International Organization for Migration
MAC	Migration Advisory Committee
MIPEX	Migrant Integration Policy Index
NGO	Nongovernmental Organization
OECD	Organisation for Economic Co-operation and Development
OHCHR	Office of the High Commissioner for Human Rights
POEA	Philippine Overseas Employment Administration
PRWORA	Personal Responsibility and Work Opportunity Reconciliation Act
PSWPS	Pacific Seasonal Worker Pilot Scheme
SAWP	Seasonal Agricultural Workers Program
TMP	Temporary migration program
UNDP	United Nations Development Program
WTO	World Trade Organization

THE PRICE OF RIGHTS

Chapter 1

The Rights of Migrant Workers
Reframing the Debate

In 1990, the General Assembly of the United Nations (UN) adopted the International Convention on the Protection of the Rights of All Migrant Workers and Members of Their Families (CMW). It stipulates a very comprehensive set of civil, political, economic, and social rights for migrants, including those living and/or working abroad illegally. Hailed as a major achievement in the struggle for improving the rights of migrants, the CMW has become a cornerstone of the human rights–based approach to regulating labor immigration advocated by many national and international organizations concerned with the protection of migrant workers. Kofi Annan, the former UN secretary general, described the CMW as "a vital part of efforts to combat exploitation of migrant workers and their families."[1]

In practice, ratification of the 1990 convention has been disappointing, both in absolute and relative terms. Although the CMW was introduced more than twenty years ago, so far fewer than fifty countries have ratified it—and the great majority of these countries are predominantly migrant sending rather than migrant receiving. This makes the CMW the least ratified convention among all the major international human rights treaties. It has a quarter of the ratifications of the Convention on the Rights of the Child (passed a year before the CMW) and less than half of the ratifications of the Convention on the Rights of Persons with Disabilities (passed sixteen years *after* the CMW). Despite having signed general human rights treaties, most nation-states, especially major immigration countries, are clearly reluctant to ratify international conventions that limit their discretion and ability to restrict the rights of migrants living and working in their territories.

The most cursory review of the rights of migrant workers around the world confirms that the majority of them, and especially those working in low-waged jobs, enjoy few of the rights stipulated in international conventions. For example, under most existing temporary migration programs (TMPs) in North America and Europe, migrants have neither the right to free choice of employment nor the access to welfare benefits given to citizens and long-term residents. In many of the Persian Gulf States in the Middle East, which have long admitted significant numbers of migrant workers, the protections of local labor laws do not apply to certain types of migrant labor. In Singapore, another major employer of

---

[1] Kofi Annan, International Migrant's Day, December 18, 2003, http://www.un.org/News/Press/docs/2003/sgsm9081.doc.htm (accessed February 1, 2011).

migrant workers, migrants working in low-waged jobs are officially prohibited from cohabiting with or getting married to a Singaporean citizen. Illegally resident migrants, whose global numbers are substantial,
have few rights regardless of what country they are working in (with few
exceptions).

Aims and Approach of the Book

This book analyzes how and why high-income countries restrict the rights
of migrant workers ("migrant rights") as part of their labor immigration
policies and discusses the implications for policy debates about regulating
labor migration and protecting migrants. It engages with theoretical debates about the tensions between human rights and citizenship rights, the
agency and interests of migrants and states, and the determinants and
ethics of labor immigration policy. The empirical analysis of the book is
global, and includes an examination of the characteristics and key features of labor immigration policies and restrictions of migrant rights in
over forty high-income countries as well as in-depth analysis of policy
drivers in major migrant-receiving and migrant-sending countries.

Based on this theoretical and empirical analysis, the book aims to contribute to normative and policy debates about the rights that migrant
workers should have when working abroad. In particular, the book explores whether there is a case for advocating a limited set of "core rights"
for migrant workers rather than the comprehensive set of rights demanded by the CMW, and if so, what these core rights should be, and
what implications might ensue for human rights–based approaches to
international labor migration. As these research questions suggest, the
book separates hard-nosed political economy analysis of the determinants of migrant rights in practice (i.e., what *is* current reality) from the
equally important normative discussion of what rights migrant workers
should have from a moral/ethical point of view.

Many UN agencies and other international and national organizations
concerned with migrant workers have responded to the widespread restrictions of migrant rights by emphasizing that migrant rights are human
rights that are universal, indivisible, and inalienable; they derive from a
common humanity and must be protected regardless of citizenship. The
key argument and starting point of this book is that we need to reframe
as well as expand current debates and analyses of migrant rights by com-
plementing conversations about the human rights of migrants with a systematic, dispassionate analysis of the interests and roles of nation-states
in granting and restricting the rights of migrant workers. This is because
the rights of migrant workers not only have *intrinsic* value as underscored
by human rights approaches but also play an important *instrumental* role
in shaping the effects of international labor migration for receiving countries, migrants, and their countries of origin.

For example, whether or not migrants enjoy the right to free choice of employment and other employment-related rights in the receiving country's labor market is likely to affect their productivity and earnings, remittances, and competition with local workers. The fiscal effects of immigration critically depend on whether and how migrants' social rights (including access to public services and welfare benefits) are restricted. Migrants' incentives and behavior in and beyond the labor market—for instance, the extent to which they acquire language and other skills relevant to employment and life in the host country—will be influenced by whether or not they have—or are on a path to acquiring—the rights to permanent residence and citizenship.

Because rights shape the effects of labor immigration, migrant rights are in practice a core component of nation-states' labor immigration policies. At its core, the design of labor immigration policy requires simultaneous policy decisions on: how to regulate the *number* of migrants to be admitted (e.g., through quotas or points-based systems); how to *select* migrants (e.g., by skill and/or nationality); and what *rights* to grant migrants after admission (e.g., temporary or permanent residence, access to welfare benefits, and limited or unlimited rights to employment). When receiving countries decide on these three issues, the impacts on the "national interest" (however defined) of the existing residents in the host countries are likely to be of great significance. Policy decisions on the number, selection, and rights of migrant workers can also be influenced by their consequences for the interests of migrants and their countries of origin, whose actions and policies can play an important role in supporting, sustaining, or undermining particular labor immigration policy decisions in migrant-receiving countries.

Viewing migrant rights as instruments of labor immigration policy has two key implications that motivate and inform the analysis in this book. First, any analysis of the reasons for migrant rights restrictions necessitates an explicit discussion of the economic, social, political, and other consequences of migrant rights (restrictions) for the national interests of migrant-receiving and migrant-sending countries as well as for migrants themselves. These consequences can include multifaceted benefits along with costs that may vary across different rights, between the short and long run as well as between migrants with different skills. Any analysis of the costs and benefits of migrant rights thus needs to be disaggregated and needs to look at the impacts of specific rights for specific groups of migrant workers.

Second, migrant rights cannot be studied in isolation from admissions policy, both in terms of positive and normative analysis. To understand why, when, and how countries restrict the rights of migrant workers, and explore what rights migrant workers *should* have, we need to consider how particular rights restrictions are related to policies that regulate the admission (i.e., the numbers and selection) of migrant workers. Do states grant skilled migrant workers more rights than low-skilled migrants, and if so, why? Are the countries that grant migrant workers near equal rights with citizens also relatively open to labor immigration, or are labor immigration policies characterized by a trade-off between openness to admitting migrant workers and some migrant rights?

These questions and the overall approach to the analysis of migrant rights in this book are, in my view, critical to fostering a more realistic debate about the protection of migrant workers in the global labor market. They do, however, raise challenging and highly sensitive issues that can easily be misunderstood or misrepresented. For example, it can be argued that any discussion of the "impacts of rights," and especially the use of the term "costs of rights," carries the danger of being misused or misinterpreted to justify or argue for more restrictions of the rights of migrant workers. It is important to emphasize at the outset that just because some rights generate costs does not mean that there is a moral justification for condoning or even advocating for such restrictions. There is also no suggestion in this book that all discussion of migrant rights should be reduced to debates about costs and benefits. The book looks at the instrumental role and consequences of rights, because I believe that we cannot hope to close the gap between human rights as expressed in international conventions and migrant rights in practice unless we understand as well as account for the reasons why nation-states grant and restrict certain rights. In other words, the current analysis and debate of what "should be" needs to be complemented (but not replaced) by a thorough discussion of "what is."

Outline of the Chapters and Main Arguments

The analysis and overall argument of the book are developed in seven relatively self-contained chapters. The discussion begins, in chapter 2, with an examination of why so few countries have ratified international legal instruments for the protection of the rights of migrant workers. The existing literature has identified a host of legal issues and complexities as well as a lack of campaigning and awareness of the CMW and other international conventions as key factors. I contend that the primary explanation for the low level of ratifications of international migrant rights treaties lies with the effects of granting or restricting migrant rights on the national interests (however defined) of migrant-receiving countries. This may sound like an obvious point, but the dearth of discussion about the multifaceted costs and benefits of specific migrant rights for receiving countries—and migrants and their countries of origin—suggests that this is an important gap in analysis and debates that needs to be urgently addressed.

If restrictions of migrant rights are used to further the national interests of migrant-receiving countries, how can we expect high-income countries to regulate the rights of migrant workers as part of their labor immigration policies? What are the likely interrelationships between nation-states' policies for regulating the number, selection, and rights of migrant workers? The analysis of these questions requires a conceptual framework for the process of labor immigration policymaking. Chapter 3 develops a basic approach that conceptualizes the design of labor immigration policy in high-income countries as a process that involves "choice under constraints." Nation-states decide on how to regulate the number, selection, and rights of migrant workers admitted in order to achieve a core set of four interrelated and sometimes-competing policy goals, including economic efficiency (e.g., maximizing the benefits of immigration for economic growth), distribution (e.g., making sure immigration does not harm the lowest-paid workers in the economy), national identity and social cohesion (concepts that are contested and hard to define in practice), and national security and public order. Although their importance and specific interpretations vary across countries, and over time, I argue that each of these objectives constitutes a fundamental policy consideration that policymakers can and do purposefully pursue in all countries.

Nation-states' labor immigration policy choices are made given a common set of potential constraints and institutional factors that limit and mediate the ways in which the pursuit of policy objectives translates into actual policies. The constraints include domestic and international legal constraints (e.g., imposed by domestic judiciaries and legal obligations arising from membership in supranational or international institutions) as well as a limited capacity to control immigration. Examples of institutional factors are the prevailing welfare state (e.g., liberal, social democratic, or conservative) and production systems such as labor market structures (e.g., liberal or coordinated). Just like policy objectives, the significance and impacts of these constraints and institutions are specific to country and time. Consequently, there can be substantial variation in the "policy space" for the regulation of labor immigration within which governments operate in different countries and at different points in time.

Based on this conceptual framework, and drawing on the existing literature on the effects of international labor migration, chapter 3 develops three hypotheses about the interrelationships between high-income countries' policies for regulating the openness, skills, and rights of migrant workers. I maintain that institutional variations across countries can be expected to affect the strength but not the existence of these three relationships.

First, high-income countries can be expected to be more open to high- than low-skilled immigration. This is partly because compared to low-skilled migrants, higher-skilled migrants can be expected to generate greater complementarities with the skills and capital of existing residents in high-income countries, greater long-term growth effects, and greater net-fiscal benefits. Second, we can expect labor immigration programs that target higher-skilled migrant workers to grant migrants more rights than those targeting lower-skilled workers. This expectation is partly motivated by the fact that the provision of some rights (e.g., social rights) creates costs and benefits that can be expected to vary with the skill level and earnings of the rights holder. For instance, granting low-skilled migrants full access to the welfare state can be expected to create greater net costs (or smaller net benefits) for the host country than affording these same rights to high-skilled migrants in high-paid jobs.

The third expectation is that there can be a trade-off (a negative relationship) between openness and some of the rights of some migrant workers admitted to high-income countries—that is, greater openness to admitting migrant workers will be associated with relatively fewer rights for migrants and vice versa. The basis for this hypothesis is closely related to the first two: if certain rights for some migrants create net costs for the receiving country (e.g., full access to the welfare state for low-skilled migrant workers), policy openness to admitting such migrants can be expected to critically depend on the extent to which some of their rights can be restricted.

To explore these interrelationships in practice, chapter 4 analyzes the characteristics of labor immigration policies and migrant rights in high- and middle-income countries. Given that there are no readily available measures of admission policies and migrant rights, I constructed two separate indexes that measure the openness of labor immigration programs in forty-six high- and middle-income countries to admitting migrant workers and the legal rights (civil and political, economic, social, residency, and family reunion rights) granted to migrant workers admitted under these programs.

My analyses of these new indicators provides strong evidence that labor immigration programs that target the admission of higher-skilled workers are more open and grant migrants more rights than programs targeting lower-skilled workers. The positive relationship between rights and targeted skills holds for many but not all rights. Economic and political rights are less sensitive to targeted skills than social, residency, and family rights. My analysis also shows that among programs in upper-high-income countries, labor immigration programs can be characterized by a trade-off between openness and some migrant rights. As expected, the openness-rights trade-offs affect only a few specific rights rather than all of them. The rights involved in this policy trade-off vary across countries and skill levels, but they most commonly include selected economic and social rights as well as rights relating to residency and family reunion. My analysis suggests that trade-offs between openness and some migrant rights can be found in policies that target a range of skills, although they generally are not present in labor immigration programs specifically designed for admitting the most highly skilled workers, for whom there is intense international competition.

Chapter 5 provides an in-depth analysis of labor immigration policy-making in a wide range of different countries to explore what drives the observed relationships between openness, skills, and rights in practice. The case study evidence discussed in this chapter shows that policy decisions on how to regulate the admission and rights of migrant workers in high-income countries are firmly based on assessments of the consequences of admitting migrants as well as granting/restricting rights for the national interests of migrant-receiving countries. With few exceptions, high-income countries are more open to high- than low-skilled migrant workers because they consider these policies to be in their best national interests. Similarly, although governments are rarely explicit about the rationales for restricting the rights of migrant workers, there is considerable evidence that considerations about the costs and benefits of rights play a powerful role in high-income countries' decisions on what rights to grant to migrant workers with different skills, and in justifying trade-offs between openness and some rights that create costs.

Chapter 6 discusses two interrelated questions: How do high-income countries' restrictions of labor immigration and migrant rights affect the interests of migrants and their countries of origin? And how have migrants and sending countries engaged with these restrictions in practice? These questions are of central importance to the analysis in this book because the interests and actions of migrants and sending countries can play a key role in supporting, sustaining, or undermining particular labor immigration policies in high-income countries. The chapter shows that migrant workers and their countries of origin are acutely aware of and engaging with the trade-off between openness and rights in practice. Every day, migrant workers are making choices about whether to stay at home, or move and work abroad under restricted rights. Large numbers are currently choosing the latter—that is, they are tolerating restrictions of some of their rights in exchange for the opportunity to migrate and work abroad. To be sure, this choice is sometimes misinformed and in many ways constrained by larger structural factors, including global economic inequalities and nation-states that restrict access to their territories through immigration control measures. Nevertheless, there is at least some minimal degree of choice in most people's decisions to move abroad for employment purposes. This points to the significance of considering the agency, "voice," and overall interests of migrants when explaining existing migration flows and policies, and when thinking normatively about whether particular trade-offs should be tolerated. Given that the human development of people is multidimensional and includes more considerations than just access to legal rights, it is not surprising to see migrant workers making "sacrifices" in some dimensions of development (e.g., limited access to some legal rights) in exchange for advancing others (e.g., opportunities to access employment at higher wages and raise the household incomes of their families).

Many low-income countries sending migrant workers abroad make a similar choice. To the extent that they can influence the labor immigration policies of high-income countries, most low-income countries are pursuing emigration policies that are, often explicitly, based on the dual objectives of sending more workers abroad and better protecting them while there. The discussion in chapter 6 shows that most low-income countries are acutely aware of the trade-off between access to labor markets in high-income countries and some migrant rights. For example, the policies of Asian countries sending migrants to the Gulf states, and Latin American countries sending low-skilled workers to the United States and Canada, clearly show that few of these countries are willing to insist on full and equal rights for fear of reduced access to the labor markets of higher-income countries. Again, this is not surprising given that labor emigration can generate large income gains for migrants and their families as well as benefit the wider development of migrants' home countries. The World Bank and other development organizations are actively promoting more international labor migration as one of the most effective ways of raising the incomes of workers in low-income countries.

There are also cases of migrant-sending countries that have explicitly rejected equality of rights for their nationals working abroad on the grounds that it constitutes a restrictive labor immigration policy measure. For example, many of the new European Union (EU) member states in eastern Europe wishing to use the European Union's Posted Workers Directive to increase the number of "migrant service providers" abroad have been critical of attempts by the old EU member states to require posted workers to be employed under exactly the same rights and conditions as citizens of the old EU member states. The new EU countries have argued that this insistence of complete equality of rights constitutes a protectionist policy that undermines their comparative advantage in cheaper labor. A similar assertion has been made by India and other low-income countries seeking to use the World Trade Organization (WTO, specifically General Agreement on Trade in Services [GATS] Mode 4) to liberalize labor migration to high-income countries. India has explicitly rejected the wage parity requirement demanded by high-income countries as a policy that makes it more difficult for low-income countries to send more migrant service providers to higher-income countries.

Chapter 7 moves the discussion from a positive analysis of "what is" to the equally important normative question of "what should be." Given what we know about labor immigration policies in practice, what can we say about how high-income countries *should* regulate the admission and rights of migrant workers? If high-income countries' labor immigration policies are characterized by a trade-off between openness and some rights for migrant workers, what rights restrictions—if any—are acceptable in order to enable more workers to access labor markets in high-income countries? It is important to emphasize that there is no one "right" answer to these inherently normative questions. I am skeptical of anybody who maintains that there are obvious or clear answers to any of these issues. Chapter 7 looks at relevant political theories and arguments to develop my own normative response, which readers can criticize and reject without rejecting the analysis in the remainder of the book.

As my intention is to contribute to national and international policy debates, I argue for a pragmatic approach that is both realistic, by taking account of existing realities in labor immigration policymaking, and idealistic, by giving more weight to the interests of migrants and countries of origin than most high-income countries currently do when designing labor immigration policies. Based on this approach, I contend that there is a strong normative case for tolerating the selective, evidence-based, temporary restriction of a few specific rights under new and expanded TMPs that help liberalize international labor migration, especially of lower-skilled workers whose international movement is currently most restricted and who would therefore reap large human development gains from employment abroad. Any rights restrictions should, in my view, be limited to the right to free choice of employment, equal access to means-tested public benefits, the right to family reunion, and the right to permanent residence and citizenship. Rights restrictions need to be evidence based in the sense that there must be a clear case that they create specific costs that the receiving country wishes to avoid or minimize to enable greater openness to admitting migrant workers. In other words, restricting these rights would lead high-income countries to be more open to labor immigration than would be the case if the rights could not be restricted. I also hold that any rights restrictions should be time limited (e.g., limited to about four years). After this period, migrants need to be granted access to permanent residence (and thus eventually citizenship) or required to leave. Finally, these rights restrictions are only acceptable, in my view, if they are accompanied by a number of supporting policies including the transparency of policies along with the effective protection of opportunities for migrant workers to exit TMPs whenever they wish and choose to do so.

Chapter 8 concludes the book by returning to the human rights of migrant workers. What are the implications of the analysis in this book for human rights debates and the rights-based approaches to migration advocated by many international organizations and NGOs concerned with protecting and promoting the interests of migrant workers? The book highlights the danger of a blind spot in human rights–based approaches to migration. Such arguments are often focused on protecting and promoting the rights of *existing* migrants without considering the consequences for nation-states' policies for admitting new migrant workers—that is, without considering the interests of the large number of *potential future migrants* who are still in their countries of origin and seeking to access labor markets of higher-income countries. The trade-off between openness and some specific migrant rights in high-income countries' labor immigration policies means that insisting on equality of rights for migrant workers can come at the price of more restrictive admission policies and, therefore, discourage the further liberalization of international labor migration. Put differently, human rights–based approaches to migration that demand all the rights stipulated in the existing international labor standards run the danger of doing good in one area (i.e., in promoting the rights of existing migrants) while doing harm in another (i.e., by making it more difficult to increase opportunities for workers to migrate and legally work in higher-income countries). Most UN agencies and other organizations advocating a human rights–based approach based on the CMW have been reluctant to acknowledge, let alone engage with, this dilemma.

I conclude that there is a strong case for advocating a rights-based approach to international labor migration that is premised on the protection of a universal set of core rights and accounts for the interests of nation-states by explicitly tolerating temporary restrictions of a few specific rights that can be shown to create net costs for receiving countries. Restricting these rights should encourage the further liberalization of international labor migration. My conclusion and recommendations imply a reframing—not a rejection—of the human rights–based approach to migration currently advocated by most UN agencies and many migrant rights organizations. The selective and temporary restriction of specific rights can be consistent with human rights that stress the agency of people. By bringing states and politics "back in," the rights-based approach to international labor migration that I propose would open up a space for legitimate and important debates about the desirability of restricting specific rights in exchange for more open admission policies in high-income countries. Rather than ignoring or shying away from these questions, human rights advocates should be at the forefront of addressing them.

Terminology and Scope of This Book

The focus of the book is on international labor migration and the rights of migrant workers, as noted above. Given the common confusion in migration research and debates caused by the various different terminologies used, it is important to be clear about the definitions used in this book as well as the scope of the analysis.

International Labor Migration and Labor Immigration Policy

I define international labor migration as migration for the primary purpose of employment. The book is not concerned with international migration for the purpose of asylum and study. Family migration—migration as a family member, partner, or dependent—is only explored whenever relevant. Consequently, where I discuss admission policies, the focus is on labor immigration policies, defined as policies for regulating the number, skills, and rights of migrants who are admitted for the primary purpose of work.

Migrant Workers

The United Nations defines migrants as people who live outside their countries of birth for more than one year. Using this definition, the United Nations estimates that there were about 214 million migrants in 2010, up from 155 million in 1990.[2] About half of the world's migrants are thought to be migrant *workers*: people born in one country and working for more than one year in another.[3] As my aim is to analyze the restrictions of the rights of migrant workers, the analysis in this book concentrates on migrant workers who are born abroad *and* do not have citizenship—and thus do not hold all the rights of citizens—of their host countries. This definition is narrower than the UN one, which includes migrants who have become—or have always been—citizens of their countries of employment.

Migrant-Receiving and Migrant-Sending Countries

Most countries experience both immigration and emigration. The book uses the terms migrant-receiving countries and migrant-sending countries, for linguistic convenience, to distinguish between net-immigration countries (i.e., countries that are receiving more migrants than they are sending abroad) and net-emigration countries (i.e., countries that are sending more migrants than they are receiving).

Scope

It is also critical to be clear about the scope of this book. Although the issues analyzed in this book are relevant to all countries, most of my theoretical and empirical analysis centers on international labor migration to higher-income countries, most of which are net receivers of migrant workers. The majority of the world's migrant workers are employed in high-income countries, especially in Europe and North America, where many countries have experienced rapid increases in labor immigration over the past twenty years. In the United Kingdom, for example, the share of foreign-born persons in the labor force increased from about 7 percent in the mid-1990s to 14 percent in 2010.[4] In the United States, migrants now constitute about 15 percent of the labor force, up from 11 percent in 1995. Although involving large absolute numbers, these shares are still relatively small compared to the proportion of foreign workers in the oil-rich Gulf states in the Middle East, another major global destination of migrant labor. Foreign nationals account for 90 percent of the labor force in the United Arab Emirates, over 80 percent in Qatar and Kuwait, and over 50 percent in Oman, Bahrain, and Saudi Arabia.[5]

My discussion of migrant-sending countries is primarily focused on lower-income countries. As shown in table 1.1 (which is based on data on migrants in general, not just migrant workers), about 60 percent of the

---

[2] UN Department of Economic and Social Affairs 2011.
[3] ILO 2010.
[4] MAC 2010.
[5] UN Department of Economic and Social Affairs 2006.

TABLE 1.1. Global number of migrants who have moved between/across more and less developed countries, 2010

	In more developed countries	In less developed countries
From more developed countries	55 million	12.6 million
From less developed countries	72.7 million	73.6 million

Source: Henning 2012.
Note: This table is based on migrant stock data.

world's migrants live in more developed countries. Of the 127.2 million migrants in more developed regions in 2010, more than half came from less developed regions. It is important to emphasize that, as shown in table 1.1, there is also considerable migration within more and less developed regions.

Unless otherwise specified, my discussion of the rights of migrant workers in specific countries focuses on the rights granted by national laws and policies. I therefore concentrate on rights in law and regulations (or rights "on paper") rather than rights in practice. In theory, migrants can be denied some rights that exist in law (e.g., if there is no effective state protection and enforcement of the existing legal right to a minimum wage) and/or enjoy rights that do not exist in law (e.g., medical doctors may in practice treat patients without the legal right to health care). Clearly, one would ideally like to measure and analyze rights in law *and* practice, but the latter would involve considerable and complex research as well as judgments that go beyond the scope of this book.

Finally, this book is about legal labor migration and the rights of migrant workers who have been legally admitted by their host countries. I do not examine illegal migration and the rights of migrants without legal residence status. While illegality in migration and employment is obviously an important issue in some countries, the vast majority of international labor migration occurs through legal channels that are regulated by nation-states.

Chapter 2

The Human Rights of Migrant Workers
Why Do So Few Countries Care?

"Migrant rights are human rights" is a common argument made by migrant rights advocates around the world. In 1990, the United Nations adopted a new human rights treaty that specifically deals with the rights of migrant workers and their families. After more than twenty years, fewer than fifty countries, none of them major immigration countries, have ratified this treaty. Even ardent supporters of the human rights approach to migration acknowledge that nation-states' response to the 1990 convention has been extremely disappointing. The great majority of countries clearly do not consider migrant rights as human rights that should be guaranteed by law.

This chapter looks at why so few countries have ratified international legal instruments for the protection of the rights of migrant workers.[1] Based on a critical review of the existing literature including the politics of the drafting process, I argue that the primary explanation lies with the effects of granting or restricting migrant rights on the national interests (however defined) of nation-states. To more explicitly link the discussion of migrant rights to the role and interests of nation-states, the chapter makes the case for studying migrant rights as a core component of countries' labor immigration policies.

International Migrant Rights Conventions

The key features and principles of human rights include: *universality*, or how human rights apply everywhere and to everyone (including migrants); *indivisibility*, or why there is no hierarchy of rights, and certain types of rights cannot be separated from others; *inalienability*, or that human rights cannot be denied to any human being, nor can they be given up voluntarily; and *equality and nondiscrimination*, or the notion that all individuals are equal as human beings. Human rights derive from a "common humanity" and the "inherent dignity of each human person" rather than from citizenship of a particular country.

The legal basis of the human rights approach to international migration comprises various international human rights treaties and separate legal instruments that specifically relate to migrants.[2] The three most significant international legal instruments that specifically address the rights

---

[1] The analysis in this chapter builds on my previous work published in Ruhs 2012.

[2] For an overview of the international human rights framework for migrants, see, for example, Weissbrodt 2008; Cholewinski 1997.

of migrant workers are the United Nations' International Convention on the Protection of the Rights of All Migrant Workers and Members of Their Families (adopted in 1990; henceforth CMW for "Convention on Migrant Workers") and the ILO's Migration of Employment Convention (1949) and the Migrant Workers (Supplementary Provisions) Convention (1975). Together with the more general human rights treaties, these instruments lay out a comprehensive set of civil, political, economic, social, and other rights for migrants, including the right to equal protections under labor laws, antidiscrimination laws, and family laws.

Briefly, ILO Convention 97 (adopted in 1949) was motivated by a concern to facilitate the movement of surplus labor from Europe to other parts of the world. It encourages countries to sign bilateral recruitment agreements (a model agreement is included in the associated ILO Recommendation 86), and includes measures to regulate the conditions under which migration occurs, general protection provisions, and, for the first time, measures to ensure equal treatment for migrant workers in various aspects of recruitment and employment. Specifically, Article 6 requires each member state for which this convention is in force to grant migrant workers equal treatment with regard to remuneration, membership in trade unions, and enjoyment of the benefits of collective bargaining, accommodation, and social security (subject to certain limitations, most notably that "there may be appropriate arrangements for the maintenance of acquired rights and rights in course of acquisition"). Article 7 stipulates that any public employment services provided to migrants must be free of charge. Importantly, ILO Convention 97 only applies to migrant workers who are legally residing and working in the host country.

In light of the radical economic and social changes during the 1960s and early 1970s (including the termination of various guest worker programs throughout Europe), ILO Convention 143 (adopted in 1975) aimed at bringing migration flows under control, focusing on the elimination of irregular migration and suppressing the activities of organizers of illegal movements of migrants. The preamble to this convention speaks of the need to "avoid excessive and uncontrolled or unassisted increase of migratory movements," which clearly reflects the concerns over immigration pressures at the time. Article 10 widens the scope of equality between migrants and nationals of the host state by requiring not only equal treatment but also equality of opportunity in respect of "employment and occupation, of social security, of trade union and cultural rights and of individual and collective freedoms for persons who as migrant workers or as members of their families are lawfully within its territory." Article 8 stipulates that host countries must not restrict a migrant's right to free choice of employment for more than two years; loss of employment will not, on its own, imply a loss of residence permit; and all migrants who have legally resided in the host country "shall enjoy equality of treatment with nationals in respect in particular of guarantees of security of employment, the provision of alternative employment, relief work and retraining." For the first time in international law, ILO Convention

143 also includes some rights for migrants in irregular status who, according to Article 9, should enjoy equality "in respect of rights arising out of past employment as regards remuneration, social security and other benefits."

Based on over a decade of negotiations, the CMW incorporates and builds on ILO conventions 97 and 143. It articulates a broad set of rights for migrants, including those living and/or working abroad illegally. The CMW includes ninety-three articles (compared to the twenty-three articles of ILO Convention 97 and the twenty-four articles of ILO Convention 143) and extends fundamental human rights to all migrant workers, both regular and irregular, with additional rights being recognized for regular migrant workers and members of their families. Crucially, the CMW is based on the principle of equal treatment of migrant and nationals rather than on a "minimum standards" approach, which characterizes many other international legal instruments.[3] Examples of rights stipulated by the CMW for both regular and irregular migrants include:

- the right to life (Article 9)
- the right to be free from forced labor (Article 11)
- the right to equality with nationals before courts and tribunals (Article 18)
- the right not to have identity documents confiscated (Article 21)
- the right to equal treatment with regard to remuneration, other conditions and terms of employment, and social security (Articles 25 and 27)
- the right to join and take part in meetings and activities of trades unions (Article 26)

Additional rights of regular migrants include:

- the right to form associations and trade unions (Article 40)
- the right to equal treatment with nationals in relation to access to education institutions, vocational training, housing (including social housing), and social and health services (Article 43)
- the right to seek alternative employment in case of the termination of a work contract prior to the expiration of the work permit (Article 51)
- the right to freely choose remunerated activity after five years of residence in the host country (Article 52)
- the right to equality of treatment with citizens in respect to protection against dismissal, employment benefits, and access to public work schemes intended to combat unemployment (Article 54)
- the right to redress in case of violation of the terms of the employment contract (Article 54)

[3] Lonnroth 1991.

The CMW also deals with the right to family reunification, but in a limited and carefully worded way. Article 44 suggests that "state parties shall take measures that they deem appropriate and that fall within their competence to facilitate the reunification of migrant workers with their spouses or persons who have with the migrant worker a relationship that, according to applicable law, produces effects equivalent to marriage, as well as with their minor dependent unmarried children."

Still, only some of the rights stipulated in the CMW are new rights. Most are included in and derived from the earlier general human rights treaties, including especially the International Covenant on Civil and Political Rights and the International Covenant on Economic, Social, and Cultural Rights (both adopted in 1966). Although the rights stipulated in all six core human rights treaties adopted before the CMW (see the list in figure 2.1) are meant to apply to all people regardless of nationality or citizenship status, their application to nonnationals had generally not been made explicit. The CMW may thus be regarded as a "more precise interpretation of human rights in the case of migrant workers."[4]

Ratification: Record and Obstacles

In practice, the ratifications of the CMW and ILO conventions on migrant workers by state parties have been disappointing (see figures 2.1 and 2.2), in both absolute terms (i.e., considering the total number of UN and ILO member states) and relative terms (i.e., compared to the ratifications of other human rights treaties and ILO conventions). With forty-six ratifications as of August 2012, the CMW is the least ratified treaty among all major human rights treaties. It has less than a quarter of the ratifications of the Convention on the Rights of the Child (passed a year before the CMW) and less than half of the ratifications of the Convention on the Rights of Persons with Disabilities (passed sixteen years *after* the CMW). The few countries that have ratified the CMW are predominantly migrant-sending rather than migrant-receiving countries.[5] The average share of migrants in their population is 3 percent, compared to over 10 percent in developed countries.[6] They are all low- or middle-income countries (based on World Bank Classifications 2012), with three-quarters having a low or medium human development index.[7] A third of the coun-

---

[4] Guchenteire and Pécoud 2009, 8.

[5] As of August 2012, the CMW had been ratified by Albania (2007), Algeria (2005), Argentina (2007), Azerbaijan (1999), Bangladesh (2011), Belize (2001), Bolivia (2000), Bosnia and Herzegovina (1996), Burkina Faso (2003), Cape Verde (1997), Chile (2005), Colombia (1995), Ecuador (2002), Egypt (1993), El Salvador (2003), Ghana (2000), Guatemala (2003), Guinea (2000), Guyana (2010), Honduras (2005), Indonesia (2012), Jamaica (2008), Kyrgyzstan (2003), Lesotho (2005), Libyan Arab Jamahitiya (2004), Mali (2003), Mauritania (2007), Mexico (1999), Morocco (1993), Nicaragua (2005), Niger (2009), Nigeria (2009), Paraguay (2008), Peru (2005), Philippines (1995), Rwanda (2008), Senegal (1999), Seychelles (1994), Sri Lanka (1996), St. Vincent and the Grenadines (2010), Syrian Arab Republic (2005), Tajikistan (2002), Timor-Leste (2004), Turkey (2004), Uganda (1995), and Uruguay (2001).

[6] UNDP 2009.

[7] Ibid.

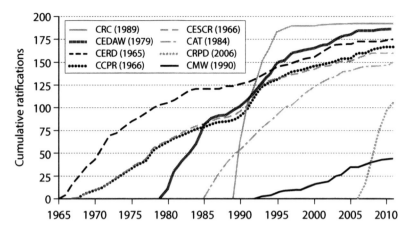

FIGURE 2.1. Ratifications of international human rights treaties, 1965–2011
Notes: CERD = International Convention on the Elimination of All Forms of Racial Discrimination; CCPR = International Covenant on Civil and Political Rights; CESCR = International Covenant on Economic, Social, and Cultural Rights; CEDAW = Convention on the Elimination of All Forms of Discrimination against Women; CAT = Convention against Torture and Other Cruel, Inhuman, or Degrading Treatment or Punishment; CRC = Convention on the Rights of the Child; CMW = International Convention on the Protection of All Migrant Workers and Members of Their Families; CRPD = Convention on the Rights of Persons with Disabilities.
Source: See http://treaties.un.org/Pages/Treaties.aspx?id=4&subid=A&lang=en (accessed in December 2011).

tries that have ratified the CMW, have added reservations. The article most commonly affected by the reservations is Article 92, paragraph 1, which provides that any unresolved dispute may be submitted to arbitration or the International Court of Justice at the request of one of the parties involved.

These figures suggest that while accepting the idea of human rights, the world's high-income countries—where migrants are most heavily concentrated—clearly do not accept that these rights should also apply to migrants living on their territories. It is also noteworthy, however, that some major sending countries have not ratified the convention.

Academic and policy analyses of the reasons for nation-states' reluctance to sign international migrant worker conventions, especially the CMW, have indicated a wide range of obstacles.[8] A commonly mentioned factor is a lack of promotion, awareness, and understanding of the CMW in many countries. For example, Patrick Taran (2000, 18) points out that "until 2001, there was not one person anywhere in the world, in any international organization, in any government, or any civil society group engaged with full-time responsibilities related to promoting this Convention." More recent analyses have confirmed that although in some countries civil society organizations have succeeded in raising the profile of the

[8] See, for example, the papers in the special issue of *International Migration Review* 25, no. 4 (1991); Hune and Niessen 1994; the papers in the special issue of *International Migration* 38, no. 6 (2000); Guchteneire and Pécord 2009.

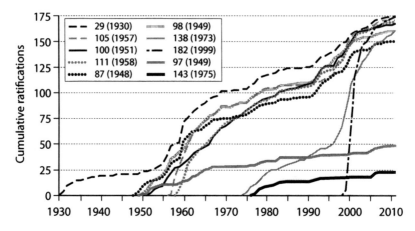

FIGURE 2.2. Ratifications of the ILO's Fundamental Conventions and Migrant Workers Conventions, 1930–2011

Notes: Freedom of association and collective bargaining: conventions 87 and 98; elimination of forced and compulsory labor: conventions 29 and 105; elimination of discrimination in employment and occupation: conventions 100 and 111; abolition of child labor: conventions 138 and 182; protection of migrant workers: conventions 97 and 143.

Source: See http://www.ilo.org/ilolex/english/newratframeE.htm (accessed December 2011).

CMW in the past decade, awareness of its existence and content remains relatively low in most countries.[9] In her analysis of attitudes toward the CMW in Asia, Nicola Piper (2009) finds that some countries do not understand all the technical details of the CMW, with many mistakenly—as Piper argues—assuming that the convention is an instrument of a liberal immigration policy that significantly limits states' ability to regulate the admission of migrants.

A second set of obstacles frequently discussed in the existing literature relates to legal issues. One argument is that because of its length and complexity, ratification would in many countries be slow, and often necessitates significant changes in national laws and legislation. Only a year after the CMW was adopted, for instance, Arthur Helton (1991) looked at the significant changes in US labor, immigration, and civil rights laws that would be required, thus raising serious doubts about the likelihood of ratification in the United States in the near future. Another analysis concluded that "technical questions, alone, therefore, may prevent many states from speedily accepting these provisions."[10] Another assertion relating to legal issues concerns the overlap of the CMW with both national and international laws including other migrant workers conventions. Some countries contend that their national laws already cover many of the rights stipulated in the CMW. They also point to the significant overlap—and some tensions—between the rights stipulated in the CMW, the ILO's migrant worker conventions, and the existing core human rights

---

[9] Guchteneire and Pécoud 2009.
[10] Cholewinski 1997, 202.

treaties.[11] For example, as a 2005 report by Germany's Ministry for Foreign Affairs suggests, "Germany will continue to work in the United Nations for the strengthening of the protection of human rights for migrants. It is convinced that this protection is thoroughly guaranteed by the implementation of the basic human rights agreements."[12]

Third, the low level of ratification of the CMW has been partly attributed to various contextual factors including, for instance, an adverse economic and social climate.[13] This argument essentially implies that economic downturns create various economic and social pressures—such as high unemployment and welfare dependency—that make it difficult for governments in high-income countries to promote the rights of migrant workers. Another contextual factor is the reluctance to "be first" to ratify the convention. For example, research has suggested that Japan and Korea are generally reluctant to take leadership in ratifying international conventions, preferring to wait for Europe to take the lead.[14] Similarly, Antoine Pécoud and Paul de Guchteneire maintain that European countries' unwillingness to ratify the convention also discouraged countries in North Africa and eastern Europe from ratifying.[15] France has claimed that it cannot ratify the convention independently of other EU member states.[16]

Some of these factors have undoubtedly played a role in discouraging high-income countries from ratifying the CMW over the past twenty years. Rather than being fundamental root causes, however, most of these factors are auxiliary issues that reflect and stem from a much more basic—and in many ways obvious—explanation of nation-states' reluctance to sign international migrant worker conventions.

The key underlying factor, now widely accepted among analysts of the CMW, relates to the national interests—however perceived—and politics of nation-states. Rights not only have intrinsic value, as emphasized by the human rights approach to migration, but they also play an important instrumental part in shaping the effects of migration. Consequently, the rights that major immigration countries are willing to grant to migrant workers critically depend on their impacts on the existing population in the host country. These impacts can involve perceived and real benefits and costs that could be economic, social, political, and/or cultural. A number of empirical studies of the CMW have confirmed that a major obstacle to ratification is the perceived cost of granting specific rights to migrant workers. In particular, many immigration countries consider the comprehensive set of rights stipulated in the CMW as being in conflict with their policies for regulating immigration, especially of low- and medium-skilled migrants, through Temporary Migration Programs that restrict some of the rights of migrants such as the rights to

[11] Böhning 1991.
[12] Cited in Hillman and Koppenfels 2009, 336.
[13] Hune and Niessen 1994.
[14] Piper 2009.
[15] Pécoud and Guchteneire 2006.
[16] Oger 2009.

free choice of employment, equal access to social welfare benefits, and family reunification.

In Canada, for example, a key obstacle to ratification of the CMW is the government's view that signing the convention would create serious problems—and may well be incompatible with—Canada's TMPs for low-skilled migrant workers, particularly its ability to restrict the employment of migrants to specific sectors and occupations that are suffering from labor shortages.[17] Similarly, the UK government has made it explicit that a critical reason for not ratifying the CMW is the associated costs for Britain and impacts on the government's ability to manage immigration in the best interest of Britain.[18] The following two excerpts from the government's statement to the House of Commons Select Committee in International Development (paragraph 22) illustrate this point:

> If the UK were to ratify the Convention, we would not be able to restrict the employment that work permit holders can do to that specified on their permit and they would have access to public funds from the date they entered the UK.[19]

> Giving all migrant workers access to public funds from the date of entry would therefore not only be costly, but also create an unnecessary "pull factor."[20]

Concerns about costs are also at the heart of many countries' reluctance to grant rights to irregular migrant workers—another major obstacle to the ratification of the CMW, which includes rights for both regular and irregular migrants. Although in some countries the argument against rights for irregular migrants is framed in terms of the importance of maintaining the "rule of law," it is clear that the perceived costs of granting rights to migrants without legal residence status is an equally important, if not decisive, obstacle.[21] The same applies to concerns about the potential costs of family reunification, which many countries—rightly or wrongly—believe to be encouraged by the CMW.[22]

If so many countries do not ratify the CMW because of the perceived costs of doing so, what explains, one may ask, the complexity, comprehensiveness, and eventual adoption of the CMW by the United Nations in the first place? The answer lies in the CMW's drafting process, which lasted for over a decade. According to Srdjan Vucetic (2007, 418), the CMW was "largely made by developing states for developing states." The drafting process formally began with the establishment of an open-ended working group in 1979, chaired by Mexico and Morocco. Crucial devel-

---

[17] Piché, Depatie-Pelletier, and Epale 2009.

[18] Ryan 2009.

[19] House of Commons International Development Committee 2004, 11–12.

[20] Ibid., 12.

[21] For an analysis of, for example, Germany's unwillingness to ratify the CMW, see Hillman and Koppenfels 2009.

[22] For a discussion of Japan's and Korea's attitudes toward the CMW, see Piper 2009.

oping countries had been successful in their attempts to entrust the drafting process to the United Nations in New York rather than to the ILO in Geneva, partly because of the ILO's tripartite structure, which means that unlike the United Nations, there was no automatic majority of developing countries.[23] The first complete draft text of a convention was submitted by seven Asian, African, and Latin Americans countries from the Group of 77 (G-77)—a coalition of developing nations founded in 1964. Although its first draft was rejected, the G-77 remained powerful during the negotiations in the 1980s. The other major players in the negotiations included a small group of major receiving states (including Australia, Canada, Denmark, Japan, the Netherlands, and the United States)—concerned about the costs of the CMW and keen on ensuring that the CMW would not interfere with their ability to regulate admission and regularization—and the MESCA group, which originally included Finland, Greece, Italy, Portugal, Spain, and Sweden, and later Norway.[24] The governments of all the MESCA countries had, according to Roger Böhning (1991, 702), a decidedly "socialist flavoring" in the early 1980s and were all sympathetic to the extensive promotion of the human rights of migrants.[25] Proposals by the MESCA group eventually became the basis for the convention's final text.[26]

A number of major high-income countries, including Australia, Germany, Japan, the United States, and the Gulf States, indicated during the drafting process that they were unlikely to ratify the convention.[27] They used various strategies that enabled them to nevertheless support the eventual adoption of the CMW by consensus. Germany followed what became known as the "German formula" during the negotiations.[28] This involved proposing alternative wordings to points that Germany objected to. After these were rejected, Germany asked for them to be noted in the protocol. This strategy enabled Germany to formally support the convention while still being able to refer back to its criticisms and concerns throughout the drafting process, thus maintaining its ambiguous position toward the CMW. Japan followed a similar strategy by submitting alternative formulations even after some of the provisions had already been agreed on by consensus.[29]

Clearly, national interests and impacts—and not concerns about protecting the human rights of migrants—were at the forefront of the politics of the CMW's drafting process. In his discussion of the drafting process, Böhning (1991, 698) noted, "It is sadly true that it is not so much the concern of the proponents of international humanitarian law as the constellation of political power relationships which is at the origin of the drafting process of international instruments." It is difficult to disagree

[23] Böhning 1991.
[24] Lonnroth 1991.
[25] Vucetic 2007.
[26] Lonnroth 1991.
[27] Cholewinski 1997, 203.
[28] See Hillman and Koppenfels 2009.
[29] Lonnroth 1991.

with Vucetic's (2007, 419) assessment that "more sensitivity to the potentially disproportional costs of the CMW in the drafting phase would have increased its chances of success."

Effectiveness

The relatively low number of ratifications of the CMW and other international migrant worker conventions does not mean that they have not had any impacts. For example, Lesley Wexler (2007) argues that even when international legal standards are not ratified, they can serve nonlegal functions by influencing nonbinding regional processes, contributing to the development and dissemination of best practices, and helping produce and codify a human rights discourse. It has also been suggested that Mexico's ratification of the CMW helps its efforts to advocate and promote the rights of Mexican migrants in the United States even though the United States has not ratified the convention.[30] In the United Kingdom, it has been argued that the convention is a useful "authoritative statement of the minimum international standards with respect to migrant workers" that is increasingly used by NGOs and migrant rights advocates, and that has become relevant to political debates on migration, even if there is a low chance of the United Kingdom ratifying the CMW in the short or medium term.[31] It has also been proposed that the CMW can enable civil society organizations to raise awareness and speak more forcefully about the rights of migrant workers.[32] The International Steering Committee for the Campaign for Ratification of the Migrant Rights Convention (2009, 7) contends that the convention has become "an instrument of reference for State parties and non-ratifying countries, including those that have stated explicitly that they do not wish to ratify it."

Despite these potential benefits, it is clear that the low levels of ratification and the nonratification by all major immigration countries severely limit the CMW's applicability as well as effectiveness in protecting the great majority of migrant workers. The twentieth-year anniversary of the CMW on December 18, 2010, was not a day for celebrating the CMW's effectiveness in protecting the rights of migrant workers. Given the low levels of ratification in its first twenty years, the CMW has undeniably been largely unsuccessful in achieving its main stated aim of providing an effective framework for protecting the rights of migrant workers in the global economy. Moreover, there is also a big question mark over the implementation of the CMW's rights among countries that have ratified the treaty. Research indicates that the ratification of human rights treaties may sometimes lead to a worsening rather than an improvement in human rights practices, especially in countries that are not fully demo-

---

[30] Diaz and Kuhner 2009.
[31] Ryan 2009, 293.
[32] Piper 2009.

cratic. This is because of the expressive role of human rights treaties. As Oona Hathaway (2002) argues,

> Ratifying a human rights treaty can relieve pressure for change imposed by international actors, who may rely more heavily on positions than effects in evaluating countries' records. This reduction in pressure may in turn lead a country that ratified to improve practices less than it otherwise might.

Although there is no evidence to claim that this effect generally applies to the CMW, some of the low-income sending countries that have ratified the convention have poor human rights records. Freedom House carries out an annual assessment of the political rights and civil liberties (of all people, not just migrants) in a large number of countries. According to the latest assessment, eight of the countries that ratified the CMW are "not free," twenty-five are "partly free," and only twelve were classified as "free."[33] It is not unreasonable to speculate that some of the low-income sending countries that have ratified the convention primarily use it for campaigning for better rights of their nationals abroad rather than to help improve the situation of migrants in their own countries.

Migrant Rights, Citizenship Rights, and Immigration Policy

The key implication of the analysis above is that the main reason for the failure of existing international conventions to achieve more ratifications and more effectively protect the rights of migrant workers stems from the instrumental role of rights in shaping the impacts of migration for the receiving country. The legal rights that migrant workers enjoy are significantly influenced by how such rights impact on the national interest (however defined) of the host country. Migrant rights cannot, therefore, be comprehensively analyzed and debated without a discussion of the role and interests of the state in granting as well as restricting migrant rights. This may sound like an obvious point, but the dearth of scrutiny about the consequences of specific migrant rights for receiving countries—and migrants and their countries of origin—suggests that this is an important gap in analysis and debates that needs to be urgently addressed.

To link the role and interests of nation-states to the rights of migrant workers it is useful to conceptualize migrant rights as a subset of citizenship rights. Citizenship can be viewed as a legal status that links individuals to states, and is associated with certain citizenship rights and duties.[34]

---

[33] Freedom House 2012.

[34] Citizenship is a complex issue that can be conceptualized and discussed in various ways. One can distinguish, for example, between citizenship as a formal status and substantial rights, legal status and practice, positive and normative uses, and more generally, "thin" and "thick" conceptualizations (see, for example, Baubock 2001).

Like human rights, citizenship rights can be classified in different ways. Citizenship rights may be broadly divided, for instance, into civic, political, and social rights.[35] They can also be classified into more detailed categories such as economic, cultural, and gender rights.[36] A crucial characteristic of citizenship rights is that, unlike human rights, they derive from a relationship with a particular state rather than from universal notions of "personhood" or "human dignity."[37]

Many migrants do not have citizenship status in the host country, and consequently, lack automatic access to the full set of citizenship rights of their country of employment.[38] In practice, nation-states have used their immigration, integration, and naturalization policies to limit and tightly regulate migrants' access to citizenship status as well as specific citizenship rights. The legal rights that migrants enjoy are typically dependent on their immigration and residence status in the host country. The immigration policies of most high-income countries create a number of different types of residence status for different types of migrants, each of which is associated with different rights and restrictions. Most countries make significant distinctions, for example, between the rights of migrants with permanent residence status (who usually enjoy most of the rights of citizens except for the right to vote), temporary migrants (whose economic and social rights are often restricted), and illegally resident migrants (who typically enjoy few rights in most countries). Further distinctions and restrictions of rights based on the migrant's nationality (e.g., member states of the European Union grant other EU nationals more rights than non-EU nationals) and purpose of residence (e.g., work, study, join family, or asylum) are common, and frequently contribute to highly complex sets of residence statuses along with associated rights and restrictions.

States not only regulate migrants' access to specific residence statuses and associated rights but also the possibilities for switching between different statuses in the host country. The state may change the legal status and associated access to rights of an individual or group over time. For instance, this could be done by creating new immigration statuses or moving people within existing statuses, as was the case when the European Union enlarged in May 2004, or more generally, under any regularization of illegally resident migrants or through naturalization policies that grant migrants full citizenship status.

Migrants' restricted and differentiated access to citizenship rights in practice makes it clear that nation-states have and do exercise significant—but as discussed in the next chapter, not complete—control over the rights of migrant workers on their territories. A key analytic starting

[35] Marshall 1950.

[36] See Castles and Davidson 2000.

[37] Although most conceptualizations are still based on the nation-state, scholars have analyzed "transnational citizenship," "global citizenship," "postnational citizenship," and "cosmopolitan citizenship" (see Bosniak 2006). There has also been some discussion about whether human rights can and should be seen as universalized citizenship (e.g., Baubock 1994).

[38] For a discussion of "denizens," see Hammar 1990.

point of this book is that policy decisions about the regulation of the rights of different types of migrant workers are, in practice, an integral part of nation-states' overall labor immigration policies. More specifically, the rights of migrant workers constitute—and can be analyzed as— one of the three core components of labor immigration policy. The design of labor immigration policy requires simultaneous policy decisions on how to regulate the *number* and *skills* of migrant workers to be admitted as well as the *rights* to be granted to migrants after admission. The issue of rights involves questions related to the rights that migrants should receive on admission, and whether and how these rights should change over time.

A critical point of this approach is that migrant rights cannot be studied in isolation from admission policy, both in terms of positive and normative analysis. Immigration challenges nation-states by raising questions about both admission and access to citizenship rights. They are interrelated policy challenges that nation-states address simultaneously. Consequently, to understand why, when, and how countries restrict migrant workers' rights, and discuss what rights migrant workers *should* have, we need to consider the potential interrelationships between migrant rights, on the one hand, and national policies for admitting migrant workers, on the other hand. The next chapter begins this task.

Chapter 3

Nation-States, Labor Immigration, and Migrant Rights
What Can We Expect?

How can we expect high-income countries to regulate the rights of migrant workers as part of their labor immigration policies? What are the likely relationships between policies for regulating the admission (openness and selection) and rights of migrant workers? Addressing these questions requires a theoretical framework for conceptualizing the potential determinants and mechanics of national labor immigration policymaking. This chapter develops a simple, flexible model of labor immigration policy and suggests testable hypotheses for empirical analysis.

The chapter is divided into three parts. It begins with a discussion of the potential objectives of labor immigration policies in high-income countries, and the extent to which nation-states can be perceived and analyzed as actors with independent "agency"—that is, with the capability of formulating and designing policy to pursue a set of national policy objectives. The second part of the chapter analyzes the major factors and institutions that constrain nation-states' capacity and formal authority to regulate the admission and rights of migrant workers, and mediate the ways in which the pursuit of certain policy objectives translates into actual policies.

Based on this conceptual framework of choice under constraints, the third part of the chapter develops three hypotheses about the relationships between high-income countries' policies for regulating the admission (openness and skills) and rights of migrant workers: labor immigration programs that target higher-skilled migrants are more open (i.e., less restrictive) to labor immigration than those targeting lower-skilled migrants; some of the rights of migrant workers are positively related to the skill level targeted by the labor immigration program under which migrants are admitted—that is, programs targeting higher-skilled migrants grant more rights than those targeting lower-skilled migrants; and there can be a trade-off (a negative relationship) between openness and some of the rights of some migrant workers admitted to high-income countries—that is, greater openness to admitting migrant workers will be associated with relatively fewer rights for migrants and vice versa.

The Objectives of Labor Immigration Policy

International labor migration generates a complex set of economic, social, political, cultural, and other consequences for individuals, communities, and countries as a whole. Consequently, the potential objectives of labor immigration policy are numerous and multifaceted. Broadly speaking, they could relate to four types of impacts on residents of the host country: economic efficiency; distribution; national identity and social cohesion; and national security and public order.

Economic Efficiency

Economic efficiency refers to the goal of maximizing the net-economic benefits (i.e., benefits minus costs) from immigration for the incomes and living standards of the residents of the host country. Many high-income countries are engaged in heated debates about whether and how immigration can be economically beneficial to the host country. Economic research suggests a wide range of impacts, some of which are better understood and more easily measurable than others. Four economic effects are most frequently discussed. First, a key insight of economic theory is that the immigration of workers whose skills and other factor endowments (e.g., capital) are, on average, different from those of existing residents, can create production complementarities that increase the national and average incomes among residents of the host country.[1]

A related second effect pertains to the role that migrant workers can play in responding to labor and skills shortages in specific sectors and/or occupations. Linking labor immigration to the "needs" of the domestic labor market is an important policy goal in most countries. What these needs are, how they vary across sectors and occupations, and how they change during periods of economic growth and downturn are highly contested. Research has shown that skills and shortages can be slippery concepts that are hard to measure, and immigration is typically only one—and not always the best—of various possible responses to shortages.[2]

Third, immigration can also generate difficult-to-measure external and spillover effects that may arise from, for example, having a bigger economy (that is, a higher GDP), a more diverse society, a greater share of highly skilled and motivated people, a higher population density, and more congested living spaces.[3] In theory, such dynamic and/or spillover effects could be positive or negative—that is, they could raise or lower the productivity and average incomes of the resident population.

Fourth, the effects of migrants on public finances also shape the net economic impacts of immigration on existing residents. Whether or not migrants are a burden or boon for the welfare state and public finances depends on the difference between the taxes they pay and the costs of public services and benefits that migrants consume—issues that are much contested and central to immigration debates in many high-income countries, especially those with extensive welfare states.[4]

[1] See, for example, Borjas 1995.
[2] See Ruhs and Anderson 2010b; Martin and Ruhs 2011.
[3] See, for example, Romer 1986; Lucas 1988.
[4] Rowthorn 2008.

Distribution

Immigration not only affects the size of national income but also its distribution. In the short run, immigration creates economic winners and losers among existing residents. The winners typically include employers who benefit from the increased supply of labor along with some consumers who may gain from the lower prices of products and services whose production/provision is intensive in the use of migrant workers. Potential losers include resident workers who are similar to migrant workers in terms of their skills and therefore may compete with migrants in the labor market. Whether and how immigration affects the wages as well as employment opportunities of resident workers, and profit margins of employers, is an empirical question that critically depends on the time frame adopted. Adverse effects that can occur in the short run, such as lower wages and reduced employment opportunities, may be partially or fully reversed in the longer run when the economy adjusts to immigration through an increase in the demand for labor.[5]

In practice, distributional considerations have played a significant and sometimes predominant role in public debates over labor immigration. This is reflected in popular concerns about "cheap migrants driving down wages" and migrants "stealing resident workers' jobs." Although the relative importance of distributional effects varies across time and place, policymakers are unlikely to be able to implement policies without considering their consequences for both economic efficiency *and* distribution. This is also reflected in the recommendations of policy-oriented research on labor immigration. For example, in the context of Canadian immigration policy, Don DeVoretz (2008) proposes a policy goal of maximizing economic gains to resident Canadians without reducing the welfare of the bottom fifth of Canadian society. Similarly, in their discussion of the objectives of EU-wide immigration policies, Tito Boeri and Herbert Brücker (2005, 673) argue that the optimal EU policy should "trade off production efficiency against a minimization of undesirable effects on income distribution in the receiving country."

National Identity and Social Cohesion

Immigration generates a wide range of social and cultural impacts that are often explored under the heading of national identity and/or social cohesion. These are ambiguous and contested concepts that are hard to define, and even harder to measure in practice. National identity may be loosely defined as the shared set of beliefs and values of a country's residents. The meaning and substance assigned to national identity—and thus the way in which international migration may impact it—largely

---

[5] See Dustmann, Glitz, and Frattini 2008.

depend on how the existing residents of countries "see themselves." For instance, in countries with long histories of immigration, such as the United States, Canada, and Australia, national identity arguably may be partly defined by cultural diversity, thus making immigration a potential tool for preserving or even increasing that diversity. In contrast, a receiving country that sees itself as culturally homogeneous, such as Japan and Korea, may view the immigration of people with different cultural backgrounds as "diluting" its national identity. Importantly, the construction of a country's national identity can go beyond collective outcomes and include the protection of individuals' rights, sometimes as one of the defining features. The Unites States is one of many examples.

Social cohesion is an equally ambiguous concept that has nonetheless become a standard term in immigration debates in a wide range of high-income countries, especially but not exclusively in Europe. As is the case with national identity, there is no one definition of social cohesion, whose meaning as well as interpretation—and hence how immigration is perceived to impact it—can be variable and context specific. A recent book on social cohesion in Australia suggests that "social cohesion reflects the strength of shared values, a sense of common identity and of belonging to the same community."[6] The United Kingdom's Commission on Integration and Cohesion (2006, 38) defined cohesion loosely as "principally the process that must happen in all communities to ensure different groups of people get on well together."

In theory, immigration may have positive or negative effects on social cohesion, however defined. In practice, debates in high-income countries have usually focused on the potential adverse effects of the arrival of newcomers. For example, the United Kingdom recently debated whether immigration is making Britain too diverse to sustain the mutual obligations behind a good society and the welfare state.[7] A commentary by Samuel Huntington (2004), titled "The Hispanic Challenge," ignited a similar debate in the United States. There is a growing body of research, with mixed conclusions, on the relationship between immigration, diversity, and social cohesion.[8]

National Security and Public Order

Although not new, concerns about the impacts of immigration on national security have gained in importance in many high-income countries over the past decade. For example, the 9/11 terrorist attacks in New York, the 7/7 bombings in the United Kingdom, and the recent mass killings in Norway have had significant impacts on immigration policy debates in North America and Europe. Efforts to "localize" the predominantly foreign labor force in most oil-rich Gulf states of the Middle East are partly

[6] Jupp, Nieuwenhuysen, and Dawson 2007, 2.
[7] See Goodhart 2004.
[8] See, for example, Putnam 2007.

motivated by security concerns about hosting a foreign population that is larger than the citizenry. In the European Union, "border management" is a key aspect of "ensuring the security of Europe," as described in the recent Action Plan for the Implementation of the Stockholm Program, which sets the priorities for developing the European area of freedom, security, and justice in the next five years.

Related to national security, the impact of immigration on public order and especially crime is another frequently discussed, controversial topic of public debate in most high-income countries. There are many instances of how specific criminal incidents involving migrants have triggered heated debates about the alleged adverse impacts of immigration on crime. In some cases, allegations of crimes committed by migrants have directly led to policy initiatives. For example, in the United States, Arizona's recent bill granting police officers wide-ranging powers to stop and check the immigration status of individuals was critically influenced by the murder of an Arizona rancher allegedly committed by an illegally resident immigrant in March 2010.

Public perceptions that immigration increases crime and is a threat to national security are common.[9] Research suggests that whether and how immigration impacts crime critically depends on the characteristics of migrants, which makes the selection of migrants and other policies aimed at shaping immigration flows important considerations from a domestic crime perspective. Similarly, while it is clear that international migration can provide new opportunities for transnational criminal networks and international political movements that use violence and terror to achieve their goals, it cannot simply be assumed that immigration has negative impacts on national security.[10] There are a number of ways in which immigration may enhance national security and defense capacities through, say, increasing GDP (and thus potential military spending) and the number of people (migrants and citizens) available for recruitment to the military.[11] Migrants can also enhance a state's military strength by providing technical and intelligence expertise.[12]

Objectives Relating to the Interests of Migrants and Their Countries of Origin

All of the four broad objectives discussed above relate to the impacts of labor migration on migrant-receiving countries. The logic of nation-states and citizenship implies that countries must prioritize the interests of their own citizens over those of noncitizens and nonresidents. Yet the objectives of labor immigration policy in receiving countries could, and many argue *should*, also take at least some account of the interests of actual and

---

[9] See, for example, Transatlantic Trends 2010.
[10] See the discussion in Adamson 2006.
[11] Mirilovic 2010.
[12] Adamson 2006.

prospective migrants as well as their countries of origin. These interests could include, for example, the economic and social integration of migrants in the host country, the maximization of the benefits of migrants' remittances, and the minimization of costs arising from the loss of skilled workers ("brain drain") for sending countries.

As explored in more detail in chapter 6 of this book, there is a large and rapidly expanding literature on the consequences of migration for migrants and their countries of origin. Richard Freeman (2006) suggests that wages of workers in high-income countries typically exceed those of workers in similar jobs in low-income countries by four to twelve times. These international wage differences mean that migrants can significantly raise their productivity and make large financial gains from employment abroad. Although it is clear that emigration cannot be a magic bullet to address deep-rooted development problems, if used effectively, remittances and other transfers that migrants make back to their home countries can be of great benefit to migrants' families and/or the overall economies of migrants' countries of origin.[13]

The potential impacts and objectives of international labor migration identified above are likely to be interrelated and potentially conflicting, which means that the relationship among them may be characterized by trade-offs. Trade-offs may exist when comparing the interests of the receiving country, migrants, and migrants' countries of origin (e.g., the international migration of highly skilled workers from low-income countries may generate significant benefits for migrants and receiving countries, but have adverse impacts on migrants' countries of origin); between the interests of different groups of people within countries (e.g., in the short term, immigration may benefit employers but harm some domestic workers in receiving countries); and between different types of impact (e.g., the level and kind of immigration that maximizes economic benefits may not be perceived to be compatible with considerations about national identity and social cohesion).

Defining and Pursuing the National Interest

Defining the national interest with regard to labor immigration policy may be conceptualized as a process of putting weights on the various interrelated impacts and objectives discussed above. How different objectives are prioritized and trade-offs managed is specific to time as well as place, historically contingent, and typically influenced by public opinion. For example, during an economic downturn, distributional considerations may play a greater role than during times of economic growth. After major security incidents involving migrants, national security and public order may become more prominent determinants of immigration policy.

[13] See, for example, UNDP 2009.

Despite differences in the importance of the various policy objectives in different countries and within countries over time, the key argument underlying my analytic approach is that the four objectives of economic efficiency, distribution, national identity/social cohesion, and national security/public order are fundamental building blocks that constitute the national interest in labor immigration policymaking in all countries. These four objectives are, to borrow a term from Christina Boswell (2007, 75), "functional imperatives" of the state. To explore whether and how nation-states restrict the rights of migrant workers as part of their overall labor immigration policies, we therefore must examine the impacts of migrant rights and related migrant admission policies on these four objectives.

A crucial assumption of this approach to the analysis of migrant rights and immigration policy is that nation-states are and can be analyzed as actors with independent "agency"—that is, with the capability of designing and implementing policies that are aimed at achieving a set of national policy objectives. Although common in the international relations and broader political science literature on migration and the state, the premise that states are actors with at least some capability of pursuing independent policy can and has been contested, particularly within the political economy approach to theorizing immigration policy.[14] In the political economy model by Gary Freeman (1995), for instance, immigration policies are the outcome of the relative powers of domestic interest groups such as employers, trade unions, and migrant community groups. The role of the nation-state is limited to that of a broker between different organized interests, without any place for national policy objectives. Freeman contends that migration creates benefits that are relatively concentrated (among employers and migrant groups), and costs that are much more diffuse across the economy and society. Consequently, employers have much greater incentives to organize and thus are much more effective in influencing policy than domestic workers. The result, according to Freeman (ibid., 886), is "client politics," where immigration policy is captured by employers who lobby the government to expand rather than restrict immigration despite adverse (but diffuse) impacts on domestic low-skilled workers.

There is no doubt that employers and other interest groups can play a powerful role in determining as well as constraining nation-states' immigration policies in practice. The argument that states are simply passively reacting to different interests and have no substantive policy objectives of their own is, however, difficult to defend in practice.[15] The economic interests of employers may well be the driving force of immigration policy in certain countries at certain times, especially during economic growth where concerns about distribution and national identity may be less of a priority, but it evidently does not describe policymaking

---

[14] See, for example, Zolberg 1999; Weiner 1995; Hollifield 2000.
[15] See also Boswell 2007.

processes in all countries and at all times. In times of economic downturn, for example, states are likely to increase the importance of protecting low-skilled workers. Some countries' immigration policies (e.g., in Australia, Canada, Japan, and Korea) are explicitly driven by noneconomic considerations such as a concern with maintaining a particular form of diversity or multiculturalism. It seems quite clear, then, that nation-states are purposeful actors whose labor immigration and other public policies are significantly influenced by national policy objectives.

Constraints and Variations in the Migration State

Nation-states are not unitary, rational, all-powerful actors that are completely free to design and implement policies in a way that maximizes a well-defined set of policy objectives.[16] In practice, there can be a wide range of factors and institutions that limit nation-states' capacity and formal authority to regulate immigration, and that mediate the ways in which the pursuit of certain objectives translates into actual policies. The three most important potential constraints and intervening factors relate to: nation-states' capacity to control immigration and the employment of migrant workers; the "liberal constraint" on immigration policymaking; and the effects of key institutions including the prevailing political system, labor market structures, and welfare state systems. Just like policy objectives, these constraints and institutional factors vary across countries as well as over time. As a result, there can be significant variation in the policy space for the regulation of labor immigration within which governments operate in different countries and at different points in time.

The Capacity to Control Immigration

Nation-states' capacity to control immigration and the employment of migrant workers is clearly incomplete. The presence of significant numbers of illegally resident migrants, who have either illegally entered the country or overstayed their legal residence permits, is at least to some extent a reflection of a limited state capacity to control the border and police migrants' actions after entry. Comparative analyses of immigration policies in high-income countries have provided many examples of the large gaps between the stated aims of states' migration policies and outcomes in practice.[17] "Unintended consequences" is a common theme in the academic and policy literature on immigration policies around the world. There are many instances of migration policy failures, and few (and some would argue, no) best practices in immigration control.

---

[16] The term *migration state* was originally coined in Hollifield 2004.
[17] Cornelius et al. 2004; see also Castles 2004.

States' capacity to control immigration varies across countries. Geography, say, obviously matters. Being an island (e.g., Australia and the United Kingdom) or sharing a long land border with a lower-income country (e.g., the United States and Germany) are important determinants of the relative ease and financial costs of border control along with the pressures for illegal entries. The complexity and strength of the state bureaucracy is another critical factor that influences both how migration policy is made as well as the extent to which laws and policies are effectively implemented. As institutional analyses of the internal working of the migration state have pointed out, different government departments have varying responsibilities, interests, and capacities in the making and implementation of public policies.[18] Policy decisions thus can be significantly influenced by negotiations, power struggles, and compromises made within the state bureaucracy. As a consequence, policies can sometimes be vague or internally contradictory, and there can be significant gaps between policy design and implementation. Depending on the institutional complexity and strength of the state bureaucracy, the capacity to rationally design and implement policies can be expected to be specific to country and time.

The porousness of international borders along with the gaps between policy aims and outcomes do not mean, however, that we are witnessing a general and continuous decline in nation-states' capacity to regulate immigration, as some have argued.[19] The policies of nation-states clearly continue to play a paramount role in influencing the scale and type of international labor migration, conditions under which it occurs, and rights of migrants after admission.[20] Immigration restrictions imposed by nation-states are the primary reason why the share of migrants in the global population (an estimated 3 percent in 2010) is relatively low despite vast differences in average earnings in different countries.

It is also still true, as Gary Freeman (1998) suggested more than a decade ago, that it is hard to find systematic empirical evidence for the thesis of a declining state capacity to control immigration. It is plausible to make the opposite argument: the introduction of new technology has, at least in certain countries, increased states' capacity to successfully implement external and internal immigration enforcement policies. Furthermore, it cannot simply be assumed that all the various unintended consequences of immigration control, and the gaps between migration policies and outcomes in practice, are due to the limited capacity of states to regulate immigration. In particular, what looks like a failure to control immigration due to a declining state capacity to control borders, such as the existence of a sizable population of illegally resident migrants, may in practice be the result of domestic politics of migration.[21]

---

[18] See, for example, Calavita 1992.
[19] See, for example, Sassen 1999.
[20] See also Zolberg 1999.
[21] Freeman 1998; Joppke 1998.

It is also important to recognize that nation-states may have differential levels of control over different components of labor immigration policy. For example, although their control over regulating the admission of migrants may be limited in various different ways, nation-states have considerably greater capacity to define the legal rights of migrants.[22] States use their legal frameworks and immigration policies to create different types of immigration status, including various types of temporary and permanent residence status. Most high-income countries are characterized by a multitude of different immigration statuses, each associated with different employment restrictions and economic and social rights.

The Liberal Constraint

The development of immigration and other public policies in liberal democratic nation-states can in practice be limited by two types of liberal constraint. The first stems from the protections provided by domestic liberal institutions, especially independent judiciaries and national constitutions.[23] There are many examples where migration policies proposed by governments could not be implemented, or were eventually overturned, because independent lawmakers considered them to violate existing laws and rights protections.[24] In 2008, for instance, the UK government attempted to tighten the rules that regulated the acquisition of permanent residence of highly skilled migrants, including a planned increase in the qualifying period for settlement from four to five years. The policies, which potentially affected about fifty thousand doctors, engineers, and other professionals, were overturned in 2009 because Britain's high court declared them unfair and unlawful. Christian Joppke (1998) maintains that the legal process, specifically statutory and constitutional residence and family rights, was a key factor in explaining why European states continued to accept migrants even after they imposed recruitment stops of guest workers in the early 1970s.

There is no doubt that domestic liberal institutions can and do impose real constraints on the development and implementation of immigration policies. As with the capacity to control immigration, though, the degree to which domestic laws and institutions protect the rights of migrants against restrictive government policies is an empirical issue that varies across countries and over time. It is important to be precise about the differential protections provided for different kinds of rights (e.g., civil and political rights are typically more strongly protected than economic and social rights), and distinguish between rights that migrants are granted on arrival and the rights acquired over time. Many of the constraints and protections supplied by the domestic laws of liberal democra-

---

[22] Cornelius and Rosenblum 2005.
[23] See, for example, Hollifield 2000.
[24] See, for example, Hollified, Hunt, and Tichenor 2008.

cies relate to the rights of medium- to long-term migrants, rather than to migrants who have just recently arrived, and are residing and working on temporary permits. The implication is that states are typically less constrained in their ability to restrict some of the rights of newcomers, particularly their social rights.

A second and related type of liberal constraint stems from international commitments to supranational bodies and rights regimes. Some scholars suggest that these commitments severely restrict and diminish nation-states' authority to regulate the admission as well as rights of migrants.[25] While it is indisputable that membership in supranational institutions and global rights regimes exerts some limits on national immigration policymaking, these "international constraints" are in practice relatively limited and often only affect a subgroup of migrants. For example, while it is true that membership in the European Union removes nation-states' formal control over the immigration and employment of migrants from other EU countries, EU member states are still in complete control over regulating the admission of migrants from outside the European Union. Progress with harmonizing immigration policy across the EU member states has been extremely limited and much slower than in other policy areas.[26]

At a global level, governance structures for regulating international migration are limited. There is no "World Migration Organization" that influences global migration in a way that is comparable to, say, the way in which the WTO regulates international trade. Efforts to use the WTO's GATS Mode 4 agreement to regulate the international migration of highly skilled workers multilaterally have had limited success. It is telling that efforts to move toward more global governance of migration, such as through the discussions at the Global Forum on Migration and Development, are almost all focused on the effects of migration on sending countries as opposed to the impacts on and policies in the major receiving countries. Immigration clearly remains a public policy issue that most countries consider to be an inherently domestic matter.

A similar conclusion can be drawn about the impacts of international or supranational rights regimes. As discussed in chapter 2, with fewer than fifty ratifications, the CMW is the most underratified UN human rights treaty. In the European Union, which has its own legally binding human rights regime, the application of most EU laws and instruments is limited to the nationals of contracting states. The impacts of EU laws on the rights of non-EU nationals thus has been limited, especially with regard to social rights, which remain strongly linked to national citizenship.[27] Virginie Guiraidon and Gallya Lahav's (2000) analysis of the effects of the European Court of Human Rights (ECHR) on national policymaking in European countries suggests a limited impact that has been

---

[25] See, for example, Sassen 1999; Soysal 1994; Jacobsen 1996.
[26] See Givens and Luedtke 2004.
[27] Dell'Olio 2002.

focused on the right to family life and protection against inhumane treatment, which in practice primarily affects European countries' expulsion policies. Guiraidon and Lahav find little evidence that the ECHR has played a role in expanding the social rights of foreigners.

Institutional Variations: Political Systems, Production Regimes, and Welfare States

Governments do not make labor immigration policy in an institutional vacuum. There are at least three institutional factors that can—at least in the short to medium term—constrain and give rise to considerable variation in the policy space for the regulation of labor immigration across countries and over time. These factors relate to differences in political systems and institutions, production regimes (including labor market policies), and welfare systems.

Whether or not a country is a liberal democracy has important implications for its labor immigration policy space and the prevailing politics of labor immigration policy. For example, the ruling elites of dictatorships are much less constrained by distributional considerations than liberal democracies where there is much greater pressure to implement redistributive policies.[28] Within liberal democracies, political institutions can play a critical intervening role in determining how specific interests translate into political power and policies. Jeffrey Togman (2001), for instance, explores why the immigration policies of the United States and France reacted so differently to the world economic crisis of the 1970s, which led to considerable increases in unemployment in both countries. France significantly reduced labor immigration in response to the changed economic situation, while the United States continued to increase the admission of migrant workers. Togman shows how the statist-corporatist institutional framework enabled the French government to change immigration policy in response to rising unemployment, according to the perceived national interest. In contrast, in the United States, "pluralist institutions have negated the impact of economic factors on immigration laws, rendering policy outcomes highly unpredictable."[29]

The prevailing production regime along with the associated labor market structure and policies constitute another important intervening factor that shapes the policy space for regulating the number, selection, and rights of migrant workers.[30] The "varieties of capitalism" literature, which has in recent years become the most influential approach to the comparative analysis of economic performance and policy, makes a broad distinction between liberal and coordinated market economies based on whether the key spheres of production are coordinated by market or nonmarket

---

[28] Mirilovic 2010.
[29] Togman 2001, 19.
[30] See, for example, Borang 2007; Devitt 2010.

mechanisms.[31] In liberal market economies, immigration policy can become a tool of promoting the flexibility of the labor market by providing employers with highly mobile migrant workers who can help maintain relatively low-cost production systems. In contrast, in coordinated market economies there are likely to be strong pressures, partly through the involvement of unions in the design and implementation of labor immigration policies, to employ migrants at the collectively agreed-on wage. As a result, governments of coordinated market economies can be expected to find it much more difficult, for example, to encourage labor immigration as a way of moderating wage growth and inflation compared to the governments of liberal market economies.

Welfare state policies are a third determinant of the policy space for regulating labor immigration, especially but not exclusively through impacting on the social rights of migrant workers. Gøsta Esping-Anderson's (1990) seminal typology and discussion of welfare regimes distinguishes between liberal, conservative, and social democratic welfare states. The type of welfare regime, which is in many ways interrelated with the prevailing production regime, shapes the space for developing labor immigration policy in two ways.[32] First, it affects the fiscal costs of immigration. Including migrants in the welfare state of social democratic countries, which are based on the principles of universalism and equality of standards, can create more costs than under liberal welfare states with a minimum of social rights. Second, it may influence the extent to which immigration is perceived as a threat to the welfare state, and consequently, the degree to which it is possible to exclude migrants from selected social rights. Restricting migrants' access to some social rights, for example, may be regarded as unproblematic in liberal and even conservative regimes, but it may be perceived as a threat to maintaining social democratic welfare states that are based on principles of universality and inclusion.

In the short run, we can expect the prevailing production regime and welfare system to constitute relatively strong and binding constraints on the policy space for the regulation of labor immigration. Any short-term changes to labor immigration policy are thus likely to be characterized by "path dependencies"—that is, by incremental changes that are strongly influenced by past policies and prevailing institutions of the labor market and welfare state. This expectation is in line with the varieties of capitalism approach, which suggests that effective public policies need to be "incentive compatible"—namely, they need to be in line with and complement the mode of coordination inherent to the prevailing institutional structures.[33] In the medium to long run, though, the institutional framework, and therefore the policy space for regulating labor immigration,

---

[31] See, for example, Hall and Soskice 2001.
[32] Ibid.; Schroder 2009.
[33] Hall and Soskice 2001.

may change.[34] For instance, governments can deregulate labor markets, change welfare state policies, make the political system more (or less) democratic, and so on. Immigration itself may contribute to changes in institutions—say, through changes in trade unions' membership rates. In other words, although binding in the short run, institutional constraints are not a fixed straitjacket for labor immigration policymaking.[35] States, firms, and other actors can bring about institutional change that results in new labor immigration policy options becoming available, and/or old ones disappearing from the prevailing policy space.

Three Hypotheses

Based on the model of labor immigration policy outlined above, the remainder of this chapter draws on the existing literature on the effects of labor migration to explore, from a theoretical perspective, the likely interrelationships between nation-states' policies for regulating the admission (openness and skills) and rights of migrant workers. I propose and discuss three hypotheses about labor immigration programs in high-income countries:[36]

1. labor immigration programs that target higher-skilled migrants are more open to labor immigration than those targeting lower-skilled migrants
2. programs that target higher-skilled migrants grant migrants more rights than programs that target lower-skilled migrants
3. there can be a trade-off (a negative relationship) between openness and some of the rights of some migrant workers admitted to high-income countries—that is, greater openness to admitting migrant workers will be associated with relatively fewer rights for migrants and vice versa

I argue that these relationships—which are interrelated—are fundamental and can be expected to apply to labor immigration policies in most high-income countries, including countries with different policy spaces (i.e., with different constraints and institutional characteristics) for the regulation of labor immigration. Institutions such as the prevailing political system, welfare state, and production system (including labor market regulations) can be expected to affect the *degree* or strength of the three relationships in different countries as well as at particular points in time—but not the existence of the relationships themselves. As discussed above, the primary impact of institutional differences is to limit—at least

---

[34] Hall and Thelen 2009.
[35] See also Bucken-Knapp 2009.
[36] Parts of the analysis in the remainder of this chapter build on Ruhs 2010a; Ruhs and Martin 2008.

in the short run—the policy choices available to policymakers in different countries at different times.

Hypothesis 1: Positive Relationship between Openness and Targeted Skills

Labor immigration programs in high-income countries can be expected to be characterized by a positive relationship between openness to admitting migrants and the targeted skill level of the migrant workers—in other words, labor immigration programs that target higher-skilled migrants are more open (i.e., impose fewer restrictions) to labor immigration than those targeting lower-skilled migrants. Within the model of labor immigration policy developed in this book, there are five reasons for expecting this relationship. The first three are based on economic considerations and effects that relate to the objectives of economic efficiency and distribution, or more specifically, to the goals of maximizing the overall net benefits from immigration and minimizing adverse impacts on the lowest paid among the existing population.[37]

For one, research suggests that skilled migrants can be expected to generate greater complementarities with the skills and capital of the existing population. George Borjas (1995), for instance, contends that in the United States, the wages of skilled workers are more responsive to supply shifts than the wages of low-skilled workers, partly because skilled workers are more highly complementary to capital than low-skilled workers. Consequently, the United States would maximize the net gains from immigration by admitting skilled rather than low-skilled workers. Such a policy would also reduce inequality among workers and ensure that the incomes of the lowest paid are not adversely affected. Boeri and Brücker (2005) make a similar argument for increasing the skill content of migration to the European Union.[38]

The economic case for admission policies that favor skilled over low-skilled migrants is further supported by economic models that explore the long-term growth and spillover effects of immigration. Various endogenous growth models emphasize the importance of human capital, knowledge, and research and development for long-term economic growth.[39] In a recent model developed by Stephen Drinkwater and colleagues (2007), skilled immigration increases the incentives to engage in more skill-

---

[37] Compare to Borjas 1999, which discusses these issues in the context of US immigration policy.

[38] The assessment that skilled migrants will generate greater complementarities with the skills and capital of the existing population in high-income countries can be expected to be relevant for most high-income countries, but an important caveat must be added. Since the economic impact of immigration critically depends on the skills of residents *and* the characteristics of the host economy, the optimal skill mix of immigrants is always highly specific to the country and time (Dustmann, Glitz, and Frattini 2008). It therefore must be assessed through empirical analysis that critically interrogates the key assumptions made in generalized economic models in the context of the specific economy and time under consideration.

[39] See, for example, Romer 1986; Lucas 1988.

intensive research and development activity, thereby increasing long-term growth. A recent study in the United States has shown that skilled migrant entrepreneurs have made a major contribution to the creation of engineering and technology businesses as well as intellectual property in the United States.[40]

The fiscal effects of immigration can provide a third reason for high-income countries to be more open to skilled rather than low-skilled migrants. The net fiscal impact of immigration—the difference between the taxes that migrants pay and the costs of public services and benefits that migrants consume—largely depend on migrants' age, earnings, and eligibility for along with take-up of government benefits and services; the nature of the welfare system, especially the extent to which it redistributes income from high- to low-income earners; and how immigration affects nonmigrants' contribution to and use of the welfare state, such as through positive or negative impacts on the employment rates of nonmigrants. Everything else being equal, skilled migrants employed in high-paid jobs can be expected to pay more taxes and be eligible for fewer welfare benefits than low-skilled migrants in low-paid jobs.[41] Alan Barrett and Yvonne McCarthy's (2008) finding that education is inversely related to welfare receipt among people in Ireland and the United Kingdom supports this assertion. Although the fiscal effects of immigration are highly country specific, empirical research indicates that the net fiscal effects of low-skilled migrants are often negative.[42]

Taken together, these three effects provide an economic rationale for high-income countries to be more open to admitting skilled rather than low-skilled migrant workers. This does not mean that there is no economic case or incentive to admit low-skilled migrants. There clearly can be cases where the employment of low-skilled migrant workers in specific sectors suffering from labor shortages that cannot be met through other means may generate economic benefits for existing residents, such as through lower prices of commodities and services whose production/provision makes intensive use of low-waged migrant workers. A common key argument against low-skilled labor immigration is the adverse impacts—at least in the short run—on low-skilled domestic workers competing with migrants for jobs. If labor markets are highly or even completely segmented—that is, most domestic workers do not compete for certain jobs—some of these distribution concerns about low-skilled labor immigration will play a smaller role.

While the general preference for admitting skilled over low-skilled migrant workers is likely to hold for most high-income countries, institutional differences can be expected to lead to differences in the degree or

---

[40] Wadhwa et al. 2008; see also Saxenian 1999.

[41] As my wording suggests, this argument assumes that high-skilled migrants do high-skilled work. Skilled migrants who fail to get jobs or work in low-paid jobs that do not correspond to their skills may have a negative net impact on public finance.

[42] See the review in Rowthorn 2008.

strength of this preference.[43] For example, countries with liberal market economies and flexible labor markets can be expected to create more lower-paid jobs, and thus may have a relatively greater demand for migrant workers in these jobs than economies with coordinated market economies and more regulated labor markets. Similarly, the magnitude of the difference between the net fiscal contributions of low- and high-skilled migrants will depend on the nature of the welfare state. Countries with large and inclusive welfare states that generate significant redistribution from high- to low-income earners, for instance, can have greater fiscal incentives to accept skilled over low-skilled migrants than countries with smaller welfare states that lead to less income redistribution.

In addition to economic considerations, high-income countries' preference for skilled over low-skilled migrant workers also may be driven by concerns about the impacts of immigration on crime. There is significant evidence that important determinants of crime are education, relative wages, and income inequality. For example, Paolo Buonanno and Daniel Montolio (2008) find that education has a large and significantly negative effect on property crime in Spain; the more educated people are, the less likely they are to engage in criminal activities. A second and related key finding that is fairly consistent across empirical studies in different countries is that crime is significantly linked to low-wage labor markets. Relative falls in the wages of low-wage earners and the resulting greater income inequality have been shown to increase property crimes.[44] These findings suggest that the immigration of low-skilled migrant workers, which is likely to increase inequality by lowering the relative wages of low-skilled domestic workers, can be expected to have a worse effect on crime than the immigration of skilled migrants.

The skills of migrants can also be expected to shape the impacts of immigration on national identity and social cohesion as measured, for one, by "social capital." It is well established in the literature on social cohesion that education has positive impacts on key dimensions of social capital such as involvement in community affairs.[45] Socioeconomic class and socioeconomic inequalities have also been found to be critical determinants; poverty, low socioeconomic status, and income inequality all erode trust among people.[46] Paola Grenier and Karen Wright (2006, 50) thus emphasize the importance of policies that "seek to minimise the social divisions of class and income that undermine the potential for the 'overlapping networks of relative equality' and general social trust that form the core of social capital."

As Fiona Adamson (2006) points out, the mobilization of skilled and highly skilled migrants can enhance a nation-state's ability to project power and influence in the international arena. For some countries, this

---

[43] See the discussion in Devitt 2010.

[44] See, for example, Freeman 1999; Machin and Meghir 2004.

[45] Hall 1999.

[46] Letki 2008; Putnam 2007.

may provide another reason for focusing their admission policies on attracting skilled rather than low-skilled migrants.

Hypothesis 2: Positive Relationship between Some Migrant Rights and Targeted Skills

A second, related hypothesis is that a positive correlation exists between some of the rights and targeted skills of migrant workers admitted under labor immigration programs in high-income countries. In other words, we can expect programs that target more highly skilled workers to be associated with more rights for migrant workers than those targeting lower-skilled workers and vice versa.

Before discussing the reasons for this hypothesis, it is crucial to reemphasize that there are significant constraints on the scope and policy space for restricting the rights of migrant worker in liberal democracies. In most liberal democratic countries, migrants with permanent residence status are typically granted almost all the rights of citizens, with the important exception of the right to vote in national elections. Restrictions of migrant rights require temporary rather than permanent immigration programs. The decision concerning whether the admission of migrants (or particular groups of migrants) should be permanent or time limited therefore is a fundamental policy issue that directly affects whether and whose rights can be restricted.

When deciding on whether and how to restrict the rights of migrant workers, receiving countries must take into account the impact on the potential migrant labor supply. Highly skilled migrants are relatively scarce in the global economy. A significant number of high-income countries are competing for a relatively small pool of highly qualified workers willing to migrate. As a result, qualified migrants are able to choose among competing destinations, and their choice of destination is likely to depend on both expected earnings and expected rights in destination areas. In order to attract highly skilled workers, countries need to offer not only high wages but also substantial rights. Given the international competition for highly skilled migrant workers, we can expect a "race to the top" where high-income countries must offer internationally competitive packages in terms of wages and rights.[47]

In contrast, there is an almost-unlimited supply of potential migrants in low-income countries willing to accept low-skilled jobs in higher-income countries with wages, employment conditions, and rights that are significantly lower than those mandated by local laws and international norms. Migrants may not demand equal treatment in the labor markets of higher-income countries, especially if they are recently arrived, plan a limited and relatively short spell of employment abroad, and/or consider

[47] Shachar 2006.

the wages and employment conditions in the labor markets in their countries of origin as their primary frame of reference.[48] The "excess" supply of low-skilled migrant labor means that it is possible to increase the admission and employment of low-skilled migrants while at the same time reducing their wages and rights. This out-of-equilibrium situation will remain as long as national borders prevent the free flow of international labor migrants seeking low-skilled work.

Why should we expect high-income countries to restrict the rights of low- and medium-skilled migrant workers, and what are the reasons for expecting restrictions to increase as the targeted skill level of the labor immigration program declines? The obvious—but nevertheless rarely discussed—answer is that all rights, including those of migrant workers, cost money. As Stephen Holmes and Cass Sunstein (1999) persuasively argue, rights cannot be protected or enforced without public funding. The costs of rights vary across different types of rights and are likely to be context specific. In most liberal democracies, for example, the average cost of protecting one (more) person's right to free speech can be expected to be lower than the average cost of providing one (more) person with free health care. It is also important to add that rights can create costs as well as benefits (economic, social, cultural, and others), which can differ between the short, medium, and long run. The short-run costs of supplying some rights, such as the right to free education for children, may be outweighed by longer-term benefits, such as greater taxes because of a more highly educated labor force that earns higher wages. High-income countries' willingness to pay for specific rights can be expected to vary over the business cycle. As Holmes and Sunstein (ibid., 94) contend, "Rights will regularly be curtailed when available resources dry up, just as they will become susceptible to expansion whenever resources expand."

If, as argued in this chapter, migrant rights are instruments and the result of a policy choice, it is plausible to expect high-income countries to selectively and strategically restrict some of the rights of migrants in a way that maximizes the net benefits for the receiving country.[49] The cost of some rights (e.g., some social rights) is inversely related to the skill level (and thus earnings) of the migrant. For instance, as mentioned above, *all else being equal* low-skilled workers in low-skilled jobs can be expected to make smaller tax contributions and greater demands on the welfare state than higher-skilled workers in higher-paying jobs. This is why some—but not all—of the rights granted to migrants under labor immigration programs can be expected to critically depend on their skills.

The discussion below looks at some of the likely costs and benefits of granting (or restricting) different types of rights for migrant workers, and the implications for whether and how high-income countries can be expected to restrict these rights for migrants with different skills. I focus on economic rights, social rights, and the rights to settlement and family reunion.

[48] Piore 1979.
[49] See also Cox and Posner 2009.

It is important to underscore at this point that in contrast to most civil and political rights, there is considerable variation in the economic and social rights *of citizens* across countries as well as within countries over time. Differences in labor market structures and welfare states mean, for example, that British citizens enjoy different rights in the labor market and welfare state than citizens of Sweden. Crucially, nation-states frequently redefine and/or reduce access to specific economic and social rights *for citizens, not just migrants.* The substance and scope of social rights in particular can vary significantly over time, often in response to cost pressures. Economic downturns, for one, can accelerate long-term trends of welfare state retrenchment that some social policy scholars have identified. Downsizing the welfare state involves a tightening of the eligibility rules (i.e., a reduction in the number of people eligible for, say, unemployment benefits or income support) and/or a reduction in the level of benefits conferred by particular rights (e.g., a reduction in the amount of unemployment benefits). Although reductions in social rights for citizens are obviously unpopular with the electorate, they are not uncommon.

Economic Rights

To facilitate a level playing field in the labor market and avoid adverse impacts on resident workers, we can expect high-income countries to grant migrant workers most of the economic rights granted to citizens including the right to equal wages and working conditions. The reason is that some employment-related rights can create costs for employers. Therefore, all else being equal, migrant workers who can be employed under restricted rights will be preferred by employers to resident workers with full employment rights. In the extreme case, the employment of different groups of workers that can be offered different wages and/or employment conditions for the same work could lead to a complete segmentation of the labor market. To avoid such developments requires equality, or near equality, in pay and other work-related rights.

Institutional differences matter in this case, at least in the short run. The assertion that equal rights are required to protect local workers from unfair competition may not apply in countries where parts of the labor market have become completely segmented and dominated entirely by migrant workers. As discussed in chapter 5, labor markets in many of the Gulf Cooperation Council (GCC) countries in the Persian Gulf are a good illustration.

The major exception to the expectation that most high-income countries will grant migrants equal labor rights relates to the right to free choice of employment. As explained in the discussion of the first hypothesis, an important rationale for admitting migrant workers, especially at the lower end of the skills spectrum, is to fill vacancies in specific sectors and/or occupations that are deemed to be experiencing a shortage of domestic workers rather than to admit workers who are free to take up any job, including in those sectors that are not suffering from shortages. Restricting migrants to specific sectors and/or occupations requires a restriction of the right to free choice of employment. Concerned about avoiding adverse distributional consequences of immigration, high-income countries can be expected to restrict this right for most low- and medium-skilled migrant workers, and potentially also some skilled workers, but not for the most highly skilled, whose choice of destination country may be influenced by whether or not their employment is in any way restricted.

Social Rights

To maximize the fiscal net contribution of migrants, high-income countries can be expected to restrict some migrants' access to some public services and welfare benefits. As the usage and receipt of welfare benefits is likely to be inversely related to migrants' skill level and earnings, there is an economic case for selectively restricting some of the lower-skilled migrants' access to equal social rights such as public housing and other income-based welfare benefits (e.g., low-income support). The lower the skills and earnings of migrants in the host country, the greater will be the strictly economic case for restricting some of their welfare rights in order to minimize the fiscal costs for existing residents. These restrictions need to be selective and limited, since the denial of the most basic social rights—such as the rights to emergency and other basic health care—could create more costs than benefits for the existing population. For example, migrants without any health care benefits may not use medical services if they are carrying infectious diseases. Migrants without any welfare benefits may also feel compelled to work at below-standard wages to survive.

Rights to Settlement and Family Reunion

Given that most restrictions of migrant rights are only feasible under TMPs, we can expect most high-income countries to regulate labor immigration through policies that grant migrant workers temporary rather than permanent residence status on arrival. Programs that target the most highly skilled workers, who will prefer and thus may choose countries that offer permanent as opposed to temporary status, are again likely to be an important exception.

A key question in the design of a TMP in high-income countries is whether migrants are expected to leave the country after their work permits expire or if there should be a mechanism that enables them to acquire permanent residence rights that may eventually lead to citizenship status. From an economic point of view, the argument for strictly temporary migration (i.e., without the possibility for upgrading to permanent residence) primarily stems from the possibility of restricting migrants' rights under a TMP. Once migrants acquire permanent residence, these restrictions would need to be lifted. This could lower the net benefit of immigration for residents by, for instance, increasing the number of migrants accessing public services and welfare benefits and competing for jobs in sectors and/or occupations where there is a sufficient supply of resident workers. Temporary residence status that is dependent on having a job in the host country also may benefit the host country in terms of flexibility over the business cycle. For example, during an economic downturn with significant job losses, it is likely in the receiving country's interest for unemployed low- and medium-skilled migrants to leave the country rather than remain resident on unemployment benefits, as could be the case if migrants had permanent residence status. Temporary residence status, in other words, gives receiving countries an element of flexibility that is lost when migrants acquire permanent residence status.

The right to family reunion also can be expected to critically depend on the skill level of the migrant. Denying high-skilled migrants the right to family reunion is likely to have significant adverse effects on a country's attractiveness. We therefore can expect that most high-income countries will grant highly skilled migrants this right. In contrast, assuming that spouses and families of low-skilled migrants are in a similar socioeconomic group as the primary applicant, family reunion for low- and medium-skilled migrants may result in increased costs arising from further pressures on access to, say, the welfare state and low-wage sectors of the domestic labor market.

Institutional differences will impact on the policy choices available. For example, countries that are not liberal democracies will find it easier than liberal democratic countries to restrict the right to settlement and family reunion. Welfare states and social models that place a high value on inclusiveness and try to avoid creating a group of second-class citizens with fewer rights than full citizens, as has been the case in Sweden, may find it more difficult to restrict rights to settlement and family reunion compared to countries with different welfare states and social models.

Hypothesis 3: Negative Relationship between Openness and Some Migrant Rights

The third hypothesis suggests that there can be a trade-off (a negative relationship) between openness and some of the rights of some migrant workers admitted to high-income countries—that is, greater openness to admitting migrant workers will be associated with relatively fewer rights for migrants and vice versa. The basis for this hypothesis is closely related to the first two: if certain rights for some migrants create net costs for the receiving country, policy openness to admitting such migrants can be expected to critically depend on the extent to which some of their rights can be restricted.

This trade-off will likely affect some social rights. In order to minimize the fiscal costs of low-skilled migrants for existing residents, high-income countries can be expected to admit either relatively low numbers of low-skilled migrants with full or close-to-full social rights, or larger numbers with more restricted rights. As discussed earlier in this chapter, although the fiscal effects of immigration are necessarily context specific, granting low-skilled and low-waged migrant workers equal access to social rights can create net costs for the receiving country, especially in countries with large welfare states. Restricting low-skilled migrants' rights to welfare benefits and public services removes some (but not all) of the arguments for selecting skilled rather than low-skilled migrants in high-income countries.

There is some evidence from existing research that supports the hypothesis of a trade-off between openness and access to some social rights. For instance, contending that "states that provide immigrants with far-ranging rights may have greater incentives to reduce immigration levels," Brian Gran and Elizabeth Clifford (2000) empirically test this hypothesis by exploring the relationship between immigration and access to social welfare programs in nine Organisation for Economic Co-operation and Development (OECD) countries during 1960–85. They focus on two specific groups of migrants: "young" migrants (nine years or younger), and "old" migrants (fifty years or older). These two groups were chosen because of their perceived economic vulnerability and greater likelihood of receiving social welfare benefits than other age groups. The scholars' empirical analysis finds a trade-off between immigration and social rights for the old but not for the young migrants. Gran and Clifford (ibid., 440) conclude that "the costs associated with less restrictive eligibility conditions to social welfare programmes magnify the pressures and incentives to limit and reduce the entry of older immigrants."

Nikola Mirilovic (2010) makes a similar argument in his analysis of the effects of being a democracy or dictatorship ("regime type") on migration flows and stocks in over 150 countries during 1980 and 2000. He finds that being a rich dictatorship has statistically significant and positive impacts on net-migration flows along with the share of migrants in the population. Mirilovic maintains that one of the key reasons why dictatorships find it easier to admit more migrant workers than democracies is that dictatorships find it easier to deny migrants access to the welfare state. So this is another illustration of how institutions—in this case, the prevailing political system—matter in determining the available policy choices as well as the strength of the relationship between openness and rights.

The right to free choice of employment is another right that can be expected to be restricted as part of a policy trade-off between openness and rights. As mentioned above, to minimize adverse distributional consequences for domestic workers, especially but perhaps not only in low- and medium-wage jobs, high-income countries have an interest in limiting the immigration and employment of migrant workers to specific sectors and/or occupations that are deemed to be suffering from domestic labor shortages. Admitting migrants without any employment restrictions would increase competition with—and hence put pressure on the wages and employment prospects of—domestic workers in jobs that are not suffering from labor shortages. Consequently, high-income countries can be expected to admit most migrant workers (highly skilled migrants are again the likely exception) only if their right to free choice of employment can be restricted, at least temporarily. Since migrants on permanent residence permits are typically given all the economic rights of citizens, this restriction requires a TMP. Countries that, for whatever reason, cannot or will not operate TMPs with restricted employment rights for low-skilled migrants can be expected to admit significantly fewer low-skilled migrant workers than those that do.

The suggested trade-off between openness and restrictions on some social rights as well as the right to free choice of employment is based on the likely effects of immigration on residents in high-income countries. It is, however, also reflected in public opinion toward immigration. Research evidence on the determinants of attitudes toward immigration suggests that social and other rights for migrants can reduce public support for more open admission policies, especially among skilled (and well-paid) residents whose taxes would contribute to covering most of the costs of providing public services and benefits for low-skilled migrants.[50] Jim Dolmas and Gregory Huffman (2004, 1155) claim that "apparent opposition to immigration may in fact not be disapproval of immigration per se, but instead might be opposition to the benefits that immigrants will subsequently receive after having emigrated." Gordon Hanson (2005, 1) thus argues for the United States that "generating greater political support for open immigration policies would require reducing immigration's adverse effects on the labor market-earnings and fiscal burdens on US residents." As one of the policy options, Hanson (ibid., 2) proposes that the country "expand temporary migration programs and phase in immigrant access to public benefits more slowly over time."

The political economy considerations noted above—based on nation-states' concerns about fiscal impacts and, to some extent, also the labor market effects of immigration—are likely to be a key driver of the expected openness-rights trade-offs in high-income countries' labor immigration policies.

It is important to clarify and reemphasize at this point that my discussion of openness refers to "policy openness," defined as the number, scope and strength of restrictions that nation-states put in place to regulate the inflow of migrant workers—something that is not necessarily the same as the actual scale of migration to a particular country. For example, in labor immigration programs that aim to attract high-skilled migrants, high degrees of policy openness will not always result in a corresponding high number of inflows of highly skilled workers. Given the global com-

---

[50] Hanson, Scheve, and Slaughter 2007.

petition for highly skilled workers, there can be many reasons (e.g., culture, language, climate, geographic location, etc.) that can discourage highly skilled workers from moving to specific countries despite legal possibilities to do so. In contrast, given the almost-unlimited supply of low- and medium-skilled workers willing to move and take up employment at higher wages abroad, high-income countries that are willing to open their borders and labor markets to low-skilled workers from abroad are likely to be able to attract as many workers as intended by policy.

Although the focus of my analysis is on policy openness along with the potential costs and benefits of rights for the national interest of the state, it is important to add that certain rights can also create costs for—and hence affect the recruitment decisions of—employers. Just like the fiscal effects of immigration create incentives for states to implement policies that involve a trade-off between openness and some social rights of low-skilled migrant workers, the costs of certain employment rights may generate incentives for employers that result in a trade-off between rights and the number of workers recruited.

Employers face a downward-sloping demand curve for labor, meaning that ceteris paribus, higher labor costs will be associated with fewer workers employed. Certain employment rights for workers—such as the right to a minimum wage, work-related benefits, and health and safety standards—increase labor costs for employers, thereby generating a trade-off between numbers and rights. In other words, employers' demand curve for labor is downward sloping with regard to certain rights. The trade-off between the rights and number of employed workers is familiar, as when employers oppose minimum wage increases because they assert that higher labor costs will mean fewer jobs. The analogy to migrants' rights is clear: if migrants have all the economic and social rights laid out in ILO and UN conventions, including the right to equal wages and all work-related benefits, their cost to employers will be higher and fewer people will be employed. On the other hand, more limited migrant rights may mean lower costs for employers and more migrants employed. In this sense, increasing the rights of migrants can affect their employment in the same way that a higher minimum wage can reduce the number of jobs (for all workers, not just migrants). Of course, it needs to be added that not all rights create significant costs for employers. It is nevertheless clear that some rights do create costs and that *significant* increases in labor costs will, ceteris paribus, encourage profit-maximizing employers to reduce the number of jobs on offer.

To avoid unintended confusion, it is worth reemphasizing that by suggesting the theoretical possibility of a trade-off between the openness and some of the rights of migrant workers admitted to high-income countries, I am not arguing or assuming that it is normatively desirable to restrict migrant rights (an issue that I examine in chapter 7). I am asserting that there are economic effects and mechanisms that potentially lead to an inverse relationship in high-income countries' policies between openness to admitting migrant workers and some of the rights granted to migrants after admission.

Trade-offs are, of course, ubiquitous in life, and preoccupy large parts of social science and public policy analysis. For example, the social policy literature concerned with welfare state retrenchment has highlighted "cost containment" as a key dimension.[51] Social policy debates have explored the various modes of fiscal retrenchment, which typically involves a tightening of eligibility rules (i.e., a reduction in access) and/or a reduction in benefits (i.e., a lower level of entitlements including social rights). Note that these trade-offs are about policy choices that affect all residents (including citizens), not only migrants.

To summarize, this chapter has provided a basic theoretical framework and testable hypotheses for an analysis of how nation-states regulate the admission as well as rights of migrant workers. The regulation of labor immigration can be described as a matter of choice under constraint. Nation-states decide how to regulate the number, selection, and rights of migrant workers admitted in order to achieve a common set of potential objectives—economic efficiency, distribution, social cohesion and national identity, and national security and public order—given a common set of potential constraints and institutional factors that limit and mediate the ways in which the pursuit of policy objectives translates into actual policies. These constraints and institutional factors stem from nation-states' incomplete capacity to control immigration; domestic liberal institutions and international rights regimes; and the prevailing national political system, production regime (including labor market policies), and welfare system. Taken together, these constraints and institutions define as well as circumscribe the policy space for the regulation of labor immigration in particular countries. The relative significance assigned to each of the policy objectives, the ways in which competing goals are managed, and the strength and impacts of the constraints and institutional factors are all highly specific to country and time. Variation in objectives and constraints leads to different national policy spaces and labor immigration policy regimes that vary both across countries and over time.

Based on this conceptual approach, and drawing from theories and research on the effects of labor immigration, the chapter has identified three basic hypotheses about the relationship between high-income countries' policies for regulating the openness, skill requirements, and rights of migrant workers. These hypotheses suggest that programs designed to admit and employ higher-skilled migrants are more open and grant more rights than do programs targeting lower-skilled migrants, and that labor immigration policies can be characterized by a trade-off (i.e., an inverse relationship) between openness and some rights for specific skill groups of migrants (i.e., programs that are more open to admitting migrant workers also impose greater restrictions on specific migrant rights). Insti-

[51] See, for example, Pierson 2001.

tutional variations can be expected to affect the strength but not the existence of these relationships in different countries and at particular points in time.

Whether these relationships can be observed and applied in practice, and what drives them, are important empirical questions that are explored in the next three chapters.

Chapter 4

An Empirical Analysis of Labor Immigration

Programs in Forty-Six Countries

This chapter analyzes the key features of labor immigration programs in high and middle-income countries in practice. I construct and scrutinize two separate indexes that measure the openness of labor immigration programs in forty-six high- and middle-income countries to admitting migrant workers, and the legal rights (civil and political, economic, social, residency, and family reunion rights) granted to migrant workers admitted under these programs. The term *labor immigration program* refers to a set of policies that regulate the admission, employment, and rights of migrant workers. Most but not all countries operate multiple and different labor immigration programs for admitting different types of migrant workers. The analysis distinguishes between programs that target low-, medium-, and high-skilled migrant workers. In addition to providing an international comparative data source for identifying the primary features of labor immigration policies, the indexes facilitate an empirical study of the three hypotheses about the relationship between openness, skills, and migrant rights developed in chapter 3.

It is important to emphasize at the outset that the construction of any index poses a number of methodological challenges and necessarily relies on numerous assumptions. The use of policy and rights indexes in particular can be contentious as they aim to provide quantitative measures of complex issues that do not easily lend themselves to the kind of simplification and rigid description associated with an index. The approach in the analysis below is to be as open and transparent as possible about the methodology along with its limitations, and carefully explain all the assumptions and decisions made at various stages of the analysis. The first half of the chapter explains the methodology, and the second half presents the empirical results. The aim is to make an initial contribution to the debate about an issue that has so far received little systematic empirical analysis.

Existing Research and the Scope of My Analysis

Indexes of Immigration Policy and Migrant Rights

There is considerable academic and policy literature that comparatively discusses labor immigration policies in different countries, but few studies have constructed indexes to systematically measure policy differences across and/or within countries.[1] The exceptions include studies by Lindsay Lowell (2005) and Lucie Cerna (2008), both of which focus on policies toward highly skilled migrant workers in about twenty countries, and Ashley Timmer and Jeffrey Williamson (1996), who constructed an index to study immigration policy change during 1860–1930 in six countries. Most recently, the United Nations Development Program (UNDP) carried out an assessment of migrant admissions, treatment, and enforcement policies in twenty-nine developed and developing countries.[2] The ongoing IMPALA (International Migration Policy and Law Analysis) project aims to measure immigration policies in twenty countries over time.[3] Some broader public policy indexes include limited evaluations of immigration policy as a subcomponent.[4] There are also more narrow indexes focusing on asylum policies.[5]

Despite the increasing interest in measuring human rights, there are also few studies that systematically measure the scope and variation of the legal rights of different types of migrants across high-income countries.[6] Notable exceptions include Harald Waldrauch's (2001) work, which constructs a "legal index" that measures the integration of migrants in six European countries, and the more recent Migrant Integration Policy Index (MIPEX), which uses a mix of legal and outcome indicators to measure policies for integrating migrants in EU member states and three non-EU countries.[7] Specifically, MIPEX measures the extent to which each country's policies conform to European directives and European standards of best practice in six areas: labor market access, family reunion, long-term residence, political participation, access to nationality, and antidiscrimination. The migration policy indexes developed by Lowell (2005), Cerna (2008), and Jeni Klugman and Medalho Pereira (2009) also include an evaluation of a small number of migrant rights.

The indexes constructed in this project differ from existing indexes on immigration policy and migrant rights in four major ways. First, they have a more clearly defined focus on rights and openness than most existing indexes. Although some migrant rights are captured by some of the existing indexes (e.g., some of the indicators used in MIPEX, the Migrant Accessibility Index, and the UNDP's policy assessment measure some legal rights of migrants), none of the existing indicators were designed to measure the rights of migrant workers. Similarly, the focus on openness, straightforwardly interpreted as the degree to which a country restricts the admission of different types of migrant workers, is less ambiguous as well as easier to conceptualize and measure than "competitiveness," as used in some of the existing studies. Second, the indexes developed and

---

[1] See, for example, Cornelius et al. 2004; OECD 2010.

[2] See Klugman and Pereira 2009.

[3] See http://projects.iq.harvard.edu/impala/home.

[4] See, for example, the *Commitment to Development Index* (Center for Global Development 2010) and the *Global Migration Barometer* (Economist Intelligence Unit 2008).

[5] See, for example, Thielemann 2004; Hatton 2004.

[6] For a review, see, for example, Carr Center for Human Rights 2005.

[7] British Council and Migration Policy Group 2011.

analyzed below differentiate between low-, medium-, and high-skilled migrant workers, thereby facilitating analysis of the variation of rights and policies according to skill, and the interplay among rights, skills, and openness. Third, rather than mixing policy and outcome indicators, the index of rights in this project centers on the legal rights granted by national laws and policies to migrant workers after admission. Although this approach has some limitations (discussed below), it has the advantage of more clearly measuring the rights granted to migrants by law and regulations in the host countries. Finally, the indexes developed in this project cover a larger number and broader range of high- and middle-income countries than existing studies.

Countries, Programs, and Skills

The analysis includes all high-income countries (i.e., those with gross national incomes [GNI] per capita that exceed US$11,905 in 2008, as defined by the World Bank) with a population exceeding two million, and, to ensure broad geographic coverage, a selection of upper- and lower-middle-income countries. In total, the sample comprises forty-six countries, including thirty-four high-income countries (thirty states in this group are upper-high-income countries defined by me as states with GNI per capita exceeding US$20,000 in 2008), nine upper-middle-income countries, and three lower-middle-income countries (China, Thailand, and Indonesia). The complete list of countries is shown in table A.1 in appendix 1.

In most but not all countries, migrant workers are admitted under various different labor immigration programs (e.g., many countries operate different policies for low- and high-skilled migrants), which are typically associated with different sets of admissions criteria and rights for migrant workers. The units of my analysis are thus labor immigration programs rather than countries as a whole. The period under consideration in this chapter is 2009, and—unless indicated otherwise—*all discussions of policies here refer to that year*. Altogether, the analysis includes 104 labor immigration programs, or an average of 2.3 programs per country. This average masks considerable variation. Some countries, such as Sweden and Belgium, only operate one major labor immigration program. In contrast, the United States has six different programs for admitting migrant workers, while Canada and Australia each have four.

To explore the potential variation of openness and rights across labor immigration programs that aim to admit migrants with different skills, each of the programs included in the analysis is assigned one or more targeted skill levels. The targeted skill level of a labor immigration program reflects the skills required in the (specific or range of) jobs that migrants are admitted to fill. It also allows for the common phenomenon of skilled migrant workers taking low-skilled jobs abroad. Just because a particular labor immigration program aims to attract low-skilled migrant workers (for low-skilled jobs) does not necessarily mean that in practice, higher-skilled migrants will not apply and be admitted to fill the jobs. There is considerable evidence showing that skilled migrants often do lower-skilled work in high-income countries. This particularly applies to new (i.e., recently arrived) migrants, who sometimes view their first job abroad as a stepping-stone to a better job that more closely corresponds to their skills.[8]

The analysis distinguishes between four broad skill levels: low-skilled (LS), defined as migrant workers with less than high school education and no vocational skills; medium-skilled (MS), defined as migrants with high school, vocational training, or trades qualifications, such as electricians, plumbers, and so on; high-skilled (HS1), defined as migrants with a first degree from a university or the equivalent tertiary training; and very high-skilled (HS2), defined as migrants with second- or third-level university degrees, or equivalent qualifications. These distinctions are necessarily artificial and not always directly applicable, as immigration policies may define skills in terms of education, occupation, work experience, and/or pay of the job in the host country. Some flexibility and judgment is required when assessing what types of skill levels specific programs are designed to target.

Importantly, some programs may target more than one skill level. Sweden, for example, has one common labor immigration program that is open to admitting migrants of any skill level. The United Kingdom has two programs: Tier 2 of the United Kingdom's points-based system admits medium- and high-skilled workers, whereas Tier 1 admits very highly skilled workers only. In the United Kingdom there are currently no programs for admitting low-skilled migrant workers from outside the European Union.

Table 4.1 gives an overview of the targeted skill levels of the labor immigration programs analyzed in this chapter, by income classification and region. Over three-quarters of all programs are in high-income countries, and over 40 percent are in Europe. Table A.1 in appendix 1 indicates the skill levels that are targeted by all the immigration programs in all the countries in the sample. The sample includes twelve seasonal programs, most of which are in Europe and target the admission of low-skilled migrant workers only.

Types of Migrants Not Covered by the Indexes

It is crucial to emphasize that as this chapter is concerned with legal labor immigration and the rights of migrant workers, the discussion focuses on *labor* immigration programs that admit migrants for the primary purpose of employment. The analysis excludes various other groups including: migrants admitted for the purpose of study, family union or reunion, or hu-

---

[8] For the United Kingdom, see, for example, Drinkwater and Clark 2008.

TABLE 4.1. Labor immigration programs in the sample, 2009

	Only LS	LS	MS	HS1	HS2	Only HS2	Number of programs	Share in Total
U-HIC (30 countries)	11	30	28	40	41	10	71	68.3%
L-HIC (4 countries)	4	7	4	5	5	0	9	8.7%
U-MICs (9 countries)	2	9	11	12	14	5	21	20.2%
L-MICS (3 countries)	0	0	0	3	3	0	3	2.9%
Europe (18 countries)	6	17	17	22	23	6	39	37.5%
Eastern Europe (3 countries)	4	5	2	3	3	0	7	6.7%
North America (2 countries)	2	4	3	4	7	3	11	10.6%
Latin America (6 countries)	2	6	7	9	11	4	15	14.4%
East Asia (3 countries)	1	2	1	3	4	1	6	5.8%
Southeast Asia (6 countries)	1	4	5	7	6	1	12	11.5%
Western Asia (6 countries)	0	6	6	6	6	0	7	6.7%
Australia and New Zealand	1	2	2	6	3	0	7	6.7%
Total (46 countries)	17	46	43	60	63	15	104	

Notes: U-HIC: upper-high-income countries with GNI per capita exceeding US$20,000 in 2008; L-HIC: lower-high-income countries with GNI per capita less than US$20,000 in 2008; U-MICs: upper-middle-income countries; L-MICs: lower-middle-income countries; onlyLS: programs that target only low-skilled workers; LS: programs that target low-skilled workers and possibly others; MS: programs that target medium-skilled workers and possibly others; HS1: programs that target high-skilled workers and possibly others; HS2: programs that target very high-skilled workers and possibly others; onlyHS2: programs that target very high-skilled workers only.

manitarian protection; migrants admitted under various channels that include an employment component but not as the primary purpose of immigration, such as au pair programs and "working holidaymakers"; migrants admitted under specific work-related immigration programs that are internationally negotiated (such as "intracompany transfers," which are regulated by GATS Mode 4) and/or that do not treat migrants as employees (e.g., programs that admit self-employed migrant entrepreneurs); and migrants who entered and/or are working illegally in the host country.

Of course, many migrants not admitted for the primary purpose of employment may nevertheless take up work in the host country and eventually become classified as migrant workers. This analysis is only concerned with migrants who are *admitted* as workers rather than for other reasons. This choice can be justified on two grounds. First, there is significant variation in the considerations that inform high-income countries' policies for regulating the admission and rights of migrant workers, students, family members/dependents, asylum seekers, and refugees. Economic considerations are likely to have a greater impact on labor immigration policies than, for instance, on asylum policies, where humanitarian considerations can be expected to play a bigger role. This chapter's analysis of the relationship between labor immigration policy and the rights of migrant workers cannot be expected to automatically apply to migrants who have not been admitted for the purpose of employment. A second and related reason is the complexity of the project: including other categories of migrants in the index would make an already-complicated measurement and analysis even more involved.

The discussion also excludes migrants admitted under free movement agreements such as that operating among EU member states. For EU countries, the index only includes policies toward non-EU (third-country) nationals. Under the European Union's free movement directive, a citizen of any EU member state has the right to freely migrate and take up employment in any other EU member state without any restrictions. In other words, EU member states are fully open toward admitting migrants from other EU member states, and are also obliged to grant them most of the rights of citizens (except for the right to vote in national elections). There are three reasons why migrants who benefit from free movement agreements are excluded from the analysis. For one, although significant in some countries, free movement agreements account for a minority of international labor migrants moving to most high- and middle-income countries. There are, however, some exceptions. For example, in the United Kingdom in 2009, labor immigration from within the European Union (which increased significantly since EU enlargement in May 2004) was eighty-six thousand compared to fifty-four thousand from outside the European Union.[9] In most other countries, free movement migration accounts for a much smaller share. Across the European Union as a whole, citizens of other EU member states constitute about a third of all migrants.[10] Second, most free movement agreements cannot be considered labor immigration policies as they are typically part of larger harmonization policies or regional projects that involve a wide range of policies as well as objectives (e.g., free trade and investment policies). A third and related point is that free movement agreements are mostly one-off policies that are difficult or impossible to reverse without changing the nature of or membership in the wider policies. For example, by implementing the free movement directive, EU member states have effectively relinquished control over the admission of other EU nationals. Unilaterally imposing restrictions on the admission and employment of EU nationals would be extremely difficult politically, and might require leaving the European Union altogether.

It is important to keep the exclusion of the groups described above in mind when analyzing and interpreting the results of the labor immigration policy indexes in this chapter. Depending on the country, high- and middle-income countries' policies toward the groups excluded from this analysis are potentially significant for explaining the labor immigration programs and policy choices analyzed in this chapter.

[9] MAC 2010.
[10] Münz 2009.

Indicators for Measuring Openness to Labor Immigration

The openness index aims to measure the degree to which labor immigration programs restrict the admission of migrant workers. A program with a high (low) degree of openness is characterized by few (many) restrictions on the legal immigration and employment of migrant workers. The indicators of the index thus aim to capture the presence and, whenever relevant, relative strength of particular restrictions. In principle, it is desirable to aim for a relatively small and parsimonious set of indicators. At the same time, it is important to identify a set of indicators that is broad enough to allow for different "modes of immigration control"—that is, different types of policies that regulate the admission of migrant workers. Different countries with different welfare states, production structures, and industrial relations systems can be expected to operate different types of restrictions on labor immigration. The set of indexes must be broad and flexible enough to capture this variation.

To conceptualize and identify the relevant indicators of openness, it is useful to broadly distinguish between three types of restrictions: quotas; criteria that employers in the host country need to meet to legally employ migrant workers ("demand restrictions"); and criteria that potential migrant workers need to meet to be admitted to the host country ("supply restrictions"). This distinction is obviously somewhat artificial as some restrictions may, for example, affect both demand and supply. Nevertheless, it is a useful general approach to identifying the relevant indicators. The overall openness index comprises a total of twelve indicators, each of which is briefly discussed below (for a list of openness indicators, see appendix 2).

Quotas

The most direct way of restricting labor immigration is through quotas: numerical limits set by the government on annual immigration or net-migration flows, or on the stock of migrants, either expressed in absolute numbers or as a share of the population or labor force of the host country. In practice, quotas can take a variety of forms. They could constitute "hard" annual caps that cannot be surpassed (i.e., the government stops admitting migrants when the quota is reached), or "soft" target levels that can be exceeded and therefore act as a guide rather than as a fixed ceiling on the annual number of admissions (as is the case, say, for Canada's programs for admitting skilled migrant workers). Quotas may be set for the country as a whole (for example, the H-1B program for recruiting skilled and specialized migrant workers in the United States); the country's various regions or administrative districts (see, for instance, Switzerland's Auslaenderausweis B program for issuing one-year work permits); or certain sectors of the economy, for specified occupations, and/or individual employers or enterprises (e.g., Singapore imposes sector-specific "dependency ceilings" that specify the maximum share of foreign workers with work permits in the total company workforce). For the purpose of this index, the quota indicator distinguishes between hard quotas that are relatively small (the most restrictive type), hard quotas that are relatively large (where the distinction between small and large is based on the share of the quota in the population), soft quotas, and no quotas (the most open policy).

Demand-Side Restrictions

Job offer. Most temporary work permit programs, such as the United Kingdom's Tier 2 program or Ireland's work permit program, require migrants to have a firm job offer before they can be admitted to the host country. In these programs it is typically the prospective employer rather than the migrant worker who initiates the work permit application process. In contrast, permanent labor immigration programs and some temporary ones for highly skilled migrants do not strictly require a job offer. For example, Canada's Federal Skilled Migrant Worker Program, Australia's Skilled Independent Visa Program, and New Zealand's Skilled Labor Immigration Program are all permanent immigration programs that admit skilled migrants without a job offer. All these programs, however, grant applicants with job offers extra points in their points-based admissions processes. Denmark's green card scheme and the United Kingdom's Tier 1 program are examples of temporary labor immigration policies that admit highly skilled migrants without a prior job offer. Designed to attract the "best and brightest" in the global competition for talent, both programs allow migrants to look for employment after they have been admitted on an initially temporary basis, but with an opportunity to upgrade to permanent status after a few years (five years in the United Kingdom, and seven years in Denmark). For the purpose of this index, the indicator "job offer" distinguishes between programs that do not admit migrants without a job offer (the most restrictive policy); do not strictly require a job offer, but use it as a factor influencing admission; and programs where a job offer does not influence admission at all (the most open policy).

Labor market test. Many—but not all—temporary work permit programs operate labor market tests, which aim to ensure that employers recruit migrant workers only after having made every reasonable effort to recruit local workers (where local is defined differently across countries).[11] The rationale of labor market tests is to protect the employment prospects of the resident workforce. Most labor market tests require employers to advertise their vacancies in the domestic labor market for a mini-

---

[11] For instance, in countries of the European Economic Area (EEA), which includes the EU countries plus Liechtenstein, Norway, and Iceland, labor market tests strive to ensure that no EEA workers are available to do the work before a non-EEA national is admitted to fill the vacancy.

mum period of time. One can broadly distinguish between two types of labor market tests: a relatively weak test based on employer "attestation," and a stronger test based on "certification." Attestation-type tests simply require employers to attest that they have unsuccessfully searched for local workers without any checks by a government agency (or other institution) into the employers' local recruitment efforts before the migrant is admitted. Tier 2 for admitting skilled workers under the United Kingdom's points-based system operates on this basis. Reflecting a "trust-the-employer approach," attestation requirements are a relatively weak restriction as they are usually associated with limited enforcement measures *after* the admission of the migrant workers.[12] In contrast, labor market tests that are based on certification require employers to obtain confirmation/certification from a particular body—typically a public employment agency—that the requirements of the labor market test have been met *before* the work permit application for employing a migrant worker can be submitted. In Ireland, for instance, employers are required to obtain a certificate from the public employment service (FÁS) to certify that they have advertised the vacancy and that no local workers were matched to the job before they apply for a work permit. The labor market test indicator in the openness index distinguishes among very strong certification-based labor market tests in all sectors/occupations covered by the program (the most restrictive policy); strong certification-based labor market tests, but with some sectors/occupations exempted (e.g., through shortage occupation lists that include jobs where the government suspends the labor market test requirement because of a known shortage of domestic workers); weak attestation-based tests; and no labor market tests (the most open policy).

Sectoral/occupational restrictions. It has become increasingly common for labor immigration programs to be restricted to specific sectors and/or occupations in the host country. Many countries, for example, operate specific programs for the seasonal employment of migrant workers in agriculture.[13] The index distinguishes between programs that restrict the employment of migrants to specific sectors and/or occupations (the restrictive policy) and those that do not (the open policy).

Economic work permit fees. All programs that admit migrants on the basis of a job offer require employers to pay administrative work permit fees. Some countries—most notably Singapore and Malaysia—also charge employers economically oriented fees as a way of "micromanaging" employers' incentives and the recruitment of migrant workers. Singapore's so-called foreign-worker levies are payable by the employer per migrant employed. The levies are flexible (i.e., regularly revised), specific to the migrant's skill level and sector of employment, and rise with the share of migrants employed at a company. For example, in 2008 the

---

[12] See, for example, MAC 2009.

[13] See, for example, Canada's long-standing Seasonal Agricultural Worker Program, or the more recent program in New Zealand for employing low-skilled migrants from the Pacific Islands in agricultural activities.

monthly levy for employing a skilled migrant in Singapore's construction sector was S$150; the corresponding levy for employing an unskilled construction worker from abroad was S$470, which was equivalent to just under 20 percent of the average monthly wages in the sector at the time.[14] The economic fees indicator distinguishes between programs that charge employers economic fees (the restrictive policy) and those that do not (the open policy).

Wage restrictions. Restrictions on the wages and other employment conditions at which migrants must be employed can constitute a powerful limit on the legal inflow and employment of migrant workers. One can broadly distinguish between three types of wage restrictions, ranging from the most open to the most restrictive. The most open policy is to simply require migrants to be employed at the legal minimum wage (if one exists) prevailing in the country. In a few countries in the Middle East, certain types of migrants are exempted from minimum wage legislation. The great majority of countries analyzed here are liberal democratic countries that all require employers to pay migrants at least the minimum wage. The most restrictive policy is to require employers to comply with wages and employment conditions stipulated in collective wage agreements. Such agreements are common in coordinated market economies, and they are strongest in the Scandinavian welfare states of, say, Sweden and Norway. In Sweden, any employer who wants to legally employ migrant workers must do so in strict compliance with prevailing industrial standards as determined by collective agreements. As will be discussed in chapter 5, this requirement has been a major factor why Sweden has seen few labor migrants from outside the European Union over the past three decades despite having an immigration policy that is relatively open on many other policy components. An intermediate policy on wage restrictions, operative in many countries including the United States and the United Kingdom, is to require employers to pay migrants the average or prevailing wage in the relevant occupation and/or sector. What constitutes the prevailing wage is typically highly contested, and that in turn is why this policy is a significantly weaker requirement than having to pay collectively agreed-on wages.

Trade union involvement. The sixth and final demand-side restriction considered by the openness index relates to the involvement of trade unions in individual work permit application processes. Representing resident workers in host countries, trade unions can be expected to have an interest in ensuring that immigration does not adversely affect the wages and employment conditions of domestic workers. Although not all trade unions are opposed to immigration, in countries with strong collective agreements and wide union coverage, trade unions have often played a major role in limiting the number of migrant workers admitted.[15] For

---

[14] Singstat 2008.
[15] See, for example, Watts 2002.

example, before Sweden's immigration policy reform in late 2008, any application for a work permit for non–European Economic Area (EEA) workers had to be approved by the relevant Swedish trade union.[16] In some other countries, unions do not have veto power, yet they still exert some influence over individual applications. Under Canada's programs for the temporary employment of low-skilled migrant workers, for instance, employers in certain sectors must consult unions as part of the process of obtaining a "positive labor market opinion" (a certification requirement) before the work permit application can be processed. Similarly, in Taiwan, employers wishing to recruit low-skilled migrant workers must notify and consult the relevant trade union, and provide full details about the job vacancy. The trade union indicator thus distinguishes among programs where unions have strong, some, or no involvement in individual work permit application processes.

Supply-Side Restrictions

Nationality and age restrictions. The personal characteristics of migrants can be factors limiting or influencing their admission under labor immigration programs in high- and middle-income countries. An increasing number of bilateral labor immigration programs are restricted or give preference to migrants from particular countries. Spain's Contingente program for low-skilled migrants, for one, is based on a series of bilateral recruitment agreements with a small number of countries including Ecuador and Morocco. Restrictions by migrants' age are less common, but nevertheless can be an important factor in certain countries. Singapore requires low- and medium-skilled migrants to be under fifty years of age. Under most points-based systems for managing labor immigration, including in Canada, Australia, New Zealand, and the United Kingdom, age is a factor that influences the admission of migrant workers. The indicator capturing restrictions based on nationality and/or age distinguishes among four types of restrictions, in order of increasing openness: programs that limit admission by both nationality and age; those that restrict admission by nationality or age; policies where admission is influenced (but not restricted) by nationality and/or age; and programs where age and nationality do not affect admission.

Gender and marital status restrictions. In a relatively small number of countries, gender and marital status are factors restricting or influencing the admission of migrant workers. In Saudi Arabia, for example, all women including migrants are prohibited from carrying out certain "hazardous" activities. Marital status can matter under points-based systems that grant extra points for the skills of spouses—as it is the case, say, under Australia's policies for admitting skilled migrants on a permanent

---

[16] See Bucken-Knapp 2009.

basis. The indicator reflecting gender and marital status restrictions includes the same distinctions of different types of restrictions as the indicator capturing nationality and age restrictions.

Skills requirements. Skills requirements are common and not restricted to labor immigration programs that target skilled and high-skilled migrant workers. The term *skills* is ambiguous, and can be interpreted and operationalized in many different ways. It could refer to education, qualifications, work experience, and other competencies. For the purpose of this index, the indicator measures whether skills requirements are an explicit criterion for admission, and if so, how specific these requirements are. The most open policy is one that does not specify any skills requirements. A weakly restrictive policy specifies a generic minimum skills threshold such as "vocational training," "completed high school," or "university degree." For example, under Germany's labor immigration program for admitting skilled migrant workers, residence permits are granted to "professionals with a recognized degree or a German equivalent foreign degree." A strongly restrictive policy uses generic minimum skills requirements plus specific and explicit skills as a criterion influencing but not restricting admissions. This is the case under most points-based admission mechanisms for skilled labor immigration that award points for different levels of academic qualifications (e.g., in the United Kingdom, Australia, and Canada) and in some countries also for work experience (in Canada). The most restrictive policy on skills restrictions admits only those migrants with specific skills. Denmark's Positive List labor immigration program, for example, defines a specific set of minimum qualifications for each profession/occupation. Depending on the occupation, qualifications vary, ranging from a professional bachelor's degree or three years of university studies to a master's degree, with some occupations requiring "Danish authorization" (e.g., dentists, veterinarians, and marine engineers).

Language skill requirements. In some countries, admission as a migrant worker requires at least some knowledge of the host country's language. For example, under the United Kingdom's current points-based system, migrants must have a minimum proficiency of English. A less restrictive policy is to use language skills as a factor influencing although not strictly limiting admission, as is the case, say, under Canada's and Australia's policies for admitting skilled migrants on a permanent basis.

Self-sufficiency. Many, but not all, labor immigration programs require migrants to prove before admission that they will be self-sufficient in the host country—that is, that they will not rely on public funds to support themselves and their families. This restriction can take the form of a requirement to demonstrate savings of a certain amount (e.g., workers seeking to enter the United Kingdom as skilled migrants must have £800 in available funds in their bank accounts for three months before the date of the work permit application) and/or evidence of a firm job offer in the host country that pays well enough to avoid dependence on public assistance.

Indicators for Measuring Migrant Rights

The migrant rights index aims to measure the absence/presence and scope of the *legal rights* (defined here as the rights granted by national laws and policies) granted to migrant workers on admission under a particular labor immigration program. Programs under which migrant workers enjoy more and a wider range of legal rights will score higher than countries with fewer, narrower legal rights for migrant workers.

The emphasis on legal rights means that the index will not measure the enjoyment and experience of rights in practice.[17] In theory, migrants can be denied some rights that exist in law (e.g., if there is no effective state protection and enforcement of the existing legal right to a minimum wage) and/or enjoy rights that do not exist in law (e.g., medical doctors may in practice treat patients without the legal rights to health care). Clearly, one would ideally like to measure rights in law *and* practice, but the latter would involve considerable and complex research that goes beyond the scope of this project.

There are three conceptual issues that are worth highlighting before looking at the specific rights included in the index. First, while the rights of migrant workers are typically more restricted than those of citizens, the legal rights of citizens can and do vary across countries. We may expect many/most liberal democracies to respect the civil and political rights stipulated in international human rights law, yet we are likely to find significant variation in economic and social rights across liberal democracies. Furthermore, high-income countries that are not liberal democracies may not provide their citizens (let alone migrants) all the civil and political rights stipulated by the human rights treaties. It is thus possible, for example, that neither citizens nor migrants have the right to join trade unions. When constructing and interpreting the scores of the index for a particular right it is obviously important—as I have done in this chapter—to also consider whether citizens enjoy that right.

A second and related issue pertains to the meaning as well as nature of different types of rights along with the implications for measurement. The meaning, freedoms, and benefits of some rights are relatively clear and consistent across countries and time, thereby lending themselves to consistent measurement. For instance, the right to free choice of employment generally means that people are free to apply for any job in the country (although the range and quality of jobs available can of course vary significantly across countries). Yet there are other rights—mainly economic and social rights—that primarily relate to equality of treatment rather than to some absolute and universal standard, which makes them more difficult to measure and compare across countries. The right to equal access to public health services is a good case in point. The range and quality of public health services obviously varies significantly across countries.

---

[17] For a discussion of different ways of measuring human rights, see, for example, Landman 2004.

Migrants with the right to equal access to public health care in Argentina and Sweden enjoy the same legal right, but the value of their rights—understood in terms of the actual benefits that the right conveys—differs dramatically across the two countries.

Third, time can play a key role in the analysis of migrant rights. As discussed in chapter 3, there is a general and crucial distinction between migrants with temporary or permanent residence status. In most liberal democracies, migrants with permanent resident status enjoy the same or similar economic and social rights as citizens. The scope for restricting migrants' rights is largely limited to migrants on temporary residence permits. The policy decision on whether to grant migrants temporary or permanent residence status thus has important implications for opportunities and ease of restricting migrants' rights.

Time can also matter as a determinant of access to specific rights. While some rights are typically granted (or not) on admission to the host country, other rights are sometimes acquired over time. For example, various countries including Ireland and the United Kingdom operate "habitual residency tests"—that is, minimum residency requirements—to determine eligibility for certain social benefits. The right to family reunion is sometimes granted only after the primary migrant has spent a minimum period of time in the host country. The measurement of rights therefore must allow for the consideration of time as a potential determinant of access to specific rights.

Given these conceptual preliminaries, the migrant rights index developed for the analysis in this chapter comprises indicators for a total of twenty-three different rights, selected and adapted from the CMW. Although greatly underratified (see the discussion in chapter 2), the CMW's comprehensive list of rights for migrant workers is a useful benchmark for this exercise. Since the emphasis in this analysis is on the rights of regular migrant workers, the indicators are based on rights taken from parts 3 and 4 of the CMW—excluding specific rights to be granted to irregular migrant workers (covered by part 5 of the CMW). It is essential to stress that some of the rights stipulated in the CMW are conditional/qualified and sometimes limited to certain groups. This is critical to keep in mind, but it does not directly affect the choice of indicators.

Following the human rights framework, the index includes a mix of different types of rights including five civil and political rights, five economic rights, five social rights, five residency rights, and three rights related to family reunion. Some of the indicators are measured as binary variables (such as 0 for "no, no legal right," and 1 for "yes, legal right in place"), while others involve a scale (0–2 with 0 = no legal right, 1 = restricted legal right, and 2 = full legal right in place without restrictions) to indicate restrictions and the degree to which a legal right is available. As explained below, in some cases scales are used to take account of rights that are granted after a certain period of time. Appendix 3 includes the full list of migrant rights indicators used and analyzed in this study.

Civil and Political Rights

The index includes five civil and political rights.[18] There are two indicators that capture the right to vote and the right to stand for elections in local and/or regional elections (no country offers migrants without citizenship status the right to vote in national elections). Both indicators include a time element to allow for the possibility that the rights to vote and/or stand for election are granted after some time, but without switching into a separate immigration status.[19]

The right to form trade unions and other associations along with the right to equal treatment and protections before criminal courts and tribunals are both measured relative to the rights of citizens; in both cases, there is an intermediate score of a "limited" right that falls between the extremes of no and equal rights.

The fifth right under the category of civil and political rights captured by the index is the right not to have identity documents confiscated by anyone, other than a public official duly authorized by law. The wording is taken from the 1990 UN convention. In some countries, especially but not only in the Gulf States, it is relatively common for employers to retain migrant workers' passports. This is generally considered illegal under both international human rights law and in terms of the national laws of the countries issuing the passport, which generally stipulate that passports are the property of the issuing country. The indicator aims to measure the extent to which the retention or confiscation of passports and other identification documents is declared illegal in the domestic laws (e.g., constitutions and/or labor laws) of host countries. In Spain and Mexico, for example, domestic laws explicitly state that migrant workers have the right not to have their documents confiscated.

Economic Rights

The indicators included in the category of economic rights are primarily aimed at measuring migrants' rights in the host country's labor market. A key right that is often restricted for migrant workers is the right to free choice of employment in the host country's labor market. Migrants on permanent work and residence permits typically enjoy this right in full, although some countries impose temporary geographic restrictions in order to retain migrant workers in regions experiencing the most acute labor shortages. For instance, Canada's Provincial Nominee Program for skilled migrant workers grants permanent residence on admission, but

---

[18] As was the case with the discussion of openness indicators, all examples of migrant rights in this section refer to the year 2009.

[19] Unless specified otherwise, the consideration of rights granted after a certain period of time always refers to time spent residing and working *under the immigration program in question*—that is, without switching to a different immigration program and/or immigration status.

temporarily restricts the migrant's legal employment to the region that nominated and supported the migrant's admission to the country. In contrast to permanent residents, temporary migrants' rights to free choice of employment are typically (although not always) restricted. Most temporary labor immigration programs require workers to work for the employer specified on the work permit only. Where possible, changing employers usually requires a new work permit application.

The right to join trade unions can be an important determinant of a migrant's bargaining power and security in the labor market. The United Arab Emirates are among the very few countries in the sample that do not have unions (for these countries only, the score thus reflects the fact that there are no unions rather than indicating discrimination against migrants with regard to the right to join unions). In Malaysia, migrants are explicitly excluded from unions. In Kuwait, migrants must have resided in the country for at least five years and must have a valid work permit before they are allowed to join trade unions as nonvoting members.

The other three economic rights included in the index all relate to equal access to the protections and benefits of the host country's employment laws. They include the right to equal pay as local workers doing the same work, the right to equal employment conditions and protection (e.g., overtime, hours of work, weekly rest, paid holidays, sick pay, health and safety at work, and protection against dismissal), and the right to redress, if the employers have violated the terms of the employment contract.

Social Rights

The social rights indicators measure migrant workers' rights to equality of access to unemployment benefits, public retirement pension schemes, public educational institutions and services, public housing including social housing schemes, and public health services. As shown in appendix 3, each of these indicators has four possible scores to take account of both time and other limitations. Two variations of social rights indicators have been constructed. One is premised on a scoring system that is strictly based on equality of rights regardless of whether citizens enjoy the rights or not. This means that a score of 1 ("full equality right") could either reflect complete equality in access to existing social rights or be due to the absence of a particular social right for all residents (citizens and noncitizens). This type of indicator thus measures the extent to which migrants are treated differently, not whether or not there is a particular social right in the host country.

A second, alternative indicator of social rights takes account of the fact that some countries do not provide their own citizens with certain social rights. Where this is the case, the score has been changed to 0 (no right). The advantage of this type of indicator is that it provides an absolute measure of whether migrants enjoy a particular right or not. The disadvantage is that it does not distinguish between countries and programs that do not grant migrants any access to an existing right afforded to citizens and those that do not offer any rights to citizens or migrants without citizenship. The construction of the overall index and analysis of social rights in particular will use both types of indicators of social rights.

Residency Rights

The length and security of residence status granted to migrant workers varies significantly across different labor immigration programs across and within countries. The existence and nature of restrictions on migrants' right to legal residence in the host country is a key issue that has crucial implications for possibilities for restricting a wide range of migrant rights. The indicator captures four common possibilities of regulating the right to residence. The most restrictive policy is to grant migrants a strictly temporary residence permit with no legal possibility of changing status ("upgrading") to a permanent residence status. This is common among seasonal migration programs and most general programs in the Gulf States. A less restrictive policy is to grant a temporary residence permit, but with an opportunity—possibly regulated by further selection mechanisms—to obtain permanent residence status after a certain number of years (the indicator distinguishes between programs that allow permanent residence in fewer or more than five years of residence in the host country). The temporary H1-B program for specialty workers in the United States, for example, allows migrants to apply for permanent residence status after six years of employment in the United States. In Ireland, migrants admitted on temporary green cards for highly skilled workers can apply for permanent residence after three years. The most generous policy with regard to migrants' rights to legal residence is to grant immediate permanent residence rights as is the case, for instance, under Australia's and Canada's points-based programs for admitting skilled migrant workers.

Three additional indicators aim to measure the conditionality and, more generally, security of a migrant's right to legal residence. One of these indicators measures how, if at all, criminal and administrative convictions affect residence status. Depending on the country, different types of immigration offenses may fall under either or both of the two types of convictions. Revocation of the legal right to residence on the basis of administrative convictions alone is considered a more restrictive policy than revocation on the basis of criminal convictions. A separate indicator assesses migrants' legal right to remedies/redress in case of withdrawal or nonrenewal of residence permit, or in case of a deportation order.

A third indicator of security of residence considers whether and how a migrant's right to legal residence is affected by loss of employment in the host country. Most TMPs, especially those that grant strictly temporary permits, make the right to residence directly conditional on employment. In other words, loss or termination of employment results in immediate loss of residence rights. Some countries, including Austria and Denmark, allow some migrants on temporary permits who have lost their employment to remain in the country for a limited period of time in order to look for a new job through "bridging visas." The most liberal policy is to completely decouple employment from residence status—namely, make the right to legal residence independent of whether the migrant is employed or not. This policy is usually reserved for skilled and highly skilled migrants admitted on permanent work and residence permits (e.g., Canada and Australia), but there are also some TMPs that allow migrants to remain for a certain period without a job (e.g., the United Kingdom's Tier 1 program for admitting highly skilled workers).

The fifth indicator in the category of residence rights relates to access to citizenship. The scores for this indicator are based on whether and after how many years it is possible to naturalize (i.e., obtain citizenship of the host country) on the basis of the immigration status granted under the immigration program under consideration. In other words, it is an indicator of direct access to citizenship rather than indirect access that requires the migrant to switch to another immigration status before applying for citizenship. Generally speaking, most programs that grant migrants permanent residence status immediately on admission also include a path to naturalization. Among temporary programs, some allow for pathways to citizenship (e.g., skilled migrant workers in the United Kingdom), while others do not (e.g., migrant workers in most of the Gulf States).

Family Rights

The final category of indicators included in the migrant rights index relates to family reunion and the spouse's right to work in the host country. Two indicators measure the right to family reunion. The first assesses whether migrants admitted under a particular immigration program have the right to family reunion, and how extensive the right is in terms of the definition of relatives qualifying as family and/or dependents. Many programs for low-skilled and strictly time-limited labor immigration do not grant migrants any rights for family reunion (e.g., seasonal migrant workers in Austria and Greece). Other programs allow family reunion, but it is fairly narrowly defined (e.g., only spouses and minor children, as is the case in Belgium's program for admitting labor migrants). The most liberal right to family reunion includes a wider group of family members and dependents, such as grandparents and children over the age of nineteen. For example, migrants admitted on a permanent basis under Canada's skilled labor immigration program can sponsor the immigration of parents, grandparents, brothers or sisters, nephews or nieces, and granddaughters or grandsons who are orphaned, under eighteen years of age, and not married or in a common law relationship. A separate indicator measures the existence and scope of judicial remedies available to migrants to challenge the refusal by authorities to allow family formation/ reunification.

The third indicator in this category assesses the limits, if any, on the spouse's right to work in the host country without a work permit. The indicators allow for three possible scores. Programs in some countries, such as the United Kingdom, allow spouses full and immediate work rights without any restrictions.[20] Others do not grant spouses without their own work permit the right to work in any job in the host country. The spouses of migrants admitted through the general labor scheme in the Netherlands, for instance, are not allowed to take up any employment unless they first apply for and obtain a work permit. An intermediate score is given for programs that grant spouses the right to freely accept employment in only some sectors and/or occupations, and/or are subject to quotas (as is the case under Austria's Key Worker Migrant Program).

Methods, Data, and Limitations

Normalization and Aggregation Procedures

The computation of aggregate scores for the overall rights and openness indexes requires a procedure for combining the scores for the individual indicators. There are two key questions: How, if at all, should the indicators be normalized and weighed? How should the scores for each indicator be aggregated to generate the overall index? It is essential to emphasize the fundamental importance of these issues. Different procedures for normalizing, weighing, and aggregating indicators will obviously produce different overall indexes.

The rights and openness indexes developed in this analysis are based on equal weights and a simple aggregation procedure that involves adding up the normalized scores for each indicator to produce the overall indexes. The main arguments in favor of equal weights are transparency and simplicity. Any procedure that departs from equal weights needs to be based on convincing reasons explaining why and how some indicators matter more than others. In this analysis of openness and migrant rights, there is no set of weights that would be obviously superior to the default of equal weights. It is, of course, entirely possible that in practice some indicators are more important than others, in the sense of having a greater impact on what is being measured. For example, within the openness index, the presence of a hard and small quota can be expected to have a bigger impact on a country's openness to labor immigration than the requirement to prove self-sufficiency. There is, however, no objective way of

[20] In the United Kingdom, the work rights of spouses are sometimes more extensive than the employment rights of the primary migrant, whose employment is often restricted to particular employers (see MAC 2009).

assessing this difference. Furthermore, since different countries may operate different modes of immigration control (i.e., employ different tools for restricting labor immigration), assigning a set of weights that differs from equal weights runs the risk of introducing various types of bias. A third argument against nonequal weights is that the relative impact of a given mechanism for restricting labor immigration could conceivably vary significantly across countries.

There are statistical tools, such as principal component analysis, for providing a purely mechanical solution to the problem of identifying suitable weights for the indicators. Principal component analysis is a data reduction procedure. It tries to identify the critical variables that account for most of the overall variation in the data. While useful for some purposes, the main problem with principal component analysis in the context of this chapter is that it is not based on any conceptual relevance of the indicators but instead simply on the degree of correlation between them. A further problem is that having eliminated some components, the remaining indicators after principal component analysis do not have straightforward interpretations as they are partly measuring effects of other indicators that have been excluded. For these reasons, principal component analysis is not an appropriate methodology for the construction of the rights and openness indexes. The construction of these indexes must be based on a conceptual framework and judgment of the substantive issues involved rather than purely on statistical correlations.

The procedure for normalizing and aggregating the individual scores adopted in the construction of the overall rights and openness indexes involves two steps. The first step is to normalize the scores for the individual indicators. For the sake of transparency and simplicity, I have adopted a common and simple procedure that normalizes the raw data, and ensures that all the scores for the individual indicators fall between 0 and 1:

Normalized score = (actual value – minimum value) / (maximum value – minimum value)

The second step is to simply add up the scores for the individual indicators to produce the overall rights and openness indexes and relevant subindexes. The score for the overall openness index thus ranges from 0 (closed) to 12 (completely open), and for the rights indicator from 0 (no rights) to 23 (full equality of rights). Whenever useful, these scores are again normalized to fall between 0 and 1.

Data Sources, Implementation, and Limitations

The indexes developed in this project are the first-ever measures of openness to labor immigration and migrant rights in a relatively large number of countries. A team of five researchers helped construct the indexes during March–August 2009, for the period early 2009, and to capture potential policy changes due to the economic downturn, also for early 2008. The scores are derived from a desk-based analysis of national immigration laws and regulations, labor law, and where relevant, constitutional laws. In a few exceptional cases, the scores to some indicators in some countries are based on relevant secondary literature and analysis.

The data collection and processing involved four stages. As a first step, the key labor immigration programs for each country were identified. Second, researchers spent an average of three days analyzing relevant legislation and policy documents, and suggested draft scores. As a third step, the scores were discussed and finalized for each country. Finally, the scores of each individual indicator were checked for consistency across all programs and countries.

The comparative measurement and analysis of migrant rights and immigration policy is still at a nascent stage, primarily because of the significant complexities and conceptual as well as methodological challenges involved. It is important to be clear and transparent about the limitations of the indexes analyzed below. Although every effort was made to score the indicators based on the best available information that could be accessed from Oxford University, the scores to the indicators undoubtedly include some degree of measurement error, and by the nature of the project, sometimes required a degree of judgment. In most but not all cases, researchers spoke the language of the country being analyzed. In some cases, such as Japan, Thailand, and some of the Gulf countries, the scores are based on English translations of the relevant laws and policies. The data obtained for some countries were better than for others. Countries for which data were considered too unreliable—including Egypt, India, Libya, Russia, and the Ukraine—were excluded from the analysis at this stage. Despite these caveats, the obtained scores are considered accurate and robust enough to provide the basis for an exploratory analysis of the relationship between openness, targeted skill levels, and migrant rights associated with different labor immigration programs. The scores may not be accurate for every single indicator for every program and every country in the sample, yet they do collectively provide us with reasonably robust measures. The indicators and scores used in this project are, I would argue, more reliable than some of the existing indicators, whose scores are based on subjective judgment by a small number of country experts.

There are also a number of conceptual limitations and assumptions, including generic issues that affect any index as well as particular questions that arise in the construction of policy and rights indexes. Can a policy really be quantified and measured by an index? Can the presence and scope of rights be reduced to a number? Most important, can we really compare and integrate measures of different types of rights that, some contend, are incommensurable? These are all legitimate questions. They do not invalidate the usefulness of the exercise, however; what they do suggest is that any results need to be carefully discussed and interpreted in light of the underlying assumptions and limitations.

Openness to Labor Immigration

The remainder of the chapter presents and examines some key results of the empirical analysis. Before looking at the evidence on the hypothesized relationships between migrants' rights, skills, and openness to labor immigration, it is useful to highlight six key features of labor immigration policies in high- and middle-income countries. (Table A.2 in appendix 1 provides basic descriptives of the aggregate openness index, and table A.3 gives a detailed list of all 104 programs analyzed, together with their aggregate openness scores.)

First, the great majority of labor immigration programs included in this study (just under 90 percent) admit migrants on temporary rather than permanent residence and employment permits. Yet there are significant regional variations. Almost all the programs in Europe and Asia are TMPs (i.e., they do not grant permanent residence on admission). In contrast, TMPs constitute much lower shares among the programs in the traditional "settler countries and regions" including North America (just over half are TMPs), and Australia and New Zealand (less than half are TMPs). It is important to add that the share of TMPs in a particular country or region does not necessarily reflect the share of temporary migrant workers admitted, as the size of different programs may vary considerably. In recent years, many of the traditional settler countries, especially Canada and Australia, have moved toward policies that significantly increase the number of temporary migrant workers.

Second, as shown in figure 4.1, there is a crucial inverse relationship between temporary visas/work permits and the skill level targeted by the immigration program. All the programs for admitting low-skilled migrants are TMPs, with about two-thirds issuing strictly temporary permits that do not allow upgrading to permanent residence status. As we move up the skill ladder, the share of permanent immigration programs increases while that of strictly temporary programs declines. Nevertheless, even among programs targeting highly skilled migrants with second- or third-level degree, two-thirds are associated with temporary rather than permanent residence status on arrival.

Third, as shown in figure 4.2, with the exception of the self-sufficiency requirement (included in over two-thirds of the programs analyzed here), supply-side restrictions on labor immigration are much less common than demand-side restrictions and quotas. This is not surprising in light of the dominance of TMPs in the sample. Supply-side restrictions are most common among permanent immigration programs for skilled and high-skilled migrant workers, such as points-based systems in Canada, Australia, and New Zealand. The most common demand-side restrictions are the requirement of a job offer (over 90 percent of programs include this requirement), labor market tests (used in just over half of all programs), and restrictions on the conditions of employment of the migrants (used by almost 40 percent of programs). Of all the twelve openness indicators,

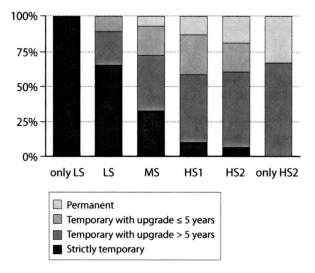

FIGURE 4.1. Temporary and permanent labor immigration programs by targeted skills, 2009
Notes: only LS: programs that target only low-skilled workers; LS: programs that target low-skilled workers and possibly others; MS: programs that target medium-skilled workers and possibly others; HS1: programs that target high-skilled workers and possibly others; HS2: programs that target very high-skilled workers and possibly others; onlyHS2: programs that target very high-skilled workers only.

restrictions by gender and marital status as well as through trade union involvement are the least commonly used tools of limiting labor immigration among the programs included in this analysis.

Figure 4.2 also shows that there are important regional variations in the types of restrictions used. Some of these differences are likely due to differences in welfare states, labor market regulations, and to some extent, political systems. For example, the requirement for migrants to prove self-sufficiency before admission is most common among programs in Europe (used by 85 percent of programs) where welfare states are larger than in other regions in the sample (the average for all programs is 70 percent). Similarly, restrictions on the migrants' wages and other employment conditions are highest in Europe, and lowest in Southeast and especially western Asia. The western Asia sample includes Israel plus four GCC countries (Saudi Arabia, Kuwait, Oman, and the United Arab Emirates) with highly segmented labor markets along with high degrees of inequality between citizens and noncitizens. A key tool for restricting labor immigration among Southeast Asian countries (used by two-thirds of programs) is economic fees, but this is much less so among programs in other regions (fewer than 10 percent of all programs in the sample use economic fees).

Fourth, although the correlations between individual openness indicators are mostly statistically insignificant, there are some types of restrictions that tend to be used as complements (i.e., in combination) while others appear to be substitutes (see table A.4 in appendix 1). For instance, labor immigration programs that require applicants to have job offers

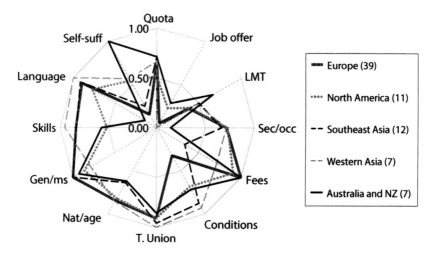

FIGURE 4.2. Openness indicators by selected regions, 2009

Notes: All indicators range from 0 (most restricted; i.e., restriction applies—the center of the spider diagram above) to 1 (most open; i.e., restriction not used at all). The numbers in parentheses indicate the number of programs analyzed in the region. For an explanation of the openness indicators in this figure, see appendix 2.

also tend to operate labor market tests (statistically significant correlation coefficient of 0.35 for all programs, and 0.40 for programs in upper-high-income countries only). Labor market tests are also positively correlated with the involvement of trade unions. There is a positive relationship between the requirement of a job offer and restrictions on the conditions of employment as well. These are expected results given that all four indicators (job offer, labor market test, restrictions of conditions of employment, and trade union involvement) reflect concerns about the responsiveness of labor immigration to shortages in the domestic labor market and the impacts of immigration on the employment opportunities of domestic workers.

Skills and language requirements tend to be used together. They are both inversely related to the requirements of having a job offer and the strength of the labor market test, suggesting that the two sets of restrictions, which reflect supply and demand factors respectively, are used as substitutes rather than in combination. Part of this negative correlation can again be explained by permanent immigration programs for skilled and highly skilled workers, which typically make heavy use of supply-side factors, but much less or no use of demand-side restrictions such as strict job offer requirements and labor market tests.

A fifth finding is that *as a group*, programs in countries in upper-high-income countries are less open to labor immigration than those in middle- and lower-high-income countries countries.[21] Arguably, the greater at-

---

[21] There is, however, no significant relationship between the gross domestic product per capita and openness within upper-high-income countries.

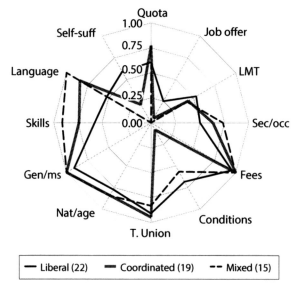

FIGURE 4.3. Restrictions by variety of capitalism, 2009

Notes: Classification (Hall and Soskice 2001): liberal market economies: Australia, Canada, Ireland, New Zealand, United States, and United Kingdom; coordinated market economies: Austria, Belgium, Denmark, Finland, Germany, Japan, Netherlands, Norway, Sweden, and Switzerland; mixed market economies: France, Greece, Italy, Portugal, Spain, and Turkey. For an explanation of the openness indicators in this figure, see appendix 2.

tractiveness and higher shares of migrant workers in higher-income countries as well as their more extensive welfare states could explain this finding.

A sixth feature of openness relates to differences in the modes of labor immigration restrictions by programs in liberal, coordinated, and mixed market economies, and liberal, social democratic, and conservative welfare states.[22]

As explained in the notes to figures 4.3 and 4.4, the countries that Peter Hall and David Soskice (2001) characterize as liberal market economies are the same as those that Esping-Andersen (1999) classifies as liberal welfare states. Figures 4.3 and 4.4 show that compared to the programs in this liberal group of countries, programs in coordinated market economies (with social democratic or conservative welfare states) are more likely to limit immigration by requiring a job offer, self-sufficiency, and restrictions on the wages and employment conditions at which migrants must be employed in the host country. The latter is a direct result of being a more coordinated economy. In contrast, programs in liberal market economies and welfare states make greater use of specific skill and language requirements.[23] These results partly reflect the fact that the lib-

[22] Market economies here are classified according to the varieties of capitalism literature; see Hall and Soskice 2001. Welfare states here are classified according to the welfare state regimes literature; see Esping-Andersen 1999.

[23] All these differences are statistically significant at the 7 percent level.

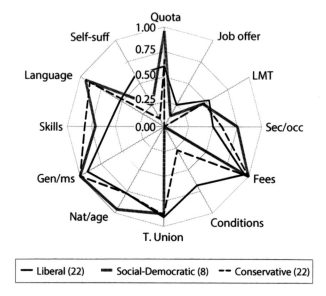

FIGURE 4.4. Restrictions by welfare state regimes, 2009

Notes: Classification (Esping-Andersen 1999): liberal welfare states: Australia, Canada, Ireland, New Zealand, United States, and United Kingdom; Social democratic welfare states: Denmark, Finland, Norway, and Sweden; conservative welfare states: Austria, Belgium, France, Germany, Italy, Japan, Netherlands, Portugal, Spain, and Switzerland. For an explanation of the openness indicators in this figure, see appendix 2.

eral market economies and welfare states in this sample include three traditional settlement countries (Australia, Canada, and New Zealand) that operate a significant number of permanent immigration programs.

Grouping restrictions by type (quotas, demand restrictions, and supply restrictions), programs in liberal economies and welfare states make less use of demand restrictions than those in coordinated economies. This is an expected result as public policies in liberal market economies are likely to be more employer led (or employer friendly) than in coordinated economies where governments, by definition, impose greater degrees of regulation on labor markets and are likely to be more concerned with the impact of immigration on the (larger) welfare state.

These results illustrate the different modes of labor immigration control across different types of market economies and welfare states. They do not suggest differences in the level of openness, though. In the sample analyzed here, there is no statistically significant difference between the openness of programs in liberal, coordinated, and mixed economies, or across different types of welfare states.

Openness and Skills

A seventh feature—which confirms the first of the three hypotheses outlined in chapter 3—is that openness to labor immigration is positively

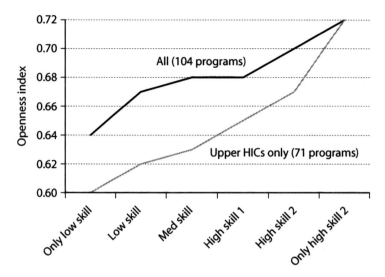

FIGURE 4.5. Aggregate openness index by targeted skill level, 2009

Notes: Onlylowskill: programs targeting low-skilled migrants only; lowskill: programs targeting low-skilled migrants (and others); medskill: programs targeting medium-skilled migrants (and others); highskill1: programs targeting high-skilled migrants (and others); highskill2: programs targeting very high-skilled migrants (and others); onlyhighskill2: programs targeting very high-skilled migrants only; upperHICs: upper-high-income countries.

related to the skill level targeted by the immigration program. As shown in figure 4.5, programs that target high-skilled workers place fewer restrictions on admission than those targeting lower-skilled migrants. The differentiation of openness by skill level is most pronounced and statistically significant for programs in the highest-income countries in the sample (upper-high-income countries). A simple regression of openness on targeted skill level and income country group (distinguishing upper-high-income countries from other countries) confirms the significance of this relationship.[24] Focusing the analysis on temporary migration programs does not substantively change the results.

More detailed study of individual openness indicators suggests that the positive relationship between the overall openness index and the skills targeted by the immigration program is primarily driven by demand-side restrictions, especially the requirement of a job offer, strength of the labor market test, restrictiveness of quotas, trade union involvement, and in upper-high-income countries, restrictions on the occupation and/or sector of employment of the migrant in the host economy (see table A.5 in appendix 1). The lower the skill level targeted, the greater these demand-side restrictions on labor immigration.

In terms of supply-side restrictions, the picture is more mixed. Restrictions by nationality and age are significantly as well as negatively correlated with targeted skills. In contrast, the host country's language and

[24] See Ruhs 2011.

general skills requirements are higher among programs that target more highly skilled workers.

Migrant Rights

There is considerable variation in the rights granted to migrant workers under different labor immigration programs, both within and across countries. As shown in figure 4.6, restrictions vary significantly across different rights (the rights index ranges from 0 to 1, with a greater number indicating fewer restrictions on rights). Among the types of rights analyzed, the six most commonly restricted rights are the rights to stand for elections and vote (two political rights), the spouse's right to work, direct access to citizenship, and time limit and security of residence (four residence and family rights). The two most restricted social rights relate to unemployment benefits and social housing. The right to free choice of employment is the only economic right that is commonly restricted. All other economic rights are granted in full under almost all programs analyzed. This is not a surprising result given that the labor laws and employment regulations in most (but not all) countries in the sample are generally applicable to all workers in the country and not just citizens.

A second key feature of migrant rights suggested by this analysis is that the rights granted to migrant workers under temporary migration programs are significantly more restricted than those granted under permanent migration programs. As shown in figure 4.6, however, there are important differences across different types of rights. Compared to permanent migration programs, TMPs place significantly more restrictions on most social rights (but not education and health), residence rights (not surprisingly), and family rights. Yet there are no statistically significant differences in terms of political and economic rights with the important exception of the right to free choice of employment, which on average is heavily restricted under TMPs, but rarely restricted under permanent programs.

The rights that migrant workers enjoy under labor immigration programs also vary across different regions of the world. As shown in figures 4.7 and 4.8, this is true for the entire group of 104 programs analyzed here and TMPs only. For example, considering all programs, labor immigration programs in GCC countries and Southeast Asia place significantly more restrictions on migrant rights than programs in Latin America, Europe, and North America. Interestingly, this ranking of regions by restrictions on migrant rights is relatively consistent across different groups of rights, and it holds regardless of whether social rights are measured in relative or absolute terms.[25] The only significant change when focusing on TMPs relates to North American programs, which impose an

[25] If we focus on social rights in absolute terms—that is, considering whether or not citizens enjoy the right—the main change compared to the data in figures 4.7 and 4.8 (which measure rights in terms of equal access) is that the difference between Latin America and Europe is significantly reduced.

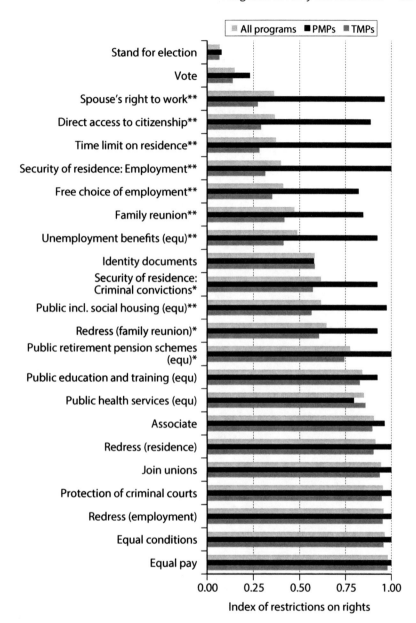

FIGURE 4.6. Restrictions of migrant rights, 2009

Notes: PMPs: permanent migration programs (i.e., programs granting permanent residence rights on arrival); TMPs: temporary migration programs; the index ranges from 0 (most restrictive) to 1 (least restrictive); * statistically significant difference between restrictions on right under PMPs and TMPs (p < 0.1); ** p < 0.05; "(equ)" after a social right means that the score measures the degree of equality of rights rather than providing an absolute measure that takes account of whether citizens enjoy the right. For more explanation of each of the rights in this figure, see appendix 3.

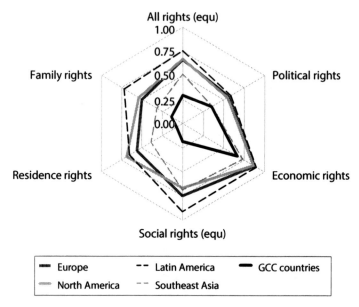

FIGURE 4.7. Restrictions of migrant rights by geographic region, all programs (N = 104), 2009

Notes: The migrant rights scores range from 0 (most restrictive) to 1 (least restrictive).

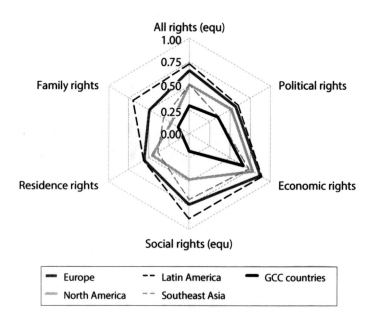

FIGURE 4.8. Restrictions of migrant rights by geographic region, TMPs only (N = 91), 2009

Notes: The migrant rights scores range from 0 (most restrictive) to 1 (least restrictive).

average level of rights restrictions that is closer to programs in Southeast Asia than in Europe.

Unlike openness to labor immigration, the overall rights index and most of the individual legal rights of migrant workers are not significantly different between programs in upper-high-income countries and other countries in the sample. Notable exceptions include the rights to family reunion, unemployment benefits, and health benefits, which are significantly more restricted under programs in upper-high-income countries.

Migrant Rights and Skills

There is a statistically significant, positive, and consistent relationship between most of the migrant rights granted and the skills targeted by the labor immigration programs included in the sample. Programs that target more (less) high-skilled workers also grant migrants more (fewer) rights. Although this finding is not unexpected, the consistency of the differentiation of most types of migrant rights by skill level is striking. As shown in figure 4.9 (all programs) and figure 4.10 (TMPs only), most types of rights increase with targeted skills except for political rights, which do not vary across programs targeting different skills. Regression analysis also confirms the significant negative relationship between TMPs and

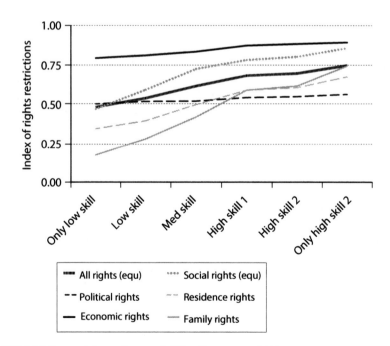

FIGURE 4.9. Migrant rights and targeted skills, all programs, 2009
Notes: 0 = most restrictive; 1 = least restrictive (no restrictions).

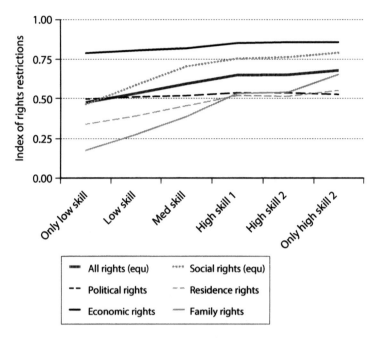

FIGURE 4.10. Migrant rights and targeted skills, TMPs, 2009
Notes: 0 = most restrictive; 1 = least restrictive (no restrictions).

rights as well as the importance of regional differences (see table A.6 in appendix 1).

Focusing on individual rights, table A.7 in appendix 1 shows that about two-thirds of the twenty-three rights analyzed are significantly and negatively correlated with the skill level targeted by the immigration program. This includes most social, residence, and family rights along with the right to free choice of employment.

Migrant Rights and Openness

The empirical analysis has confirmed that both openness to labor immigration and some of the rights of migrant workers are positively correlated with the targeted skill level of the migrants admitted under the program. The third hypothesis to be tested relates to the relationship between migrant rights and openness to labor immigration. As discussed in chapter 3, if some rights create net costs for the receiving country, there may be a negative relationship between openness and some of the rights of migrant workers.

As a first step, all 104 programs are included in the analysis. This yields no significant relationship (at the 10 percent level) between openness and aggregate rights at any skill level. If we limit the sample to programs in upper-high-income countries only (n = 71), however, a different and more

TABLE 4.2. Correlations between openness and rights (aggregate and subindexes), all programs in upper-high-income countries, 2009

			Openness			
Targeted skill level	only LS	LS	MS	HS1	HS2	only HS2
Observations	11	30	28	40	41	10
Aggregate rights (equ)			−0.341	−0.402	−0.349	
			(0.08)	(0.01)	(0.02)	
Aggregate rights (abs)			−0.324	−0.434	−0.375	
			(0.09)	(0.01)	(0.02)	
Political rights						
Economic rights			−0.372	−0.311		
			(0.05)	(0.05)		
Social rights (equ)			−0.320	−0.330	−0.339	
			(0.09)	(0.03)	(0.03)	
Social rights (abs)				−0.430	−0.410	
				(0.01)	(0.01)	
Residence rights			−0.327	−0.360	−0.300	
			(0.09)	(0.02)	(0.06)	
Family rights				−0.330	−0.310	
				(0.04)	(0.04)	

Note: p-values in parentheses; correlations with p > 0.10 are not shown. N = 71 programs.

nuanced picture emerges. Table 4.2 shows the correlation coefficients between openness and rights (aggregate and subindexes) for programs targeting different levels of skills. A number of statistically significant correlations emerge, and all of them have a negative sign, suggesting a trade-off between openness and rights. As shown by columns 3–5 of table 4.2, the overall rights index (aggregate rights) is negatively correlated with openness for programs targeting medium, high, and very high skills. There is no statistically significant correlation between aggregate rights and openness for programs targeting low skills only (column 1), low skills (column 2), and very high skills only (column 6). The sample sizes for programs targeting low skill only (11) and very high skills only (10) are small, thereby making it hard to detect statistically significant effects.

Table 4.2 also shows that economic, social, residence, and family rights are all negatively correlated with openness in programs targeting medium, high, and/or very high skills. Political rights (as a group) are the only type of rights analyzed here that are not correlated with openness at any skill level (recall that political rights were also not correlated with skills).

How sensitive are these results to the exclusion of permanent migration programs and GCC countries (see table A.8 in appendix 1)? Focusing on TMPs in upper-high-income countries changes the results in three ways. First, there is no more statistically significant relationship between openness and rights under programs targeting medium-skilled workers. Second, political rights are negatively correlated with openness for programs targeting skilled and/or highly skilled workers. Third, the trade-off between openness and family rights (as a group) disappears. Aggregate, economic, social, and residence rights remain negatively correlated with openness under programs targeting migrants with high or very high skills.

The exclusion of GCC countries from the sample of TMPs in high-income countries (n = 59) makes the statistically significant trade-offs between openness and economic rights as well as between openness and residence rights disappear. Excluding GCC countries from the sample of *all programs* (i.e., temporary and permanent) in upper-high-income countries (n = 69) leaves statistically significant trade-offs between openness and aggregate rights as well as between openness and social rights in programs for targeting high-skilled or very-high-skilled migrants.

So the relationship between openness and rights clearly varies across different types of rights. It also depends on the sample analyzed, and to some extent is sensitive to the exclusion of permanent migration programs and certain countries. Nevertheless, whatever the sample, the analysis suggests that there can be statistically significant trade-offs between openness and some types of rights for programs targeting medium, high, or very high skills.

The finding of a trade-off between openness and a specific group of rights (e.g., social rights) does not imply that all rights within that group are affected. Analysis of the relationship between openness and specific rights finds evidence of trade-offs involving some but not all rights (see tables A.9 and A.10 in appendix 1).

Considering all programs in upper-high-income countries, my analysis identifies trade-offs between openness and three social rights: access to retirement benefits, unemployment benefits, and access to public education (the latter effect becomes insignificant if GCC countries are excluded). These trade-offs are mostly observed in programs targeting medium, high, or very high skills.

The trade-off between openness and economic rights as a group is largely driven by an inverse relationship between openness and the right to join trade unions. The effect disappears when GCC countries are excluded. This is a plausible result as labor immigration programs in GCC countries are among the most open programs in the world (and analyzed here), but also among the relatively few programs that often restrict the right to join trade unions (if the right exists at all).

Among residence rights, the data for all programs in upper-high-income countries suggest a negative relationship—among programs targeting high skills—between openness and the extent to which security of residence is linked to employment and criminal convictions (the more open the program, the stronger the link). Yet these relationships disappear (i.e., they become statistically insignificant) when focusing on TMPs only, which is a plausible finding as TMPs have less variation in residence rights than a larger sample that includes permanent migration programs.

Turning to individual family rights, the data do not detect any statistically significant relationship between openness and the right to family reunion. The analysis, though, does suggest a trade-off between openness and the spouse's right to work under programs targeting high-skilled migrant workers.[26]

Finally, the right to associate and the right to equal protection in criminal courts are inversely related to openness under programs targeting high-skilled workers. Interestingly, this effect remains if we exclude the GCC countries. The right not to have identity documents confiscated is also negatively related to openness, primarily among programs targeting low-skilled workers.

Effects of the Economic Downturn

The analysis above relates to labor immigration policies in early 2009, less than a year after the onset of the global financial crisis and economic downturn that began in mid-2008. To explore the potential impacts of the downturn on labor immigration policies in a systematic way, the project collected data for all the openness and rights indicators for early 2008 as well as early 2009. Based on these indicators, relatively few and mostly only minor policy changes could be detected during this period. This result is in line with other studies suggesting that a year after the onset of the economic downturn, changes to labor immigration policies had been quite limited in most countries.[27] This does not, of course, preclude the possibility that some countries introduced more significant policy changes because of the continuing downturn after mid-2009—a period outside the scope of this study.

Because of the limited change in the indicators between 2008 and 2009, all the major results based on 2009 data also hold when using 2008 data.

Summary of Findings

This chapter has explored the main features of labor immigration programs in high- and middle-income countries. Based on an analysis of over

---

[26] Note that the way that the index has been measured means that there can be two explanations for the absence of the legal right to work for the spouse: first, the program allows family reunion, but does not grant a legal right to work for the migrant's spouse; second, the program does not allow family reunion at all. This means that the trade-off between openness and the spouse's right to work may capture some effect from denying the right to family reunion.

[27] See, for example, IOM 2010. There are instances of policy changes that did occur in late 2008 or early 2009. In early 2009, in its new points-based system, the United Kingdom raised the minimum education and earnings requirements necessary to gain admission under Tier 1 (for highly skilled migrant workers), mainly in response to the rising unemployment of British graduates. Spain reduced the annual quota of work permits issued under its Programa de Contigentes from over fifteen thousand in 2008 to less than a thousand in 2009, while at the same time eliminating the job seeker's permit that previously allowed some economic migrants to enter Spain without a prior job offer. Ireland reduced the number of jobs eligible for "green cards" (work permits for skilled migrants) and increased the minimum period that employers are required to advertise their job vacancies before applying for a work permit from four to eight weeks. Malaysia reduced the duration of some short-term work permits.

a hundred labor immigration programs in forty-six countries, the key findings include:

1. The great majority of labor immigration programs in high- and middle-income countries are TMPs (i.e., programs that do not grant permanent residence on arrival).
2. All the existing permanent immigration programs target high-skilled workers. Nevertheless, even among programs that target very-high-skilled workers, two-thirds are associated with temporary rather than permanent residence status on arrival.
3. Quotas and demand-side restrictions on labor immigration (i.e., requirements of employers in receiving countries) are much more common than supply-side restrictions (i.e., restrictions related to the characteristics of migrants). Supply-side restrictions are most common among permanent immigration programs (i.e., programs that grant permanent residence on arrival).
4. Some types of restriction on labor immigration tend to be used as complements (e.g., requirements of job offers and labor market tests), while others are used as substitutes (e.g., skills and language requirements, on the one hand, and job offer and labor market tests, on the other hand).
5. Programs in upper-high-income countries are, *as a group*, less open to labor immigration than those in the lower-income countries in the sample.
6. There are different modes of immigration control—different ways of restricting labor immigration—that vary across regions, welfare states (welfare regimes), and varieties of capitalism (i.e., liberal, coordinated, and mixed market economies). For example, programs in liberal economies and welfare states make less use of demand restrictions than programs in coordinated economies.
7. Openness to labor immigration is positively related to the skill level targeted by the labor immigration program—that is, programs that target high-skilled migrant workers place fewer restrictions on admission than those targeting lower-skilled migrants. This finding confirms the first of the three hypotheses developed in chapter 3.
8. There is considerable variation in the legal rights granted to migrant workers under different labor immigration programs, both within and across countries. Among the types of rights analyzed, the six most commonly restricted rights are the rights to stand for elections and vote (two political rights), the spouse's right to work, direct access to citizenship, and the time limit on and security of residence (four residence and family rights). The two most commonly restricted social rights relate to unemployment benefits and social housing. The right to free choice of

employment is the only economic right that was found to be commonly restricted in this analysis of legal rights.

9. Temporary labor immigration programs impose significantly greater restrictions on the rights of migrant workers than permanent migration programs.

10. The legal rights that migrant workers enjoy under labor immigration programs also vary across different regions of the world. Labor immigration programs in GCC countries and Southeast Asia place significantly more restrictions on migrant rights than programs in Latin America, Europe, and North America

11. There is a positive relationship between some of the rights granted to migrant workers and the skill level targeted by the immigration program—that is, programs that target higher-skilled migrants impose fewer restrictions on some rights than programs targeting lower-skilled migrants. This holds for many but not all rights. Political and most economic rights (except for the right to free choice of employment) are less sensitive to targeted skills than are social, residency, and family rights. This finding confirms the second hypothesis in chapter 3.

12. Among programs in upper-high-income countries in the sample, there is evidence of a trade-off (i.e., a negative relationship) between some specific rights (e.g., selected social rights) and openness to labor immigration under programs targeting specific skills (mainly medium and high skills in my analysis in this chapter). The number and type of rights affected by the trade-off depend on the types of programs included in the analysis (e.g., temporary and/or permanent) as well as the countries included (e.g., GCC included or excluded). Nevertheless, despite these important caveats, the analysis does strongly suggest that there can be a trade-off between openness and some specific rights. It is important to investigate this relationship further through in-depth case studies.

The empirical evidence presented in this chapter points to correlations, yet not necessarily causal relationships, between openness, skills, and rights. It is possible that causality is involved, but this issue has been outside the scope of this study.

It is also crucial to recall that the findings above refer to migrant rights and openness as defined in this chapter. In my analysis, the term *migrant rights* refers to the legal rights granted to migrant workers admitted under a labor immigration program, not to rights in practice and/or the rights of *all* migrant workers. I have defined *openness* as "policy openness" measured by the scale and strength of policy restrictions on the admission and employment of migrant workers, rather than by the actual number of migrant workers admitted under a labor immigration program. Expanding the analysis to cover rights in practice and account for the actual numbers of migrants admitted in an international comparative way are complex though critical areas for future research.

The results should be interpreted in light of these limitations along with the other caveats and assumptions made in this chapter. Importantly, many of the questions and issues analyzed in this chapter cannot be settled by quantitative analysis alone. The next chapter provides in-depth case studies to complement the quantitative analysis above, and better understand what drives the relationships between openness, skills, and rights identified in this chapter.

Chapter 5

Regulating the Admission and Rights of Migrant Workers
Policy Rationales in High-Income Countries

What explains the relationships between openness, skills, and rights in labor immigration policies? Why are labor immigration programs that target higher-skilled workers characterized by greater openness and more rights for migrants than programs that admit lower-skilled workers? What drives the trade-off between openness and some migrant rights? The theoretical framework and hypotheses developed in chapter 3 suggest that the answers may be found in national policymakers' assessments of the multifaceted benefits and costs of admitting migrants, and granting or denying specific rights to migrant workers of different skill levels.

This chapter explores the drivers of the relationships between openness, skills, and rights that we observe in practice. It discusses each of the three relationships—between openness and skills, rights and skills, and openness and rights—providing short case studies of where they occur, and why. It also looks at examples of policies that are not characterized by these relationships, and delves into the reasons for these exceptional cases.

The examples discussed below focus on high-income countries because this is where the quantitative analysis found the strongest evidence of relationships between openness, skills, and rights. The case studies cover a wide range of political systems, welfare states, labor markets, and geographic regions of the world. They thus include labor immigration policies that are made in different national policy spaces.

Given the focus on examining the drivers of key relationships, this chapter does not provide complete in-depth case studies of the evolution and determinants of specific policies in particular countries. Some of the examples go beyond the definitions adopted in the previous chapter and include groups that were excluded from the quantitative analysis (e.g., policies toward EU nationals).

The period under consideration in this chapter is 2011, and—unless indicated otherwise—*all discussions of policies here refer to policy developments in or before that year.*

Explaining Greater Openness to Higher-Skilled Migrant Workers

The theoretical framework developed in chapter 3 conceptualized labor immigration policy as a process that can be described as choice under constraints. National policymakers make decisions on how to regulate the admission and rights of migrant workers in order to achieve a set of national policy objectives (economic efficiency, distribution, national identity/cohesion, and national security/public order) given a series of constraints (including domestic and international legal constraints, a limited capacity to control immigration, and the prevailing welfare states and production systems). Within this approach, the discussion in chapter 3 suggested at least three reasons why high-income countries can be expected to be more open to admitting skilled rather than low-skilled migrant workers. First, skilled migrants can be expected to generate greater complementarities with the skills and capital of the existing population. Second, endogenous growth models emphasize the importance of human capital and knowledge for long-term economic growth. Third, the net fiscal impact of immigration—the difference between the taxes that migrants pay and the costs of public services and benefits that migrants consume—critically depends on migrants' earnings and thus skills. Everything else being equal, skilled migrants employed in high-skilled jobs will pay more taxes and be eligible for fewer welfare benefits than low-skilled migrants in low-skilled jobs. The empirical case studies below show that these considerations are indeed at the heart of explaining policy choices in practice.

Europe: United Kingdom, Ireland, and Germany

Most but not all high-income countries in Europe are more open to admitting skilled versus low-skilled migrant workers. Since the early 2000s, the United Kingdom's labor immigration policy for admitting migrant workers from outside the European Union has been among the most explicitly skills-based admission policies in Europe. The Labor government that came into power in 1997 drastically increased skilled labor immigration from outside the European Union (the number of work permits issued to non-EU workers increased from less than forty thousand in 1999 to almost eighty thousand in 2006 when it was announced that the policy would be reformed), but channels for low-skilled immigration from outside the European Union remained small and strictly limited.[1] In 2008, the United Kingdom introduced a points-based system, which comprised three tiers for migrant workers.[2] The UK Home Office (2006) described and differentiated these tiers based on skills along with the perceived economic contribution to Britain:

- Tier 1: Highly skilled individuals to contribute to growth and productivity

[1] MAC 2009.
[2] The United Kingdom's points-based system has a total of five tiers. Tiers 1–3 are for migrant workers, Tier 4 is for students, and Tier 5 is for a range of temporary migrants, some of whom are given permission to work part-time.

- Tier 2: Skilled workers with a job offer to fill gaps in the UK labor force
- Tier 3: Limited numbers of low-skilled workers needed to fill specific temporary labor shortages

The United Kingdom's points-based system was designed to make policy simpler and more "rational." As Tony Blair, the prime minister at the time of the development of the new policy, put it: "The challenge for the Government is to maintain public confidence in the system by agreeing [to] immigration where it is in the country's interest and preventing it where it is not."[3] The increased selection and regulation of admission by skill, with higher-skilled migrants facing fewer restrictions than lower-skilled migrants, was at the heart of the new policy. Aimed at "attracting the best and brightest" in the global race for talent, Tier 1 does not require a job offer in the United Kingdom. In contrast, Tier 2 has been much more restricted with admission requiring a firm job offer, successful resident labor market test (unless the job is on a shortage occupation list recommend by the Migration Advisory Committee [MAC], a panel of independent labor market experts), and minimum threshold of points awarded based on prospective earnings and education (the education criterion was dropped in 2011). Tier 3 for low-skilled migrants from outside the European Union has never been opened, partly because of the availability of workers from other EU countries, especially since the European Union's enlargement in May 2004, leading to a large inflow of eastern European workers.

After coming into power in May 2010, the Conservative–Liberal Democrat Coalition government essentially maintained the structure of the points-based system, but introduced an overall limit (cap) on the annual number of non-EU workers admitted to the United Kingdom. The cap on non-EU labor immigration is part of a larger policy goal of reducing the overall net migration from over two hundred thousand to "tens of thousands" by 2015. Other important policy changes included the raising of the skills threshold for Tier 2, resulting in an even greater selectivity by skill. Tier 1 for highly skilled workers was reduced from fifteen thousand to only one thousand annually, because of a concern about abuse rather than a policy of not wanting to attract highly skilled workers. As Damian Green, the immigration minister, explained at the launch of the limit: "We are sending out a clear message—the UK remains open for business and we want those who have the most to offer to come and settle here." So the emphasis on attracting the most highly skilled remains, albeit based on a much stricter definition of what the current government calls "exceptional talent."

Similar to the United Kingdom, Ireland operates a dual labor immigration system, with separate programs for highly skilled workers (the "green card permits" programs) and medium-skilled workers (a work permit

---

[3] Home Office 2005, 5.

program). In contrast to work permits, green cards do not require a labor market test and are open to a much larger number of occupations (all occupations, in fact, if the pay is over sixty thousand euros). A report commissioned by the Irish government to inform the development of its new immigration policies concluded that this dual system was justified by the greater benefits of skilled compared to low-skilled immigration, and—as in the case of the United Kingdom—the availability of other EU workers to fill low-skilled vacancies. The report suggested that "the interaction of the revised work permits system and the permanent Green Card system is intended to facilitate required high skilled migration, whilst encouraging employers to source low skills from within the EEA."[4]

Germany has recently begun to transform its labor immigration policies from focusing on limiting numbers (a policy in place since the end of the guest worker era in the early 1970s) to a more managed system of actively attracting and selecting migrants based on their skills. The Immigration Act of 2005 initiated a set of policy developments that aimed at opening up the country to skilled and especially highly skilled migrant workers, while essentially maintaining (with minor exceptions) the ban on recruiting low-skilled migrants from outside the European Union. Two key themes in German policy debates since 2005 have been the need to operate attractive and open policies for highly skilled workers in order to be competitive in the global race for talent, and the goal of linking skilled labor immigration to the needs of the economy while protecting German workers in the labor market. The Immigration Act explicitly states that the admission of migrant workers must be "geared to the requirements of the German economy, according due consideration to the situation on the labor market and the need to combat unemployment effectively."[5] Based on research suggesting future shortages of skilled and highly skilled workers, the government developed an action plan in 2008 that reinforced the policy focus on admitting skilled and especially highly skilled migrants.[6]

Canada and Australia

Canada and Australia are examples of countries where greater openness to skilled migrants has been explicitly related to the use of immigration as a nation-building tool. Throughout the twentieth century, Canada's immigration policy has been driven by the core objectives of expanding the population, boosting the economy, and developing society. Selective admission of migrants that would further these goals has been at the heart of Canada's policies.[7] Since the 1960s, when racial admission criteria were eliminated, Canada has operated a points-based system for regulating permanent labor immigration that aims to ensure that only skilled

---

[4] Expert Groups of Future Skills Needs 2005, 133.
[5] Cited in Parusel and Schneider 2010, 20.
[6] Bundesministerium des Inneren 2008.
[7] See Reitz 2004; Wayland 1997.

and highly skilled migrants are admitted as permanent residents. The focus on skilled labor immigration has been justified by the expectation and explicit argument that more highly skilled migrants would have a better chance of finding well-paid employment and therefore making a bigger contribution to the Canadian economy. As Jeffrey Reitz (2004, 106) explains, "A positive social, cultural, and political impact was also expected." The emphasis on selecting skilled migrants is also thought to be a key reason for Canada's more positive public attitudes to immigration compared to other countries.[8]

The evolution of Australian immigration policy followed a similar trajectory. In 1972, following the end of the White Australia Policy, Australia introduced a points-based system that selected migrants based on a range of economic criteria including skills. Applicants with more skills and education receive more points, and hence have a higher chance of admission.[9] In the 1990s, the points-based system was reformed in response to the relatively high unemployment rates of migrants. Australia's response was to sharpen admissions criteria—by, for instance, strengthening English-language requirements and premigration qualifications screening—in order to "select for success" among skilled applicants.[10]

Canada and Australia have in recent years introduced TMPs for both high- and low-skilled migrant workers to complement their policies for admitting skilled migrants on a permanent basis. Despite the noticeable shift toward more TMPs to fill labor shortages, including for low-skilled migrants, the focus of both countries' labor immigration policies is still on admitting skilled migrants.[11]

East Asia: Singapore, Hong Kong, and the Republic of Korea

Greater openness to skilled migrant workers is also a key characteristic of labor immigration policies in many Southeast Asian countries, some of which admit large numbers of low-skilled migrants. For example, Singapore has long admitted migrant workers of all skill levels as part of its overall population and development policies, which are increasingly framed in the context of the prospect of an aging and shrinking population. Selectivity based on skills has always been an important dimension of Singapore's labor immigration policies. There is a clear distinction between attracting and integrating "foreign talent" and regulating the temporary employment of lower-skilled "foreign workers," and this has been reflected in a set of highly differentiated policies for different types of migrant workers. In response to increasing concerns about the sustainability of the increase in immigration over time, the Singaporean government has recently committed to efforts aimed at stabilizing the share of

[8] Reitz 2010.
[9] See Castles and Vasta 2004.
[10] Hawthorne 2005.
[11] See Hawthorne 2011; CIC 2010a.

migrants in the workforce at about a third (where it is now). Given that objective, there is now even greater emphasis on more openness for skilled and highly skilled migrants. Singapore's deputy prime minister has recently stressed "*good quality* foreign workers and immigration still remain important to our sustained economic growth and are vital to address our serious longer-term population challenges."[12] An influential report by the Economic Strategies Committee (2010) recommended that better management of Singapore's dependence on migrant workers would require raising the quality of foreign workers by more actively encouraging employers to hire and retain skilled workers.

Hong Kong operates a tightly regulated labor immigration program for low-skilled migrant workers and a more open program for attracting high-skilled migrant labor. The "imported workers program" for temporary low-skilled workers requires a firm job offer and labor market test. In contrast, the "quality migrant admission" scheme, aimed at attracting highly skilled migrants "to enhance Hong Kong's economic competitiveness in the globalized market," does not require a job offer and can lead to settlement.[13]

The recent labor immigration policies of the Republic of Korea, which began to import migrant workers in the early 1990s, is also explicit about the policy preference for skilled over low-skilled workers. Throughout the 1990s, the policy approach was to admit skilled migrants as workers and low-skilled migrants as trainees.[14] The trainee program attracted heavy criticism because of concerns about its treatment of trainees and the rise in the number of irregular migrants. In the early and mid-2000s, the Korean government reformed its overall labor immigration policies. This included replacing the trainee program with a formal employment permits program for low-skilled workers under which all migrants are treated as workers. At the same time, a number of policy initiatives such as the introduction of multiple entry visas encouraged the immigration of skilled migrant workers, especially but not only for jobs related to information technologies.[15] The new labor immigration policy that emerged in the 2000s was clearly differentiated by skill, with greater policy openness toward skilled migrant workers.[16] The employment permits system for low-skilled workers, for example, is limited by a quota, while high-skilled policies do not include numerical limits.

The greater policy openness to skilled workers is clearly reflected in the Korean Ministry of Justice's (2008, 2) first five-year plan for immigration policy (2008–12), which "consolidates the fragmented policies of ministries into a comprehensive and long-term policy." In the context of low birthrates and a rapidly aging population, the plan explains that the "past government's Immigration Policy was control-oriented and focused on

---

[12] Singapore Government Press Center 2010, 7; emphasis added.
[13] Immigration Department of Hong Kong, http://www.immd.gov.hk/ehtml/home.htm.
[14] Yoo 2005.
[15] Ibid.
[16] Kim 2009.

protecting national security. The strategic value of foreign workers was not recognized. The policy line on foreign workers needs to be changed into a 'strategic opening' to tap into the talent and capital of the rest of the world" (ibid., 9). It mentioned four immigration policy objectives: "enhancing national competitiveness with a proactive openness policy," "pursuing quality social integration," "enforcing immigration laws," and "protecting human rights of foreigners" (ibid., 14). In its discussion of the first of these four objectives, the plan makes it clear that "the areas and ways of opening up are decided on the basis of national interest through cost-benefit analysis" (ibid., 11). The benefits are described as resolving labor shortages and economic contribution with the expansion of knowledge and information. The list of costs mentioned in the plan includes "social problems from a larger low-income class" along with "conflicts between local nationals and immigrants" (ibid.). As is the case in other countries, there is a strong view that Korea "needs an aggressive program for attracting highly skilled foreigners from overseas to help with technological innovation, develop value-added industries and lead global management" (ibid., 16).

While the great majority of high-income countries are more open to admitting skilled than low-skilled migrant workers, there are exceptions such as the GCC countries and Sweden. It is important to discuss the reasons for these cases. I also look at the case of the United States, a longstanding country of labor immigration with an ambiguous mix of policies toward admitting skilled and low-skilled migrant workers.

The GCC Exception

The clearest exception to the general pattern of more open labor immigration policies to skilled workers is the oil-rich GCC states (Bahrain, Kuwait, Oman, Qatar, Saudi Arabia, and the United Arab Emirates). The GCC countries operate one common type of labor immigration program—the *kafala* (sponsorship) system—for admitting migrants of all skill levels.

Since the dramatic increase in oil prices and revenues in 1973–74 and 1979, the GCC countries have admitted large numbers of what are meant to be strictly temporary migrant workers. After forty years of mass labor migration to the Gulf, migrants now constitute large majorities of the workforce in almost all GCC countries (ranging from just over 50 percent in Saudi Arabia to 95 percent in Qatar), especially in the private sector, where relatively few citizens work. The private sectors of Kuwait, Qatar, and the United Arab Emirates are effectively 100 percent staffed by migrant workers. In other GCC countries, the share of nationals in total private sector employment is higher, but it is still less than 50 percent (with Oman at 48 percent, Saudi Arabia at 46 percent, and Bahrain at 30 percent). Although doing all kinds of work, the majority of temporary migrants in GCC countries are employed in low- and medium-skilled jobs in sectors such as construction, wholesale, and retail and domestic services.[17]

The kafala system for regulating labor immigration in GCC countries is essentially an employer-led, large-scale guest worker program that is open to admitting migrant workers, but at the same time restrictive in terms of the rights granted to migrants after admission. The key feature of the kafala system is that to obtain a temporary work permit, migrant workers require a *kafeel* (sponsor), who is given considerable control over the migrant. In addition to providing employment, the kafeel essentially takes financial and legal responsibility for the migrant after admission. Each GCC citizen has the right to become a kafeel and recruit migrant workers (including domestic workers). The temporary work permit requires the migrant to work for their sponsor only. Although illegal in many GCC countries, in practice it is common for sponsors to hold migrant workers' passports and for migrant workers from different countries to be paid different wages for the same work. Mechanisms for filing grievances are limited. Migrants' rights in the labor market and access to welfare benefits are significantly restricted. In most GCC countries, there is no opportunity to obtain permanent residence. Family reunion is possible although often quite restricted.[18] Since migrants are primarily considered as strictly temporary workers, integration policies and projects are largely absent.[19] In many ways, the kafala system is the world's largest and strictest TMP.

The reasons for the kafala system's openness to admitting migrant workers of all skill levels stem from its fundamental policy objectives. The unique design and policies of the kafala system reflect three types of objectives that are broadly shared among all GCC countries: provide a cheap workforce for the low-cost provision of goods and services (including domestic services) in the private sector, and in some countries, help fill vacancies in the public sector; regulate the perceived impact of immigration on the culture and perceived national identity of the population; and address security concerns potentially arising from the fact that large numbers of migrants often outnumber citizens. Overall, the kafala system has helped develop and maintain a unique economic and social model whose primary aim is to distribute the oil wealth (which in most GCC countries accounts for the great majority of government revenues) among citizens. A key policy of this model has been to effectively guarantee citizens a job in the public sector, where employment conditions as well as benefits are much higher and working hours are much shorter than in the private sector.[20] Large-scale temporary labor immigration has thus been used to staff and develop the private sector, and do most or in some countries all the low-skilled work—including the provision of domestic services—

---

[17] Baldwin-Edwards 2011.
[18] See, for example, Shah 2005.
[19] Fargues 2006.
[20] See also Winckler 2010.

which citizens do not wish to do, and under the prevailing economic and social model, are not meant to do.

Another reason for the absence of differentiated policies toward migrant workers with different skills lies in the control and discretion granted to kafeels in determining employment conditions. The restrictions that employers impose on low-skilled migrant workers are in practice significantly greater than those experienced by more highly skilled workers. So although the kafala system constitutes one policy for admitting and employing migrants of all skills, in actuality it is flexible in facilitating differential treatment based on skills and nationality.

Given its unique design, the kafala system has had predictable consequences for the labor markets of GCC countries, giving rise in recent years to debates about policy reform, and in a few countries, some first concrete steps toward changes. By design rather than accident, the labor markets of GCC countries have become extremely segmented.[21] There is a fundamental divide between public and private sector jobs as well as high levels of segmentation within the private sector. It is not uncommon for different jobs to be dominated by workers of different nationalities and for workers from different countries to be paid different wages. Given the easy access to migrant workers, productivity levels in the private sector are often low. In the context of highly segmented markets, the employment of citizens in the public sector has become a major policy issue, mainly because the public sectors of many GCC countries are unable to continue to absorb all citizens and employ them in a productive way. Citizens' employment rates are low (less than 30 percent in most GCC countries), and their unemployment rates are relatively high.[22]

Most GCC countries have responded to the growing un- and underemployment of citizens with "localization policies" aimed at increasing the share of nationals while reducing the reliance on migrant workers in specific medium- and high-skilled occupations, but not in low-skilled occupations, where it appears to be accepted that jobs will continue to be done by migrants. Although different countries have experimented with different types of localization policies (including banning foreigners from particular occupations or imposing quotas that require a minimum share of nationals in employment in specific occupations), the general consensus is that they have so far had limited success, with the possible exception of Saudi Arabia.[23]

There is a growing recognition in most GCC countries that the success of localization policies is closely linked to reform of the kafala system and labor markets. While wages and conditions in the public sector remain significantly higher than in the private sector, and while private sector employers continue to exercise a high degree of control over migrants, it

---

[21] See Awad 2009.

[22] The unemployment rates are estimated at between 10 and 15 percent in 2008 for Saudi Arabia and the United Arab Emirates; see Baldwin-Edwards 2011.

[23] See the discussion in ibid.

is difficult to see how the share of nationals in the private sector will increase in any significant way. A few countries have taken initial steps to reform the kafala system—for instance, Bahrain modified its policies in 2009, now allowing migrants to change employers, and Kuwait announced in 2010 that it would end the kafala system sometime in 2011—but most GCC countries are currently continuing with their long-standing policies without any major reforms.

A Swedish Policy Experiment

With a population of just under nine million, Sweden is the biggest Scandinavian country with one of the world's most advanced social welfare states. It combines a liberal market economy with an extensive state-run welfare state. Most comparative analyses of social policy consider Sweden the archetypal "social democratic welfare state" that aims at universal coverage along with rights and benefit equality.[24] Most wages and employment conditions are determined by collective bargaining, and with most workers in unions, employment conditions generally adhere to industry-wide standards.

With the exception of the period 1949–71 when Sweden experienced labor immigration from Finland and southern Europe, migration to Sweden has—until recently—primarily consisted of asylum seekers and family members. Over the past thirty years, labor immigration from outside the common Nordic labor market has been minimal. In 2007, Sweden issued fewer than five thousand first-time work permits and migration for work accounted for less than 2 percent of permanent-type migration to Sweden.[25] The low numbers of labor migrants from outside the European Union were due to a restrictive labor immigration policy in place in Sweden since the early 1970s. Concerned about "social dumping," adverse impacts on collectively agreed-on wages and employment conditions, and maintaining the Swedish "economic model" more generally, Sweden's powerful trade unions have—until recently—played an important role in opposing and restricting non-EU labor immigration. The key requirement was that the Swedish Public Employment Service, in close consultation with the unions, needed to approve any application for a work permit for a non-EU national. Reflecting the highly restrictive policy at the time, in the early 2000s the home page of the Swedish Migration Board's website made it clear that "obtaining a Swedish work permit is no easy matter."[26]

In late 2008, Sweden's new center-right coalition government, in power since 2006, introduced significant reforms of its labor immigration policy for workers from outside the European Union. Contrary to previous gov-

---

[24] See especially Esping-Andersen 1990.
[25] OECD 2011.
[26] Bucken-Knapp 2009.

ernments, the new one considered a more open and flexible labor immigration policy of vital interest to the Swedish labor market and economy. The new rules made it much easier for employers to recruit workers from outside the European Union. The long-standing requirement for approval from the Public Employment Service was eliminated, thus weakening the influence of trade unions over migrant worker admissions. Meant to be "employer driven," the new labor immigration policy has four requirements for the admission of non-EU workers: an offer of employment; advertisement of the job in Sweden and the European Union for ten days; the terms of employment must be equivalent to those provided by a Swedish collective agreement, or customary terms and conditions for the occupation or industry (which constitutes the continuation of a long-standing requirement of labor immigration policy in Sweden); and the relevant union must be given the opportunity to state an opinion on the terms of employment. The temporary work permits are valid for two years and renewable. After forty-eight months, the employee will be eligible for a permanent residence permit.

Importantly, in contrast to most other high-income European countries (including other social democratic welfare states such as Denmark), Sweden's new labor immigration policy does not distinguish between workers with different skills. In the words of Tobias Billstrom (2008), Sweden's immigration minister since 2006,

> Sweden has now decided to reopen the path for those wishing to come to work. In stark contrast to immigration regulations in many other countries, Swedish policy is not based on quotas or aimed exclusively at highly qualified labor. Instead one of the main features of the reform is that it focuses on the employers' demand for labor, high- as well as low-skilled workers. In doing so, Sweden is setting an example, which hopefully others in Europe will follow.

Following the introduction of the new policy, the number of work permits issued to employees from outside the European Union increased dramatically to over fourteen thousand in both 2009 and 2010—double the figure in 2008, and triple the number for 2007. The numbers would likely have been larger were it not for the economic downturn. Permits were issued to a wide range of low-, medium-, and high-skilled occupations. In 2010, the top three occupations were agricultural, fishery, and related workers (most of whom were seasonal workers), data specialists, and restaurant and hotel workers. These three occupations accounted for almost 60 percent of all permits issued in 2010. The top three countries whose nationals received new work permits were Thailand, India, and China (together accounting for half the total that year, according to Swedish Migration Board statistics).

Although Sweden's policy appears open and employer driven on paper, in practice the strict requirement that all workers be employed at collectively agreed-on wages is likely to act as a strong deterrent for employing large numbers of migrants. Unlike employers in countries with flexible labor markets such as the United Kingdom, Swedish employers cannot easily use non-EU labor immigration to lower wages or moderate wage growth, which reduces the danger of adversely affecting the employment conditions of low-skilled (and other) Swedish workers. This—together with the Swedish language—is likely to help explain why the number of work permits issued to non-EU nationals remains relatively low despite significant policy reforms.

So in addition to the continuing role of the "Swedish model" in limiting labor immigration, how can we understand and explain why Sweden's new admission policy does not distinguish between workers of different skills? The answer arguably lies with the relatively recent introduction of the policy and its somewhat-experimental nature. As the effects of the new policy become clearer over time, it is possible that there will be further policy changes toward greater skill selectivity in admission, although there are no concrete signs yet that such a policy change is in the cards. As the immigration minister's speeches over the past few years make clear, Sweden is acutely aware that its "employers know best" policies are out of step with policies in most other high-income countries. In Billstrom's (2009) words a few months after the launch of the new policy: "Our new reform has been in place for six months. Time will tell how successful our reform will be. It is, however, my strong belief that managing high- and lesser-skilled migration through a general framework has a lot of benefits for all stakeholders involved."

It remains to be seen how sustainable the policy proves to be over time. Mindful of potential debates about policy changes, Sweden had commissioned the OECD to evaluate its new policy. In its first evaluation report, the OECD (2011, 131) notes that "the faith in employers appears to be largely justified until now, although some vulnerability in the system could be addressed, especially in monitoring workplaces not covered by collective bargaining, and marginal businesses." More stringent requirements were announced in January 2012 for employers in mainly low-skilled industries and new businesses applying for work permits to hire non-EU workers. These new requirements primarily relate to the employer's ability to guarantee the applicant's salary and other conditions set out as part of the work permit application process.[27]

The US Ambiguity

Almost all migrant workers legally admitted to the United States are admitted as "nonimmigrants" on temporary visas.[28] Over the past few years,

---

[27] See http://www.migrationsverket.se/info/166_en.html (accessed January 26, 2012).

[28] The United States makes a strict distinction between immigrants (legal permanent residents with green cards) admitted for permanent settlement and nonimmigrants admitted on temporary visas (some

the United States issued about three hundred thousand visas to temporary workers per year.[29] The key temporary labor immigration programs in the United States are: O-1 for highly skilled persons "with extraordinary ability in the sciences, arts, education, business or athletics"; H1-B for skilled migrants for employment in "specialty occupations"; H2-A for temporary workers in agriculture; and H2-B for temporary workers in other (nonagricultural) sectors. The O-1 program is demanding in terms of the skills required and has admitted less than ten thousand people annually over the past five years. The H1-B program is capped at eighty-five thousand regular visas per year, but there are a number of categories exempted from the cap including migrants who work for colleges and universities. Among the low-skilled programs, H2-B is capped at sixty-six thousand and H2-A is not capped.[30]

There is disagreement and ambiguity about whether US policies are more open to admitting skilled or low-skilled migrant workers. Some US migration scholars have argued that US policies are more restrictive to skilled than toward low-skilled migrant workers.[31] Others disagree, and have contended that the admission procedures for H1-B are easier than for H2-A or H2-B.[32] My own assessment in chapter 4 concerning the openness of these policies finds that based on the openness indicators used, the H2-A and H2-B programs (i.e., the two low-skilled programs) are slightly more open than the H1-B program and significantly less open than the O-1 program. In terms of the numbers of workers admitted, over the past few years migrants admitted on H1-B or O-1 visas (just under seven hundred thousand during 2006–10) have exceeded those admitted on H2-A or H2-B visas (just under six hundred thousand during the same period), but the difference is not large.[33]

Given that the United States is a long-standing country of labor immigration, why are US policies ambiguous and not characterized by a clear, strong policy preference for admitting skilled migrant workers? The main explanation, I argue, lies with the long-term political gridlock over immigration in US politics, which has made it impossible to introduce and implement significant reforms to migrant admission policies over the past two to three decades. While immigration is a difficult and highly

---

of which may eventually lead to permanent immigrant status). Over the past five years, the United States has admitted about half a million new migrants as permanent immigrants (green card holders) every year.

A key feature of US immigration policy is that the great majority (about three quarters) of permanent immigrants admitted every year are admitted on the basis of having close family relationships with a US citizen or green card holder. This has been the case since 1965 when the "family preference" policy was first introduced. Immigrants admitted for employment purposes accounted for less than 3 percent (12,000 people) of all new immigrant admissions in 2010 (excluding family members).

[29] US Department of State 2011, table: "Classes of Nonimmigrants Visas Issued." The figures exclude visas for intracompany transfers, which numbered seventy-five thousand in 2010.

[30] Ibid. H2-A issued fifty-six thousand visas in 2009.

[31] Orrenius and Zavodny 2011; Crook 2011.

[32] Personal conversation with Phillip Martin, one of the most prominent labor migration experts in the United States.

[33] US Department of State 2011, table: "Classes of Nonimmigrants Visas Issued."

contested political issue in most countries, the United States appears almost unique among high-income countries in its long-term political paralysis on the matter.[34]

There is consensus that the current system is "broken."[35] Moreover, there is consensus that any comprehensive immigration reform must deal with three major areas: border and workplace controls, the eleven million irregular migrants in the United States, and the admission of new migrant workers or "future flows."[36] There has been no shortage of proposals about how to reform admission policies, with many of them calling for a more skills-based labor immigration policy that prioritizes the admission of skilled over low-skilled migrant workers. For example, in addition to proposals by prominent economists,[37] the bipartisan US Commission for Immigration Reform—known as the Jordan Commission—maintained in the late 1990s that "immigration can support the national interest by bringing to the United States individuals whose skills would benefit our society. It also can help US businesses compete in the global economy. This national interest in the competitiveness of business must be balanced by an equally compelling national interest in developing a US workforce that has the skills necessary to compete in the global economy."[38] The commission recommended that US immigration policy should eliminate the admission of unskilled migrant workers, and focus on the admission of skilled and highly skilled workers. Although none of these recommendations have been implemented yet, it seems clear that the current absence of more skills-based admission policies (i.e., policies that are more open to skilled than low-skilled migrant workers) is a result of political gridlock and institutional complexities rather than an active choice made by the US government to further the US national interest.

Why More Rights for Skilled Migrant Workers?

Why do labor immigration programs that target higher-skilled workers grant migrants more rights than programs targeting lower-skilled workers? The theoretical discussion in chapter 3 suggested two potential reasons: the recognition that to be successful in the global race for talent, countries need to offer highly skilled migrants a comprehensive set of rights; and the perceived costs and benefits of rights, which vary across different rights as well as between migrants with different skills.

---

[34] Compare the discussion about the United States as a "weak state" in, for example, Jacobs and King 2009.

[35] See, for example, Bush 2007; Obama 2011; Crook 2011.

[36] See Martin and Ruhs 2011.

[37] See, for example, Borjas 1999; Hanson 2005.

[38] US Commission for Immigration Reform 1995, executive summary.

Attracting Highly Skilled Migrants in the "Global Race for Talent"

With few exceptions, high-income countries recognize that there is global competition for highly skilled migrant workers, and are explicit in their policy debates and policy decisions about the need to offer a comprehensive set of rights to help attract highly qualified migrant labor.

For example, Canada and Australia, two countries that have long been successful in attracting skilled migrants, both grant qualified migrants permanent residence and the associated comprehensive set of rights immediately on arrival. Since the early 2000s, the United Kingdom has had labor immigration programs in place that aim to attract highly qualified migrants by offering them the opportunity to migrate to the United Kingdom without a job offer and with the right to apply for permanent residence after a certain number of years of residence (five years as of 2011). In 2006, Ireland introduced a green card for highly skilled workers that allows immediate family reunification and provides a path to permanent residence after two years. France introduced skill- and talent-based permits as part of its immigration policy reform in 2006. The permits are aimed at attracting highly skilled migrants, and in contrast to France's policies toward lower-skilled migrants, grant family members a "private and family life residence permit" that allows spouses to work.

Since the early 2000s, Germany's changing policies toward highly skilled migrants illustrate the importance and growing recognition of the central role of rights in attracting global talent. Germany introduced its own version of a green card program in 2000 to attract highly skilled information technology workers from outside the European Union. It offered a five-year work permit with no clear path to permanent residence and attracted fewer than the twenty thousand visas offered.[39] Following the failure of the green card system to attract significant numbers of highly skilled migrants, Germany passed a new immigration law in 2004 that provides for unlimited residence permits for highly qualified migrants and their families.

The European Commission's (2007a) recently introduced blue card for highly skilled non-EU workers grants migrants a series of socioeconomic rights and favorable conditions for family reunification. It was specifically designed to attract highly skilled migrants to the European Union. Jose Manuel Barroso, the European Commission president at the time, explained at the launch of the debate about the blue card that "with today's proposal for an EU Blue Card we send a clear signal: highly skilled migrants are welcome in the EU!"[40]

The use of rights to attract highly skilled migrants is also an explicit part of the labor immigration programs of countries in East Asia (includ-

---

[39] For a discussion of this, see Kolb 2005.
[40] European Commission 2007a.

ing some of those that impose significant restrictions on the rights of most migrants in their countries). For example, as part of Korea's new strategy for attracting highly skilled migrants, "professionals will be classified by expertise and profession, and special benefits such as permanent residence status will be granted to those who are strategically valuable in industries," and "dual nationality can be achieved in practice by loosening foreign nationality renunciation requirements for people with exceptional talent in social, economic and cultural areas."[41]

Singapore markets itself as the "talent capital." Access to permanent residence and citizenship are considered key aspects of attracting and maintaining highly skilled workers. In light of the rising number of awards of permanent residence status to migrants in recent years (the number of Singapore permanent residents almost doubled between 2000 and 2010), the Singaporean government has come under pressure to make a greater distinction between the rights of citizens and permanent residents.[42] Although the government has responded by making some distinctions more explicit (e.g., in education and health care), it has also emphasized that access to rights is crucial to attracting global talent. According to Singapore's deputy prime minister, "We must also avoid making ourselves so unattractive that suitable foreigners are deterred from sinking roots and becoming part of Singapore. There is a global competition for good people with talent and if we make Singapore an inhospitable place, we will lose out."[43]

The Costs and Benefits of Rights

A main theme of this book is that migrant rights play an important instrumental role in shaping the effects of international migration for the receiving country as well as for migrants and their countries of origin. In other words, restricting and granting rights has consequences that include multifaceted costs and benefits for the national interest, however perceived. As discussed in chapter 3, these consequences can be expected to vary across rights and, critically, between migrants with different skill levels. For some rights, countries can be expected to perceive equality of rights with citizens as best for the national interest. For some other rights, restrictions may be perceived as beneficial with an important distinction based on migrants' skills. Granting some rights to higher-skilled migrants can be perceived to be less costly and/or more beneficial than granting the same rights to lower-skilled migrants.

Governments are rarely explicit about the rationales for restricting or granting rights to migrant workers. If clear reasons are given, they often explain equality of rights rather than why specific rights are restricted.

[41] Ministry of Justice 2008, 18–19.

[42] See http://www.singstat.gov.sg/stats/themes/people/popnindicators.pdf (accessed September 25, 2011).

[43] Singapore Government Press Center 2010.

Nevertheless, as shown in the examples below, there is considerable evidence that considerations about the costs and benefits of rights play a powerful role in high-income countries' decisions on what rights to grant to migrant workers with different skills. In line with the theoretical discussion and framework developed in chapter 3, while concerns about the costs of social rights are common among most countries, concerns about the costs of other rights vary across different countries in line with those countries' different policy spaces for restricting different types of migrant rights.

The United Kingdom's labor immigration policies in recent years have been explicitly based on a cost-benefit approach, so the rationales for specific policies, including to some extent policies toward migrant rights, are more explicit and more openly discussed than in many other countries. As part of its reform of labor immigration policies for non-EU nationals in 2011, for instance, the UK government ran public consultations on migrant workers' rights to settlement and family reunion. Although not spelled out explicitly, it is clear from both consultation papers that the governments' policy proposals were influenced by a perceived difference between the costs and benefits of rights for low- and high-skilled workers. The settlement consultation made it apparent that the impact on public services and welfare is a key reason for restricting the right to settlement to "those who make the biggest contribution to the United Kingdom"—that is, high-skilled and high-paid workers rather than low-skilled workers:

> A recent Ipsos Mori poll found that 75% of Britons believe that immigration is currently a problem and 44% thought it was a problem because of abuse of or burdens on public services. The Department for Communities and Local Government Citizenship Survey found that 78% of people thought that the number of immigrants coming to Britain should be reduced. Reserving settlement and the rights it affords, including the ability to access welfare benefits and apply for British citizenship, to those migrants who make the biggest contribution to the UK would help address these concerns.[44]

In their unique study of the rationales for restricting selected rights of migrants in the United Kingdom, Sarah Spencer and Jason Pobjoy (2011, 37) conclude that cost is the "primary consideration in denying family reunion rights to those who come to the United Kingdom to undertake low-skilled work." This assessment is confirmed by the UK government's family consultation, which underscored that the financial ability to support a spouse or partner is a key reason for granting or denying family reunification:

> It is obvious that British citizens and those settled here should be able to marry or enter into a civil partnership with whomever they

[44] UK Home Office 2011a, 11.

choose. But if they want to establish their family life in the UK, rather than overseas, then their spouse or partner must have a genuine attachment to the UK, be able to speak English, and integrate into our society, and they must not be a burden on the taxpayer. Families should be able to manage their own lives. If a British citizen or a person settled here cannot support their foreign spouse or partner, then they cannot expect the taxpayer to do it for them.[45]

In Canada, the reasons for granting low-skilled migrants more restricted rights than higher-skilled migrants are most explicit in discussion of why the Canadian government does not ratify the CMW. Although a traditional settlement country that grants many migrants permanent residence on admission, Canada has in recent years greatly expanded its TMPs, especially for low- and medium-skilled migrant workers. The aim of these TMPs is to fill labor shortages in specific sectors and occupations—an objective that requires a restriction of migrants' right to free choice of employment. A recent analysis of the obstacles to ratification of the CMW in Canada concluded that the Canadian government is "not really interested in accepting the responsibility, through ratification of the Convention, of giving more rights than currently given for low-skilled workers under a temporary work permit, in particular the 'right freely to choose their remunerated activity.' "[46]

As is the case in most high-income countries, Germany does not ratify the CMW partly because it fears that the rights granted by the convention to irregular migrants would legitimize and encourage more irregular migration as well as create pressures for the social security system.[47] The German government's answer to a parliamentary question in 2009 about the reasons for Germany's refusal to sign the CMW specifically mentioned the right to education as an example of a right that would have to be granted to migrants and their children without legal residence status.[48] The great majority of irregular migrants are low skilled. Although Germany's (and many other high-income countries') arguments against rights for irregular migrants are typically framed in terms of the importance of "discouraging irregular migration" and "maintaining the rule of law," it is clear that the perceived financial costs of granting social and other rights to low-skilled migrants are an important obstacle.

Financial costs also played a critical role in the introduction of restrictions on migrants' access to welfare benefits in the United States. The Personal Responsibility and Work Opportunity Reconciliation Act (PRWORA) of 1996 brought about major changes in access to means-tested public benefits. Although it was a general reform bill that affected access to welfare for everybody, it also included a specific section that codified (for the first time) migrants' access to welfare benefits. Until

[45] UK Home Office 2011b, foreword.
[46] Piché, Depatie-Pelletier, and Epale 2009, 205–6.
[47] See, for example, Hillman and Koppenfels 2009.
[48] See http://dipbt.bundestag.de/dip21/btd/16/116/1611603.pdf (accessed September 25, 2011).

1996, legal migrants generally enjoyed the same access to welfare rights as US citizens. The PRWORA introduced a key distinction between citizens and noncitizens. Migrants who had acquired US citizenship continued to be eligible, while the eligibility of immigrants without US citizenship was differentially restricted. The PRWORA divided legal immigrants without US citizenship into two groups: qualified and unqualified aliens. Qualified aliens included legal permanent residents and refugees (and some other smaller groups). Unqualified aliens included unauthorized migrants (many of who were unaffected by the law as they had never been eligible for welfare benefits), temporary legal migrants (especially workers and students), and applicants for permanent legal status already residing in the United States.

There is a large literature on the determinants and effects of the PRWORA in general and its immigrant provisions in particular. In understanding the rationale for the immigrant provisions of the PRWORA, it is important to emphasize the economic and political context. There was a perception that the United States had become a welfare magnet for low-skilled migrants and that public spending on immigrant welfare was increasing. The immigrant provisions in the PRWORA highlight that "self-sufficiency has been a basic principle of United States immigration policies," thus suggesting a policy intent of reducing access to benefits for newcomers and other migrants until they have proven themselves by obtaining US citizenship or at least permanent residence. Michael Fix and Jeffrey Passel (2002) describe the goals of the PRWORA's immigrant provisions as threefold: reduce immigration for the purpose of benefits rather than work; shift responsibility for the financial support of migrants away from employers to new migrants' sponsors; and reduce welfare spending on migrants.

The PRWORA did not explicitly use skills as a criterion for deciding migrant workers' access to welfare benefits. By including temporary migrant workers under unqualified aliens and permanent migrant workers under qualified aliens, however, the law in practice removed access to benefits for all low-skilled migrant workers (admitted under TMPs with no possibility of acquiring permanent residence) and maintained access for skilled migrant workers after they have acquired permanent residence. So although the explicit lines of division were centered on citizenship and permanent residence, the result of the PRWORA was that migrant workers' access to welfare benefits was clearly differentiated by skill. Arguably, this was part of the policy intent given that higher-skilled migrants are less likely to make demands on the welfare state than lower-skilled ones.

In some countries, the reasons for granting skilled migrants more rights than low-skilled migrants go beyond economic considerations, and include perceived impacts on issues related to perceptions of national identity and nation building. Policy decisions about whether to grant or deny the rights to permanent residence and citizenship are in some countries partially based on the migrants' skill level because of the perception that skilled migrants are more suitable candidates for inclusion in the citizenry or permanent resident population than low-skilled migrants. For example, Singapore's policies of offering rights to permanent residence and access to citizenship to skilled (but not low-skilled) migrants is not only driven by an economic need to attract skilled migrant workers (as discussed above) but also by a belief that skilled migrants are more likely to fit in and enhance Singapore's self-image of a multiracial global city as well as "meeting point for enterprise, talent, culture and ideas."[49] According to Singapore's deputy prime minister in a speech to Parliament in 2011:

> But not all foreigners who come here to work are allowed to sink roots. We allow only those of good quality and who share our core values to become PRs or citizens. We take into account not just factors such as the applicant's economic contributions, qualifications and age, but also whether he can integrate well into our society, and his commitment to sinking roots.[50]

Japan and Korea—countries that still see themselves as culturally homogeneous—have recently begun to adopt more proactive approaches to regulating labor immigration along with migrant workers' acquisition of permanent residence and citizenship. In both countries, the rights to permanent residence and citizenship are reserved for skilled and highly skilled workers, partly because they are considered more desirable members of a relatively homogeneous community.[51]

The examples above show that governments in different countries are making a distinction between the rights of low- and high-skilled migrant workers based on the perception that granting some rights (especially social rights, the right to free choice of employment, long-term residence rights, and access to citizenship) to low-skilled migrant workers creates greater economic and other net costs (or smaller net benefits) to the national interest of the receiving country than granting the same rights to higher-skilled migrant workers. Although the discussion was not comprehensive and there are some exceptions to this approach—for instance, Sweden grants equal social, residence, and family reunion rights to migrants regardless of their skill level—a large number of high-income countries are clearly making a distinction between the rights of low- and high-skilled migrants based on a perception of differential impacts.

It is important to stress that while some specific rights are restricted by skill level because of their perceived impacts, many other rights are granted to both low- and high-skilled migrants precisely because of their perceived economic and other net benefits for the receiving country. For

---

[49] Economic Strategies Committee 2010, 9.

[50] Singapore Government Public Service Division 2011.

[51] See http://www.immi-moj.go.jp/english/tetuduki/zairyuu/eizyuu.html (accessed November 4, 2011).

example, to facilitate a level playing field in the labor market and avoid adverse impacts on resident workers, governments in a wide range of high-income countries grant migrant workers equal or near-equal rights in the labor market (with the significant exception of the right to free choice of employment, which as noted above, is typically more restricted for low-skilled migrants). The protection of resident workers was one of the main rationales behind the European Commission's (2007b) recent proposal for a common set of rights for third-country workers in EU countries. The argument for equal rights to avoid unfair competition with resident workers is typically made most strongly in countries with strong labor market regulation such as Sweden. Equal rights to protect domestic workers is a consideration that used to apply less in GCC countries, where labor markets are completely segmented (and migrants therefore are not competing with citizens), but as mentioned earlier in this chapter, the equality of employment rights is increasingly recognized as a crucial step toward encouraging the greater employment of citizens in the private sector.

Explaining Trade-Offs between Openness and Rights

This section briefly discusses examples of tensions between openness to labor immigration and specific migrant rights. The aim is to understand the drivers of the trade-off. Meant to be illustrative rather than comprehensive case studies, the examples involve a range of different rights and different countries. The examples show that these trade-offs are not accidents or unintended consequences of policy decisions. Instead, they are the result of policymakers' choices, which are heavily influenced by the perceived costs and benefits of specific rights.

US Policy Changes in the 1990s: "Immigration Yes, Welfare No"

In 1994, President William Clinton formally appointed the bipartisan US Commission on Immigration Reform, which was created by the 1990 Immigration Act with the mandate to "review and evaluate the implementation and impact of immigration policy."[52] The commission published three separate reports with a series of recommendations for reforming US policies toward illegal and legal immigration as well as naturalization. The commission was appointed at a time when concerns about the effects of immigration—both legal and illegal—had become an increasingly important focal point of the US immigration debate. In November 1994, for instance, Californian voters approved Proposition 187, intended to deny illegally resident aliens and their children welfare ben-

---

[52] US Commission on Immigration Reform 1995, 2.

efits, nonemergency health care and public education.[53] The fiscal effects of immigration were thus an important theme of the commission's work.

In its 1994 and 1995 reports, the commission urged Congress to maintain immigrant access to social safety net programs but reduce the admission of immigrants, both permanent and temporary, including the elimination of most low-skilled labor immigration. The commission argued that while illegally resident migrants should not be eligible for public benefits except in emergency cases, legal immigrants should not be denied access to public benefits programs. As Susan Martin, the commission's executive director, explained in 1996, this recommendation was based on the idea that US policy should strike a "grand bargain" on legal immigration: reduce the growth in immigration, but maintain legal immigrants' full access to the social safety net.[54] Congress rejected this recommendation. It instead kept immigrant numbers high, and in 1996 reduced migrant access to benefits through the PRWORA discussed above. This policy outcome broadly reflected the "immigrants yes, welfare no" approach advocated by, among others, Michigan senator Spencer Abraham, a key opponent of restrictive admission policies. In his analysis of the US politics of immigration control in the 1990s, Daniel Tichenor (2002, 284) described this policy as

> a triumph for free market expansionists, who allied with pro-immigration liberals to sustain unprecedented legal admissions with anti-immigrant conservatives to trim alien substantive and procedural rights. The outcomes of 1996 suggested that large-scale immigration would flow into the United States uninterrupted for the foreseeable future, and that those who arrived would enjoy fewer membership rights until they acquired citizenship.

Opening Labor Markets and Restricting Welfare Rights for East European Workers in the United Kingdom and Ireland

A similar trade-off between openness to immigration and migrants' access to welfare rights could be observed when the United Kingdom and Ireland were in the minority of existing EU member states (together with Sweden) that opened their labor markets to workers from the new EU member states in May 2004.

Ten new countries joined the European Union in May 2004, including eight eastern European countries, also known as the A-8 (the Czech Republic, Estonia, Hungary, Latvia, Lithuania, Poland, Slovakia, and Slovenia), plus Cyprus and Malta. Under the accession agreements negotiated between the old and new EU member states, existing members could restrict A-8 workers' legal access to the labor market for a transitional pe-

---

[53] Proposition 187 was eventually declared unconstitutional by a federal court; see Tichenor 2002.

[54] See http://migration.ucdavis.edu/rs/printfriendly.php?id=110_0_3_0 (accessed November 20, 2011).

riod lasting up to seven years.[55] The transitional arrangements were mainly due to fears in existing EU member states that EU enlargement would trigger the movement of large numbers of eastern European workers to the older member states. Many member states were explicit in their concerns about the impacts on their labor markets and welfare states.

Both the United Kingdom and Ireland decided in 2003 that they would grant eastern European workers immediate unrestricted access to their labor markets. The decisions were made in the context of sustained economic growth in both countries. In the United Kingdom, EU enlargement was seen as an opportunity to meet employer demand for better access to low-skilled migrant workers—access that had been significantly restricted under the prevailing work permit system for non-EU workers.

In early 2004, the United Kingdom and, to a lesser degree, Ireland experienced heated public debates about the likely consequences of the decision to open labor markets to EU workers. Beyond the labor market effects, there was growing concern about the potential danger of a large number of low-skilled eastern European migrants moving for welfare benefits rather than work. In the face of significant political pressure as well as hostile public opinion and media coverage, the UK government decided to stick with its initial decision of opening labor markets to A-8 workers in May 2004, but to impose restrictions on migrants' access to unemployment and welfare benefits. This involved changing the law regulating access to means-tested benefits. The Social Security (Habitual Residence) Amendment Regulations 2004 introduced the new requirement that a claimant must be able to demonstrate a "right to reside" in the United Kingdom in addition to the habitual residency test.[56] Under the new rules, A-8 workers could only have a right to reside (for benefit purposes) if they were working and registered under the Workers Registration Scheme (a special scheme set up for A-8 workers), or if they had already completed a twelve-month period of continuous, registered employment. During the first twelve months of registered employment, A-8 workers were entitled to child and in-work benefits such as tax credits. Those with a low income could also be entitled to housing and council tax benefits, and become eligible for assistance under the homelessness legislation. A-8 workers who were not registered did not have access to any of these benefits. After twelve months of registration, A-8 workers gained the right to be treated the same way as other EU nationals.[57] Although Ireland did not operate a formal registration scheme, it imposed similar restrictions on eastern Europeans' access to welfare benefits.

---

[55] The possibility of temporary restrictions applied to EU nationals exercising their right to freedom of movement as *workers*, but with a few exceptions, not to the freedom to provide services. See the discussion in Engblom 2011.

[56] See the Social Security (Habitual Residence) Amendment Regulations 2004, http://www.opsi.gov .uk/si/si2004/20041232.htm. The term *habitual residence* is not defined in legislation. The most important factors for habitual residence are generally the length, continuity, and general nature of actual residence rather than intention.

[57] In line with the EU accession treaties, the United Kingdom's Worker Registration Scheme was lifted in May 2011.

The United Kingdom and Ireland's policies toward eastern Europeans thus involved a clear trade-off between facilitating openness while at the same time temporarily restricting social rights. Since May 2004, more than a million new eastern Europeans came to work in the United Kingdom for some time (many have left again), and more than two hundred thousand arrived in Ireland.

Insisting on Rights as a Way of Restricting A-8 Immigration in Sweden

Sweden was the third of the EU-15 member states to grant A-8 migrants immediate unrestricted access to the labor market in May 2004. In contrast to the United Kingdom and Ireland—and in line with the Swedish social democratic model—Sweden offered eastern European migrants unrestricted access to the social welfare system based on the assumption that Sweden's labor market structures and regulations would ensure that any eastern European workers employed in Sweden would be given the exactly same wages as well as employment rights as Swedish workers. Most wages and benefits in Sweden are set via collective bargaining, and with most workers in unions, wages and benefits adhere to industry-wide standards. At the time of EU enlargement in 2004, Sweden introduced a number of measures aimed at preventing immigration from undermining the effectiveness of existing labor market regulations and collective bargaining structures.[58]

The requirement of equal rights in Sweden's highly regulated labor market effectively meant that from the employers' view, migrant workers were as expensive as Swedish ones. To a considerable degree, this explains why Sweden has experienced relatively low levels of labor immigration of A-8 nationals (just over fifty thousand new EU workers during 2005–11).[59] The insistence on equal labor rights in practice made Sweden's policies toward admitting and employing A-8 workers much more restrictive than suggested by its formal decision to grant A-8 nationals immediate access to the labor market.

The experience of the Latvian construction company Laval un Partnery (L&P) is a good illustration of the trade-off between the openness to and rights of migrant workers admitted to Sweden. In May 2004, L&P, acting through a subsidiary (L&P Baltic Bygg AB, registered in Sweden) posted workers from Latvia to work on refurbishing a school near Stockholm. Swedish unions protested because L&P agreed to pay its Latvian workers in Sweden the equivalent of twelve euros an hour. Swedish unions demanded that L&P pay the equivalent of sixteen euros, the wage negotiated for Stockholm-area construction workers, and blocked access

---

[58] Tamas and Munz 2006.
[59] See http://www.migrationsverket.se/info/790_en.html (accessed November 13, 2011).

to the work site when L&P refused. L&P sued to stop the union's action, lost in Swedish labor courts in late 2004, and subsequently left Stockholm.[60] After L&P brought the case back to the Swedish labor court, however, the ruling was eventually sent to the European Court of Justice. In December 2007, the court ruled—to the great shock of Swedish trade unions—that the unions' blockade and sympathy actions to combat social dumping against L&P represented a restriction on the freedom to provide services. The ruling effectively restricted Swedish trade unions' right to take industrial action to force foreign companies into signing collective agreements when operating in Sweden. In light of this ruling by the European Court of Justice, the Swedish Labor Court ruled in 2009 that Swedish trade unions have to pay punitive damages of about fifty-five thousand euros to L&P.[61]

New TMPs for Low-Skilled Migrant Workers in Canada and Australia

Canada and Australia are traditional settlement countries that used to grant most migrant workers permanent residence on arrival. In both countries, temporary labor immigration programs have been on the rise over the past twenty years. Until relatively recently, the great majority of temporary migrant workers admitted to Canada and Australia were skilled. Since the early 2000s, though, Canada, and to a lesser extent also Australia, have created and expanded low-skilled labor immigration schemes. In both countries, the increased openness to low-skilled labor migrants was accompanied by considerable restrictions of some migrant rights, indicating a trade-off between openness and rights.

Canada first introduced TMPs in 1973. The number of temporary labor migrants significantly increased over time, especially during the 1990s and 2000s. The number of initial entries of temporary foreign workers doubled from 32,000 in 1990 to 63,000 in 2000, and rose to 85,000 in 2010.[62] The increase in temporary migrant workers was accompanied by a marked shift in their composition by skill. In 2001, just under two-thirds of temporary foreign workers (total entries) were skilled or highly skilled (i.e., in managerial, professional, or skilled and technical occupations). By 2010, this share had dropped to just over 40 percent.[63] The rapid increase in low-skilled migrant admissions was driven by the expansion of the Live-in Caregiver Program for domestic workers (total entries doubled from just over 4,000 in 2000 to over 8,000 in 2010) and the Seasonal Agricultural Workers Program (SAWP) (24,000 entries in 2010 compared to 18,500 in 2001) as well as the introduction and ex-

---

[60] See the discussion in Woolfson and Sommers 2006; Tamas and Munz 2006.
[61] Ronnmar 2010.
[62] CIC 2010b, 52–53.
[63] Ibid., 78.

pansion of a new low-skilled pilot program (the total entries under this new program increased from 2,000 in 2002 to 15,000 in 2010).[64]

The introduction of the low-skilled pilot program in the early 2000s was a response to employer demand for low-skilled migrant workers in a range of sectors beyond domestic services and agriculture (covered by the Live-in Caregiver Program and SAWP, respectively). The oil and gas, construction, and later also hospitality and tourism sectors in particular were demanding access to low-skilled migrant workers.[65]

A key feature of the low-skilled pilot program is that it involves a number of restrictions of migrant rights that are significantly greater than those imposed on skilled temporary migrants and permanent migrants. In contrast to skilled temporary migrants, most low-skilled temporary migrants do not have opportunities to acquire permanent residence in Canada.[66]

A recent study by Statistics Canada described the rights of low-skilled temporary foreign workers as follows:

> Other non-permanent residents, usually those coming from abroad specifically to work, receive closed permits that may restrict the type of job they hold, the location where they work and/or the specific employer for whom they work. . . .

> Non-permanent residents admitted to Canada under the Temporary Worker Program can bring spouses and close family members with them provided they can demonstrate the financial capacity to support these family members while in Canada. However, non-permanent residents working in low-wage jobs may not be able to meet this requirement. . . .

> Non-permanent residents who have permits to work in Canada have the same labor rights and access to health and social programs as other workers in Canada. However, labour standards, employee rights and access to social programs differ according to the province or territory of work and most social programs and many jurisdictions require a minimum period of work or residence in order to qualify for benefits. As a result, some non-permanent residents may not qualify for unemployment, health and social assistance benefits.[67]

The federal government's view that many employment and social rights of temporary migrant workers fall under the jurisdiction of provinces has been subject of controversy. Judy Fudge and Fiona MacPhail

[64] See ibid., 62.

[65] Fudge and MacPhail 2009.

[66] Introduced in 2008, the Canadian Experience Class program regulates the transfer of skilled temporary migrants to permanent residence, but low-skilled migrants are excluded from this program.

[67] Thomas 2010.

(2009) point out that temporary workers are not eligible for provincial social assistance in any of Canada's provinces.

It is clear that Canada's opening to a growing number of low-skilled migrant workers has been accompanied by a series of restrictions on the employment, social, residency, and family reunion rights of migrants admitted under the low-skilled pilot program.

A similar story can be told about the recent introduction of a new low-skilled TMP in Australia. Like Canada, Australia has over the past two decades shifted from its long-standing policy of granting most migrants settlement on arrival and gradually increased the number of migrants admitted on a temporary basis. Until recently, temporary labor immigration programs admitted only skilled migrants, who were then given the opportunity to transfer to permanent residence after a certain number of years. Introduced in 1996, the 457 visa program admits skilled migrants on a temporary basis. The stock of 457 visa holders doubled from 60,000 in 2005 to just under 120,000 in 2010.[68]

Until recently, migrants who enter Australia as working holidaymakers or students largely met the employer demand for low-skilled migrant workers. Both groups are not admitted for the primary purpose of employment, but students and working holidaymakers are legally allowed to work part-time during their stay in Australia. Most of the employed students and working holidaymakers do low-skilled work. The number of working holidaymakers (stock) increased from 70,000 in 2005 to 114,000 in 2010, and the number of international students rose from 150,000 in 2005 to just under 300,000 in 2010. Peter Mares (2011) argues that the increase in working holidaymakers was used instrumentally to help fill low-skilled labor shortages.

In 2008, the Australian government introduced its first formal labor immigration program for low-skilled migrant workers. Partly based on a similar scheme introduced in New Zealand in 1997, Australia's new Pacific Seasonal Workers pilot scheme initially provided twenty-five hundred visas for workers from four Pacific Islands countries (Kiribati, Papua New Guinea, Tonga, and Vanuatu) to work in the Australian horticulture industry for up to seven months a year. Workers are recruited by "labor hire companies" selected by the Australian government, rather than by individual growers. In September 2011, the scheme was expanded to include more countries (Nauru, Samoa, Solomon Islands, and Tuvalu) and more sectors (the tourism sector for workers from East Timor).

Australia's Pacific Seasonal Workers scheme includes various safeguards aimed at protecting migrant workers from exploitation.[69] The scheme, however, does restrict some migrant rights in important ways—and it is apparent that these restrictions were instrumental to the government's decision to open up immigration to low-skilled migrant workers.

---

[68] Mares 2011.
[69] See the discussion in MacDermott and Opeskin 2010.

The workers admitted under Australia's low-skilled temporary immigration program do not have the right to free choice of employment; workers are tied to labor hiring companies (rather than individual employers) and cannot leave the sector to take up employment in other sectors. There is also no right to transfer to permanent residence and no right to bring family members. The Australian government made it clear that these restrictions were instrumental to ensuring that workers will return home after their temporary work permits expire: "The fact that they will not be able to bring dependents, such as family members, over to Australia provides further incentive to return home after their period of work has concluded. In addition, a 'no further stay' condition will be imposed on all visas issued under the pilot."[70]

The World Bank was influential in encouraging the introduction of low-skilled labor schemes in both New Zealand and Australia. In analyzing the pros and cons of such schemes, the World Bank (2006, 136) explicitly recognized the trade-off between increased openness and restricting some migrant rights.

Trade-Offs between Openness and Rights in the GCC Countries

GCC countries are the most extreme examples of countries operating high openness–low rights labor immigration policies. As discussed earlier in this chapter, the GCC countries combine an employer-led admissions policy that brings in large numbers of temporary migrant workers with significant restrictions on migrants' economic, social, and residency rights as well as, in some cases, their civil and political rights. Some GCC countries have recently initiated efforts to grant migrants better protection.[71] Yet there are numerous reports documenting the denial and abuses of migrant workers' rights—in some cases involving basic human rights violations—especially (but not exclusively) of construction and domestic workers.[72]

What drives the trade-off between openness and rights in the GCC countries? The primary factor is economic. As described above, the kafala system has provided a cheap migrant workforce that has facilitated the low-cost provision of goods and services in the private sector along with the development as well as maintenance of a generous welfare state whose benefits and services are largely limited to citizens. This system has clearly been of significant short-term economic benefit to GCC citizens as employers in the private and domestic service sectors, and as consumers of public services and products/services supplied by the private sector. As discussed above, though, it has also created long-term economic problems including especially increasing un- and underemployment of citizens who can no longer be absorbed in the public sector. There is an increasing

[70] Australian government 2009.
[71] Baldwin-Edwards 2005.
[72] See, for example, Human Rights Watch 2004.

recognition that localization policies—that is, policies aimed at reducing the reliance on migrant workers in certain occupations—can only be successful if migrants are given greater economic and social rights, thus reducing the gap between the rights of—and costs associated with employing—citizens and migrants. For example, according to Mohammed Ebrahim Dito (2008, 8), "Extending social protection to include migrant workers will contribute toward levelling the gap between national and migrant workers." In other words, granting more rights to migrants can be expected to result in lower openness and numbers.

Especially in countries with small populations and where citizens constitute a small minority of the population, a second reason for restricting migrant workers' rights in GCC countries stems from concerns about maintaining the national identity and national security. The policy of strictly temporary migration with few or no opportunities to acquire permanent residence and citizenship has aimed at maintaining the identities of the citizen population without having to actively pursue policies of reducing the number of migrant workers.

Singapore

Singapore's policies for admitting low-skilled migrant workers are another example where a relatively high degree of openness to admitting migrants has been combined with considerable restrictions of migrants' rights, including some of their civil and political rights (as is the case in some of the GCC countries). Singapore's work permit system for low-skilled migrant workers (excluding Malaysians, who are treated differently) requires employers to ensure that their migrant workers have "acceptable accommodation," and take responsibility for (and bear the costs of) migrants' "upkeep and maintenance in Singapore," including any costs of medical treatment. It also includes the following conditions "to be complied with by the foreign employee":

- The foreign employee shall undergo a medical examination by a Singapore registered doctor as and when directed by the Controller. If the foreign employee is certified medically unfit, the Work Permit of the foreign employee shall be revoked.
- The foreign employee shall not go through any form of marriage or apply to marry under any law, religion, custom or usage with a Singapore Citizen or Permanent Resident in or outside Singapore, without the prior approval of the Controller, while the foreign employee holds a Work Permit, and also after the foreign employee's Work Permit has expired or has been cancelled or revoked.
- If the foreign employee is a female foreign employee, the foreign employee shall not become pregnant or deliver any child in Singapore during and after the validity period of her Work Permit,

unless she is a Work Permit holder who is already married to a Singapore Citizen or Permanent Resident with the approval of the Controller.
• The foreign employee shall not be involved in any illegal, immoral or undesirable activities, including breaking up families in Singapore.[73]

As is the case in the GCC countries, the rationales for these restrictions clearly go beyond economic considerations. They are aimed at tightly controlling the perceived impacts of a large number of low-skilled migrant workers in relation to the social fabric and cohesion of the country. As discussed by Brenda Yeoh (2006) Singapore's overall social objectives and model of nation building involve a dual approach to regulating labor immigration. High-skilled migrants need to be attracted and included as potential future citizens in Singapore's society. In contrast, low-skilled migrants are admitted in large numbers, but they are intentionally excluded from becoming full and equal members of society. As Yeoh (ibid., 23) argues, low-skilled migrants' "structural position within multicultural Singapore society is carefully excluded. Unskilled contract workers are admitted into the physical terrain of the nation state primarily as temporary workers, rather than as social and political subjects." It is thus clear that Singapore's openness to low-skilled labor immigration is perceived to be dependent on restrictions of migrants' rights.

The National Interest: Expected Impacts Drive Labor Immigration Policies

The case study evidence explored in this chapter shows that policy decisions on how to regulate the admission and rights of migrant workers in high-income countries are firmly based on assessments of the consequences of admitting migrants and granting/restricting rights for the national interests of migrant-receiving countries. With few exceptions, high-income countries are more open and grant more rights to high- than low-skilled migrant workers because they consider these policies to be in their best national interests. Given the disagreements about the multifaceted consequences of immigration for the receiving country, it is no surprise that the impact assessments of specific admission policies and rights restrictions are commonly contested as well as continuously evolving in different countries. While the degree to which policy decisions are informed by evidence about real effects versus perceptions of likely effects varies across countries, it is clear that assessments of the impact on the national interest are a core factor explaining the policy choices observed in high-income countries in practice.

---

[73] Ministry of Manpower 2011.

The policy examples discussed in this chapter also provide further evidence for the existence of trade-offs between openness and some specific rights in labor immigration policies, especially for admitting low- and medium-skilled migrant workers. While the rights restricted as part of this policy trade-off vary across countries to some extent (access to social rights are most commonly restricted), it is apparent that the trade-offs are based on a calculus made by national policymakers about the associated costs and benefits for the receiving country. As the next chapter will show, these trade-offs are in important ways sustained by global inequalities, which affect the interests and choices of migrants along with their countries of origin.

Chapter 6

Labor Emigration and Rights Abroad
The Perspectives of Migrants and Their Countries of Origin

Labor immigration policies are "made" in migrant-receiving countries, but they have important consequences for migrants and their countries of origin. This chapter looks at two interrelated questions. How do high-income countries' restrictions of labor immigration and migrant rights affect the interests of migrants along with their countries of origin? How have migrants and sending countries engaged with these restrictions in practice?

These questions are of central importance to this book's analysis because the interests of migrants and sending countries can play a crucial role in supporting, sustaining, or undermining particular labor immigration policies in high-income countries. Understanding how migrants and sending countries are affected by—and respond to—particular restrictions on migration and rights is also critical to any ethical/normative evaluation of particular policy regimes. The ethics of labor immigration policy will be examined in the next chapter.

The discussion in this chapter is divided into two parts. The first explores how emigration and rights impact on migrant workers, and how migrants have in practice responded to the labor immigration policy regimes they face. The second half of the chapter concentrates on the effects for sending countries, and reviews selected examples of major sending countries' engagements with high-income countries' policies on the admission and rights of migrant workers.

Migrants: Emigration, Rights, and Human Development

Any study of the impacts of particular labor immigration policies on migrant workers requires a conceptual framework for capturing the multifaceted and multidimensional interests of and outcomes for migrants. The discussion below employs a human development approach.

Building largely on the capability approach developed by Amartya Sen (1980, 1999), human development can be defined as a process of "enlarging people's choices and enhancing *human capabilities* (the range of things people can be and do) and *freedoms*, enabling them to: live a long and healthy life, have access to knowledge and a decent standard of living, and participate in the life of their community and decisions affecting their lives."[1] A capability approach is "people centered" in the sense that it focuses on agency and choice.

[1] UNDP 2010.

The concept of human development is inherently multidimensional.[2] Theoretical discussions and empirical applications of the human development approach have identified various different dimensions of well-being and development. Martha Nussbaum (2000), for example, lists central human functional capabilities related to life, bodily health, bodily integrity, senses, imagination, thought, emotions, practical reason, affiliation, other species, play, and control over one's environment. A World Bank study of how poor people perceive and experience poverty distinguished between material, bodily, social, psychological, and emotional well-being; security; and freedom of choice and action.[3] Although Sen has not followed others in trying to identify a definite list of universally applicable capabilities, he has highlighted the importance of basic capabilities such as "the ability to move about," "the ability to meet one's nutritional requirements," "the wherewithal to be clothed and sheltered," and "the power to participate in the social life of the community."[4]

The idea of human development shares a common motivation with human rights. Both approaches "reflect a fundamental commitment to promoting the freedom, well-being and dignity of individuals in all societies."[5] Despite their basic compatibility, however, it is crucial not to conflate human development with human rights. As Sen points out, for instance, although it can support many human rights, the capability approach cannot adequately take account of "process freedoms" such as the right to due process in legal proceedings.[6]

A key feature of the human development approach, which is particularly significant in the context of this book, is its explicit recognition of the possibility of conflicts and trade-offs between different dimensions of development (or between different components of capability), and the consequent need to engage in public debate and reasoning about how to value and prioritize competing capabilities and objectives. The emphasis on the need for valuation and public debate of the potential trade-offs distinguishes the human development approach from both traditional economic approaches that focus on income as the only measure of well-being and human rights approaches that consider rights indivisible, and therefore find it more difficult to engage in debate about trade-offs and priorities.[7] As the UNDP's (2000, 23) report on human rights and human development argues:

Human rights advocates have often asserted the indivisibility and importance of all human rights. This claim makes sense if it is un-

[2] See the discussion in Alkire 2002.
[3] Narayan et al. 2000.
[4] Sen 1980, 218.
[5] UNDP 2000, 19.
[6] Sen 2005.
[7] The concept of "decent work," which has informed the recent work of the ILO, is similar in its emphasis on the multidimensionality and potential trade-offs between different dimensions of labor market outcomes for individuals. For example, Martin Godfrey's (2003) discussion of decent work explicitly mentions the potential trade-offs between the quantity and quality of work available.

derstood as denying that there is a hierarchy of different kinds of rights (economic, civil, cultural, political and social). But it cannot be denied that scarcity of resources and institutional constraints often require us to prioritize concern for securing different rights for the purposes of policy choice. Human development analysis helps us to see these choices in explicit and direct terms.

In the context of the effects of migration and migrant rights, the human development approach is particularly useful because it can distinguish— and requires critical exploration of the potential conflicts—between the capability to move and work abroad, and the capabilities while working and living abroad.

Access: The Capability to Move and Work Abroad

Because international labor migration is much more restricted than international trade and capitals flows, the wage differences across countries are much larger than differences in commodity prices and interest rates.[8] Richard Freeman (2006) estimates that the wages of workers in high-income countries typically exceed those of workers in similar jobs in low-income countries by four to twelve times. A more recent study finds that the ratio of wages earned by workers in the Unites States to wages earned by "identical" workers (with the same country of birth, years of schooling, age, sex, and rural/urban residence) abroad ranges from 15.45 (for workers born in Yemen) to 1.99 (workers born in the Dominican Republic), with a median ratio of 4.11.[9] These international wage differences mean that migrants can significantly raise their productivity and make large financial gains from employment abroad. The wage differences and relative income gains are largest for low-skilled workers whose international movement is the most restricted.

Emigration is of course not without financial costs for migrants. These costs can include visas fees, travel expenses, payments to recruitment agencies, and in some cases a range of illegal payments such as bribes and other "kickbacks" demanded by different actors involved in facilitating the migration process. These costs vary considerably across different migration corridors and also across different types of migrants within the same corridor. Legal migration costs can be multiples of monthly earnings abroad.[10] If illegal payments are involved, the cost of migrating can in some cases exceed annual earnings.

Although there clearly are some migrants for whom, at least in the short run, the costs outweigh the benefits, the majority of labor migrants can be expected to reap large financial benefits from employment in higher-income countries even after all the costs have been deducted. The

[8] Rodrik 2002.
[9] Clemens, Montenegro, and Pritchett 2009.
[10] UNDP 2009.

increase in migrants' net earnings (i.e., after deducting any costs) can also lead to increases in the economic welfare of migrants' families, either directly if they are with the migrant in the host country or indirectly through remittances. There is debate about the impacts of remittances on sending countries as a whole, but there is no doubt that remittances can play a powerful role in improving the living standards and human development of migrants' families.

While there are relatively few systematic empirical analyses of the impacts of emigration on the human development of migrants and their families, two recent studies by the World Bank (both authored by David McKenzie and John Gibson) provide evidence of the potential benefits for migrants. The two studies evaluate the development impacts of participation by migrants from Tonga and other Pacific Islands countries in the Recognized Seasonal Employer (RSE) program in New Zealand launched in 2007, and the Pacific Seasonal Worker Pilot Scheme (PSWPS) in Australia started in 2008. The evaluations of both schemes show large financial benefits—and improvement in a range of human development indicators—for participating migrants and their families in their countries of origin. For example, Tongan migrants participating in the PSWPS in Australia received after-tax earnings of AUD12,200 for six months' work, which is more than five times greater than their previous incomes for a comparable period in their countries of origin. The migration costs were estimated at AUD6,300. They included payments for half the airfare, passports, police clearance, medical checkups, visas, internal travel within the home country, clothing, accommodation, food, health insurance, transport, and telephone calls while in Australia. Of the remaining AUD5,900, the average Tongan migrant remitted AUD4,600, which led to a 39 percent increase in the per capita household income of the migrants' family in Tonga.[11]

In comparison, a Tongan worker's participation in New Zealand's RSE (which runs for less than six months) increased per capita household income by about 33 percent.[12] In addition to raising household income and consumption, the program has allowed households to purchase more durable goods and led to an increase in child schooling in Tonga. The World Bank's evaluation of the RSE observes, "This should rank it among the most effective development policies evaluated to date."[13]

There is thus a strong economic rationale for workers in low- and middle-income countries—especially low-skilled workers whose international movement is currently the most restricted—to seek better access to labor markets in higher-income countries. Importantly, better access to employment opportunities in high-income countries has the potential to not only increase the economic welfare of workers and their families but also improve other dimensions of human development such as education and health. Based on an in-depth analysis of the impact of migra-

[11] Gibson and McKenzie 2011a.
[12] McKenzie and Gibson 2010.
[13] Ibid., abstract.

tion on human development, in 2009 the Human Development Report concluded that "outcomes in all aspects of human development, not only income but also education and health, are for the most part positive—some immensely so, with people from the poorest places gaining the most."[14] This is why "opening up existing migration barriers" was among the report's core recommendations for national and international policymakers.

Rights Abroad: Capabilities While Living and Working Abroad

How and to what extent migration improves human development outcomes for migrants critically depends on their legal rights while working and living abroad. As human development is defined as enlarging choice, capabilities, and freedoms, we can generally expect that the economic, social, political, and cultural rights that migrants *effectively* enjoy will have a positive impact on their human development. For example, the right to public health care and education will promote good health as well as the development of knowledge and human capital. Cultural rights enable migrants to practice their own cultures and traditions. The right to family reunion enables a family life. Access to the welfare state could, among other things, offer support in times of economic hardship. And many employment rights, such as the right to free choice of employment (rather than being tied to specific employers of occupations), can be expected to enable migrants to achieve better outcomes in the labor market.

Conversely, restrictions on migrant rights will lower migrants' human development gains from employment abroad. The denial of basic rights, such as the right not to have identity documents confiscated and the right to redress if the terms of the employment contract have been violated by the employer, can lead to situations where migrants' welfare and capability to act become highly dependent on their employer, thereby leading to "unfree" living and working conditions.

Various national and international institutions concerned with migrants have published a large number of reports and case studies documenting how a lack of rights can have highly adverse impacts on migrants' personal safety, physical and mental health, ability to participate in social life, and outcomes in the labor market. Most academic analyses do not consider specific rights but instead distinguish between the four major types of immigration status: illegally resident, temporary (legal) resident, permanent (legal) resident, and citizen.

Their "deportability" can put illegally resident migrants in a vulnerable position in the host country.[15] Some employers may offer illegally resident migrants lower wages and inferior employment conditions, either

---

[14] UNDP 2009, v.
[15] De Genova 2002.

because they take advantage of migrant's deportability and/or simply to account for the increased risk associated with employing migrants without legal residence rights. Research by J. Edward Taylor (1992) suggests that cost-minimizing employers will allocate illegally resident migrants to jobs where the expected cost of apprehension is lowest, and that such jobs are likely to be relatively low-skilled ones. Deportability may also impact on migrants' earnings through mechanisms that are not directly related to employer discrimination. Significantly, illegal residence status may alter migrants' behavior in the labor market.[16] Migrants without the right to reside may, for example, have lower reservation wages than workers with the right to legal residence. The fear of being deported could also discourage migrants from investing in the development of host-country-specific human capital.[17] Illegal residence status could also impact on the kinds of social networks that migrants may access, which in turn may affect migrants' access to well-paying jobs.[18]

Although not at constant risk of removal, migrants employed on legal temporary work permits in low-skilled occupations may also experience lower earnings because of their immigration status. Temporary work permits for low-skilled workers typically restrict migrants' employment to the sector and employer specified on the document. Where a change of employer is allowed, a new application for another work permit is usually required. This requirement naturally restricts migrants' choice of employment in the labor market and may make it difficult to leave jobs offering adverse employment conditions. Furthermore, a temporary migrant's right to legal residence is usually tied to ongoing employment in the host country. As can be the case with illegally resident migrants, unscrupulous employers may take advantage of temporary migrants' employment restrictions and offer employment conditions that are lower than those enjoyed by migrants with permanent residence status.

Most of the limited empirical research on the impacts of immigration status on migrants' labor market outcomes has focused on the effects of illegality. Most studies have been carried out in the United States, especially in the aftermath of the 1986 Immigration Reform and Control Act, which gave amnesty to undocumented immigrants—about 1.7 million outside agriculture—who could prove continuous residence in the United States since 1982. Francisco Rivera-Batiz (1999) concluded that legalization led to significant wage growth for legalized migrants. Sherrie Kossoudji and Deborah Cobb-Clark (2002) also found that the act had positive earnings effects for legalized migrants, mainly because of increased returns to human capital.[19]

Most of the existing research confirms the expectation that immigration status and the associated rights (restrictions) can be a significant determinant of migrants' outcomes within and outside the labor market.

[16] Kossoudji and Cobb-Clark 2002.
[17] Chiswik 1984.
[18] Massey 1987.
[19] See also Tienda and Singer 1995.

Expanding rights thus generally can be expected to have beneficial effects on the economic welfare and human development of migrants and their families.

Migration Decisions and Trade-Offs in Practice

International labor migration can be associated with trade-offs between different dimensions of human development. As shown in chapters 4 and 5, except for policies directed toward the most highly skilled migrant workers, labor immigration programs in high-income countries often present migrants with a trade-off between access to labor markets, on the one hand, and restrictions of some of their rights while working and living abroad, on the other. How have migrant workers responded to and engaged in this trade-off in practice?

At the most fundamental level, the fact that large numbers of migrant workers move to and take up employment in countries that severely restrict migrants' rights can be seen as an indication—although as discussed further below, not necessarily as stand-alone proof—that many workers are willing to tolerate, at least temporarily, a trade-off between better economic outcomes, such as higher wages and family income, and fewer rights.[20] As will be explored in chapter 7, the mere presence of migrant workers in countries with high openness–low rights policies of course does not mean that such policies are in the migrants' best interests, and therefore desirable or ethical from a normative point of view. Nevertheless, it is important to recognize that there is large-scale labor migration to countries that severely restrict migrant rights. Low-skilled labor migration to the GCC countries and Singapore is the most extreme case in point. Despite significant restrictions of their rights while working and living abroad, millions of migrant workers pay substantial recruitment fees and other costs to move to these countries in order to improve their incomes as well as raise the living standards of their families.

Global survey data confirm that there is an enormous "excess supply" of workers who would like to migrate and take up employment in higher-income countries, including countries where their rights are restricted. A recent global GALLUP survey of adults' desires to permanently migrate and take up employment abroad found that 15 percent of the world's adults (seven hundred million people) say that they would like to permanently move to another country if the opportunity arose.[21] Unsurprisingly, the most desired movement is from low- to high-income countries. As shown in table 6.1, Saudi Arabia, the United Arab Emirates, and Singapore are among the fifteen top-desired destination countries. Saudi Arabia ranks above Australia and Germany, and the United Arab Emirates is a more desired destination than Switzerland.

[20] See also Abella 2008.
[21] Esipova et al. 2010–11.

TABLE 6.1. Top desired destination countries of potential migrants, GALLUP migration intentions survey, 2010–11

	Percentage of potential migrants who would like to move to these countries	Millions of adults (projected numbers based on percentages who would like to move)
United States	24%	166
Canada	7%	46
United Kingdom	7%	46
France	6%	39
Spain	4%	31
Saudi Arabia	4%	28
Australia	4%	26
Germany	4%	26
Italy	3%	22
Japan	2%	17
United Arab Emirates	2%	12
Switzerland	1%	10
South Africa	1%	9
Russia	1%	8
Singapore	1%	8

Source: Esipova et al. 2011, 3.

Of course, any survey data on desires to move abroad must be interpreted cautiously as most migration desires or intentions do not translate into actual decisions to move. Still, it is interesting that when given the choice to mention any country in the world as their preference, large numbers of adults mention countries that are known to severely restrict the rights of migrant workers.

To what degree can labor migration to countries with restrictions on the rights of migrant workers be discussed in terms of workers making a deliberate choice to trade some of their rights for higher wages and, in many cases, considerable remittances for their families? This question goes to the heart of long-standing debates about the roles and interrelations between agency—the capacity to act independently and make reasoned choices—and structure—factors that limit the choices or opportunities available—in human behavior and decision making.[22]

For most migrant workers, both factors are likely to be at play. There are clearly important structural factors that impact on and in many ways circumscribe the set of options that individual workers have in their home countries as well as at different points in the migration process (such as departure, movement, or stay abroad). These factors include, for example, the global economic inequalities between different countries and regions of the world, social norms prevailing in home and destination countries, the migration and other policies of nation-states, and the activities

[22] See, for example, Emirbayer and Mische 1998; Archer 2000; Goddard 2000.

of employers and recruitment agencies. The collective interests of families and households may influence individuals' decisions too.[23] Workers with different characteristics, motivations, and resources (e.g., low or high skilled, single or married, living in large or small households, men or women, and employed or unemployed) in different countries (e.g., low or high income), and at different points in time (e.g., during economic growth or crisis) clearly face different structural constraints on the options and opportunities available to them. In other words, the degree of individuals' agency in decision making about migration is specific to the individuals' characteristics as well as the time and place. Workers with different characteristics in different countries and situations can also be expected to attach different degrees of importance to the various dimensions of human development. For example, low-skilled workers in Bangladesh may prioritize, at least temporarily, getting a higher-paid job over enjoying access to particular social rights while working abroad in a way that might be unacceptable to a higher-skilled worker in Bangladesh, or even to low-skilled workers in other higher-income countries.

Despite these real and omnipresent structural constraints, international labor migration involves—in most but not all cases—at least some element of choice. Migrant workers are, to put it another way, not simply helpless victims of larger structural forces but to some extent also active agents that make decisions on whether to stay or leave. The degree of choice is variable, and related to the extent to which migration is forced or voluntary. As Thomas Faist (2000, 24) and others have suggested, it is useful to think about the popular distinction between forced and voluntary migration "as a graded scale and not as a dichotomy. . . . [I]t then makes sense to think of degrees of freedom as ranging from high to low, from involuntary or forced to voluntary." There are clearly some migrants whose only choice to survive is to leave. This group includes people fleeing from life-threatening persecution (e.g., refugees under the Geneva Convention), or natural disasters such as extreme floods or drought. But the great majority of migrant workers—people leaving with the primary purpose of finding employment abroad—retain some power to decide whether or not to leave (as opposed to forced migration, when migrants do not have this power).[24]

There is almost always some element of choice even among the poorest and least skilled labor migrants, who typically have the fewest options and are often moving to places that generate the greatest trade-offs between different dimensions of human development.[25] This is one of the key conclusions of a recent, rare study of migrant workers' decisions and rationalizations before, during, and after migration:

> Even among the poor, decision-making surrounding whether or not to migrate has to take place. Even after they leave, they have to

---

[23] As suggested by the new economics of migration literature, see, for example, Stark 1991.

[24] Compare to William Petersen's (1958, 261) notion of "impelled migration."

[25] See also Agustin 2003.

make decisions about what kind of work to do, how to earn money, whether to send the money home, how much to send, how to send it, as well as whether and after how much time, to go home. Therefore, poverty does not operate in an automatic, unmediated way to simply push people out. People have to decide where to go and, after going, whether to stay away or come home.[26]

Empirical research concerning the motivations and experiences of different types of migrant workers at various stages of the migration process and in a wide range of countries provides evidence that migrant workers' decisions are typically (although not always) based on an awareness about the actual and potential trade-offs involved in migration and employment abroad. For example, a study of eastern European migrants working in the United Kingdom before and after their countries joined the European Union in May 2004 found that migrants frequently recognize and rationalize the trade-offs involved in employment abroad.[27] Most of the five hundred migrants interviewed worked in jobs that offered low wages and poor working conditions. Working hours were longer than the average for the occupation, and many migrants did not receive paid holidays or written contracts. Many migrants had far more skills than required to do the job, but in contrast to the usual portrayal of bad employer–exploited migrant, most migrants saw themselves as making tough choices and trade-offs. The migrants tolerated low-skilled work and poor conditions because the pay was significantly better than at home, and they could also learn or improve their English. Most important, migrants were prepared for poor conditions because the job was perceived as temporary, with most expecting to eventually move into better jobs or return home. Although sometimes leading to insecurity, the absence of a written contract was not always perceived as disadvantageous.

Choice and awareness of trade-offs are also emphasized by a range of studies of migrant workers employed under guest worker programs, including those that pose significant restrictions on the rights of migrant workers (especially in GCC countries and East Asia). In her review of guest worker programs in a global and historical perspective, Cindy Hahamovitch (2003, 71) concludes that although guest workers have sometime been reduced to slavelike status, "we can still state, though not without some trepidation, that these were exceptions not the rule. Though slavery is alive and well in the global economy of the 21st century . . . guestworkers are generally volunteers."

In their study of the experiences of migrant workers in the United Arab Emirates, Sulayman Khalaf and Saad Alkobaisi (1999, 295) observe that "all the migrants now work and live under non-egalitarian conditions, yet it is they who made their own journeys to this global world because they

---

[26] Ullah 2010, 191.
[27] Anderson et al. 2006.

saw and still see opportunities for them lying there to be exploited, and dreams to be realized." Similarly, Akm Ahsan Ullah's (2010) study of Bangladeshi labor migrants working in low-skilled jobs in Hong Kong and Singapore demonstrates that migrants' decisions before, during, and after migration are based on an assessment of a wide range of perceived costs and benefits that go beyond economic concerns, and include, for instance, psychological impacts, especially costs associated with being separated from their children and families.

There also is a considerable body of academic research that suggests elements of choice and awareness of trade-offs in types of labor migration that are popularly discussed in terms of forced migration and/or exploitation. In her book *On the Move for Love*, for example, Sealing Cheng (2010) discusses the experiences of Filipina migrants who work as entertainers in US military camp towns in Korea. Often depicted as hyperexploited, trafficked persons by the media, governments, NGOs, and international organizations, the book argues that these women have mostly made their choice to migrate with a broad understanding of the likely risks involved in their profession. Cheng contends that migrants have accepted these risks as preferable to the alternative: poverty at home. She (ibid., 11, 222) maintains that "Filipinas make their deployment to South Korea 'their own,' as migrant women do not merely obey the call of global capital and leave home as commodified labor or sex objects but are also moved by their capacity to aspire, their will to change, and their dreams of flight," and calls for "considering their agency in tandem with structural vulnerabilities."

Migrants who are residing and/or working illegally outside their countries of origin typically experience the most extreme trade-off between employment abroad and rights. As noted earlier in this chapter, illegality is typically associated with few legal rights in the host country. Nevertheless, many high-income countries experience growing populations of illegally resident migrant workers who either entered illegally or overstayed their temporary visas. Illegally resident migrants are vulnerable to a wide range of different types of disadvantages and exploitation—and yet research has shown that illegality in the employment of migrants is the result not only of structural factors (especially income inequality and the immigration policies of receiving countries) but also of the decisions of migrants and their employers.[28] There are clearly many workers who consider illegal employment abroad as their best option.

The argument that migrant workers, even those frequently described as experiencing exploitation, are aware of and actively engage in trade-offs between access to higher-paid jobs and restrictions on their rights does not deny that migrants sometimes make decisions based on incomplete or wrong information. Migrants may not be fully aware of the actual wages and living conditions that they are most likely to experience

---

[28] See, for example, Ruhs and Anderson 2010a.

abroad, or they may be victims of unscrupulous employers and/or recruitment agents who engage in "contract substitution," where migrants agree to specific wages and conditions before departure, and then are presented with a new contract with worse terms and conditions after arrival in the host country. For example, Ullah's (2010) qualitative study shows how in some cases, the premigration perceptions about potential trade-offs are correct in the sense of materializing once migration takes place, while in other places they are incorrect in the sense that expectations about, say, wages, housing, and life abroad are not realized in the host country. In this study, most Bangladeshi respondents in Hong Kong justified their migration decision and continuing stay by the fact that they earned ten to fifteen times more than was possible in their own country. Half the respondents in Hong Kong said that their initial migration decision was correct in the sense that it was based on information that turned out to be broadly accurate. In contrast, only a minority of the study's respondents in Malaysia said that their initial migration decisions were correct. They rationalized their continued stay in Malaysia with the hope of recouping the unexpectedly high costs they had incurred in financing their migration. The way in which employment abroad is rationalized thus can change after migration because the facts have changed—which is why assessments of how migrants rationalize their decisions cannot rely on the revealed preference argument alone.[29]

While some migrants undeniably make choices that they might not make if they had better information, it is hard to claim that this applies to the majority of migrant workers. Migration is critically influenced by networks between communities in sending and destination countries, which help provide information for workers considering a move for the first time. Moreover, a considerable share of migrant workers employed under significantly restricted rights comprises repeat migrants in the sense that people engage in circular migration between their home and destination country. Circular migrants who return to their destination countries make this choice based on the experiences and information gained from previous employment abroad.

A key factor that helps explain the choices that migrant workers make, both at the point of deciding whether to stay or move abroad as well as while working abroad, is migrants' "dual frame of reference"—the idea that migrants—especially those recently arrived and intending to stay temporarily—compare the conditions of their employment and life abroad to standards in their home countries rather than to those enjoyed by citizens of the host country. As Michael Piore (1979, 54) asserts in his classic work *Birds of Passage*, as many new migrants' social identity remains located in their place of origin, "the migrant is initially a true economic man, probably the closest thing in real life to the Homo economicus of economic theory." Employers are often acutely aware of the

---

[29] See also the discussion in Faist 2000, 37.

different frames of reference among different groups of migrants, which helps explain why migrant workers, especially those working in low-waged jobs, are frequently praised by employers as having a superior "work ethic" compared to domestic workers.[30]

Trade-offs between access and rights are also increasingly recognized by many NGOs concerned with defending the interests and rights of migrant workers. For instance, Daniel Bell and Nicola Piper (2005) found that NGOs representing domestic helpers in Hong Kong and Singapore were reluctant to promote equal rights for fear of sharply reduced admissions. Manuel Pastor and Susan Alva make a similar argument in the context of the US debate on guest workers. Activists and migrant advocates traditionally oppose guest worker programs, but according to Pastor and Alva (2004, 94), "behind the scenes, there was some support for such a guest worker program, including one based on a certain hierarchy of rights, ranging from those considered baseline for humane existence, such as labour protections, to more extensive provisions, such as the rights to vote, that might be more reasonably limited." The scholars contend that the main reason why some activists have begun to support guest worker policies is the perceived transnational existence of many migrants, so that they are moving between countries with different rights.

Sending Countries: Interests and Policy Choices

The remainder of this chapter discusses the interests of lower-income migrant-sending countries with regard to the labor immigration policies—openness, selection, and rights—of high-income countries. The analysis below first looks at this question in theory: What does research about the effects of emigration tell us about what sending countries' interests might be with regard to how high-income countries regulate immigration and the rights of migrant workers? This is followed by three empirical examples of how sending countries have engaged with high-income countries' labor immigration policies, including trade-offs between access and rights in practice.

Before this exploration, though, it is important to emphasize three crucial contextual points about the constraints on and determinants of labor emigration policy. First, along with being constrained by a wide range of factors in their power to restrict immigration, nation-states face even greater constraints on their formal authority and power to regulate labor emigration as well as the rights of migrant workers abroad.[31] While there is no right to migrate to any specific country, there is a human right to leave and return to one's country of origin or citizenship.[32] While exit

---

[30] Waldinger and Lichter 2003; Anderson and Ruhs 2010.

[31] See the discussion in chapter 3.

[32] Specifically, "everyone has the right to leave any country, including his own, and to return to his country," as per Article 13 of the Universal Declaration of Human Rights; see also Article 8 of the CMW.

controls were common in the past, they have been on the decline, and there are now few countries that still use them.[33]

At the same time, countries can and do implement a wide range of policies that are aimed at influencing the scale and composition of labor emigration as well as the rights of their workers abroad. Examples of such policies include: the promotion of "labor export" through the establishment of government departments tasked with facilitating recruitment and employment abroad; bilateral recruitment agreements with immigration countries; regulation of the recruitment industry; direct lobbying of foreign governments and/or through supra- and international institutions; and a range of diaspora engagement policies such as the extension of dual citizenship rights and the right to vote in the home country while residing abroad. The effectiveness of these policies in influencing the scale, type, and conditions of labor emigration and employment abroad is variable, and depends on a range of factors that are specific to the country and time.

A second important point to underscore is that just like immigration policy, a range of constraints and factors circumscribe the available policy space for regulating labor emigration. For instance, the prevailing political system (e.g., democratic versus nondemocratic states) and historical relationships with receiving countries will influence the availability as well as effectiveness of specific policy instruments. So we can expect significant differences in the policy space for regulating labor emigration across countries and over time.

Third, as is the case with immigration policy, the extent to which "the state" exercises agency plus is in a position to formulate and implement policies based on a given set of objectives varies across countries and over time. We know that in practice, different parts of the state may have different interests and different aspects, and dimensions of emigration policies are not always consistent. For example, in his analysis of the determinants of Mexico's policies toward emigration to the United States, David Fitzgerald (2006, 260) argues for a "'neopluralist' approach disaggregating 'the state' into a multilevel organization of distinct component units in which incumbents and other political actors compete for their interests."[34] My defense of a national interest approach to the analysis of emigration policies mirrors the argument I made in my conceptualization of immigration policy in chapter 3. Any emigration policy needs to be justified in terms of basic functional imperatives of the state that are reflected in broad policy objectives (the national interest) that countries can and do formulate as well as pursue in practice. As the discussion in this chapter will show, many sending countries clearly do articulate and attempt to pursue national policy objectives with regard to labor emigration and the rights of citizens abroad, so it makes sense to analyze policies in light of an examination of their national interests.

[33] See the discussion in Zolberg 2007.
[34] Fitzgerald 2006, 260.

Sending Countries, Emigration, and Migrant Rights: What Can We Expect?

Low-income countries have strong economic incentives to send more workers to take up employment in higher-income countries. The World Bank estimates that increasing the share of migrants in high-income countries by 3 percent would generate a global real-income gain of over $350 billion, exceeding the estimated gains from global trade reform by about 13 percent.[35] If migrants transfer some of their benefits back to their home countries—in the form of remittances, investments, and/or knowledge transfers—migrant-sending countries may reap a significant share of these global gains from migration. According to the World Bank, remittance flows to developing countries amounted to about US$351 billion in 2011 (more than triple the figure from 2002).[36] Global remittance flows are more than twice as large as the total development aid and represent the largest source of foreign exchange for numerous countries.

It is important to emphasize that more emigration does not automatically translate into faster development within migrants' countries of origin. The effects of remittances, and emigration more generally, can be mixed in both in theory and practice.[37] Research and the experiences of countries experiencing large-scale emigration—such as Egypt, Mexico, and the Philippines—suggest that sending workers abroad cannot, on its own, be an effective development strategy.[38] Yet it is clear that, if used effectively, remittances and other transfers migrants make back to their home countries can be of significant benefit to migrants' families and/or the overall economies of migrants' countries of origin.

Regarding selection policies, there are three economic reasons why we can expect low- and middle-income countries to particularly favor the liberalization of international flows of low-skilled workers. First, low-income countries have relatively more low-skilled workers and the international wage differentials between low-skilled workers are significantly higher than those between skilled workers.[39] The liberalization of low-skilled migration consequently would generate greater global efficiency gains than that of skilled migration. A related point is that the emigration of low-skilled workers can be expected to raise the wages of nonmigrant low-skilled workers in migrant-sending countries.[40] This would increase the economic welfare of the lowest-income earners rather than those of skilled and highly skilled middle- and high-income earners, and thus decrease inequality in poor countries.

[35] World Bank 2005.

[36] See http://siteresources.worldbank.org/TOPICS/Resources/214970-1288877981391/Migration andDevelopmentBrief17.pdf (accessed January 26, 2012).

[37] See, for example, Lucas 2005.

[38] ILO 2004.

[39] Freeman and Oostendorp 2000.

[40] See, for example, Boyer, Hatton, and O'Rourke 1994; Kaczmarczyk and Okólski 2008.

Second, in some but not all low- and middle-income countries, the emigration of skilled workers can create significant costs because of the training and other investment in the migrant along with, more generally, the decline in productive capacity. Costs of this brain drain are likely to be particularly pronounced in small countries with relatively underdeveloped public health care and other sectors that require skilled workers. For example, more than 80 percent of the tertiary educated workforce in Suriname, Jamaica, and Haiti has emigrated abroad.[41] It is important to stress, however, that skilled emigration is not always a net drain on the sending country. Some countries aim to produce an oversupply of skilled labor and consider the export of skilled workers as an opportunity rather than as a threat.[42] There is also some empirical research evidence to support the idea that high-skilled emigration can, under certain conditions, increase—not decrease—the stock of human capital in sending countries. In theory, this "brain gain" can happen when the future prospect of emigration raises individuals' incentives to acquire human capital and when only a share of those getting education with a view to future employment abroad end up actually emigrating. Educational institutions' capacity to expand their training in respond to rising demand is a key condition for this process to work in practice—a condition that is likely to hold only for some countries. A recent review of empirical research indicates some, although relatively weak, evidence supporting the existence of such positive brain-gain effects.[43]

Third, just as high-skilled migrants can be expected to make a bigger net fiscal contribution than low-skilled migrants in migrant-receiving countries, the emigration of high-skilled workers can be expected to create a greater fiscal loss for their countries of origin than would the departure of low-skilled workers. A recent study of the fiscal impact of high-skilled emigration from India to the United States found that the annual net fiscal impact to India was about 0.5 percent of India's gross national income or 2.5 percent of India's total fiscal revenues.[44]

Finally, what are the potential interests of sending countries with regard to the rights of their nationals working abroad? In principle we can expect any country to strongly want to promote the rights of their workers abroad. Due to economic incentives, however, sending countries, may not always insist on more or equal rights. For one, in high-income countries where labor immigration policies are characterized by a trade-off between admission and rights, an insistence on rights may jeopardize sending countries' objective of sending more workers abroad. Second, while many rights will improve the human development of both migrants and those "left behind" (family members and/or others) in migrants' countries of origin, it is important to consider potential exceptions and trade-offs where an increase in certain rights for migrants may lead to a

[41] World Bank 2008b.
[42] Bhagwati 2008.
[43] Gibson and McKenzie 2011b.
[44] Desai et al. 2009.

reduction in the benefits of migration for migrants' countries of origin. Migrants on temporary residence permits, for example—especially those with families in their home countries—can be expected to remit more of their wages than migrants with permanent residence status abroad. Although the overall empirical evidence on this issue is mixed, there is some evidence that remittances initially increase, yet eventually decrease with a migrant's duration of stay in the host country, reflecting the counteracting forces of wage increases (which increase remittances), on the one hand, and increased detachment from the home country and family reunification (lowering remittances) over time, on the other hand.[45] Acquiring the right to permanent residence will benefit migrants' human development, but the associated decline in remittances (and if migrants are highly skilled, the potential permanent loss of human capital) could lower human development in migrants' countries of origin. Of course, the impact of rights on remittances is just one type of effect that may be outweighed by other beneficial impacts for sending countries. The research on this issue is limited.

The critical conclusion from these basic theoretical considerations is that while the interests of sending countries can be expected to favor more open admission policies, especially for low-skilled workers, in higher-income countries, sending countries' interests toward the rights of their nationals working abroad—especially for those rights that are perceived to be inversely related to openness—are much more ambiguous. How sending countries engage with and respond to trade-offs between openness and rights is an important question for empirical research.

A global review of guest worker programs concluded that at least to some extent, all of them involved sending countries that were afraid of insisting on rights of their workers abroad for fear of losing access to labor markets.[46] "The more remittances pour into banks, the less inclined sending governments have been to protest too much."[47] The remainder of this chapter reviews four examples of sending countries' engagements with trade-offs between access to labor markets in higher-income countries and the rights of migrant workers abroad. As was the case in chapter 5, the period under consideration here is 2011, and—unless indicated otherwise—*all discussions of policies below refer to policy in or before that year.*

Low-Income Countries Sending Migrant Workers to the GCC Countries and Southeast Asia

The trade-offs between openness to labor immigration and migrant rights are most pronounced in GCC countries, such as Saudi Arabia and the United Arab Emirates, and in some Southeast Asian countries, such as

---

[45] See, for example, Carling 2008.
[46] Hahamovitch 2003.
[47] Ibid., 92.

TABLE 6.2. Emigration, remittances, and foreign direct investments in major Asian sending countries, 2010

Sending countries	Emigrants (millions)	Top destination countries	Remittances (US$ billion)	Net foreign direct investment inflows (US$ billion)
Bangladesh	5.3	India, Saudi Arabia, United Kingdom, Kuwait, Oman, United States, Malaysia, United Arab Emirates	11.1	1.0
India	11.3	United Arab Emirates, United States, Saudi Arabia, Bangladesh, Nepal, United Kingdom, Canada, Oman	55.0	41.2
Indonesia	2.5	Malaysia, Saudi Arabia, Netherlands, Singapore, United States, Jordan, Australia, Japan	7.1	9.3
Pakistan	4.7	India, Saudi Arabia, United Arab Emirates, United Kingdom, United States, Qatar, Canada, Kuwait	9.4	5.4
Philippines	4.3	United States, Saudi Arabia, Canada, Malaysia, Japan, Australia, Italy, Qatar	21.3	1.4

Source: World Bank 2011.

Singapore and Malaysia. How are countries that are sending large numbers of migrant workers to these countries perceiving and responding to these trade-offs?

The majority of migrant workers employed in GCC countries and Singapore are from Asian countries, many of which are heavily dependent on labor emigration and remittances (see table 6.2).

Most sending countries in Asia have created specific government departments tasked with working toward two objectives: promoting labor emigration and remittances; and protecting the rights and welfare of migrants abroad. There is a widespread perception that these two aims are often competing. According to Piyasiri Wickramasekara (2011, 31), one of the foremost experts of Asian labor emigration, "Origin countries in Asia are generally confronted between the dilemma of promotion and protection." This dilemma is reflected in the formal labor emigration strategies and plans recently developed in various countries. For instance, the Sri Lanka National Labor Migration Policy enacted in 2008 makes the trade-off explicit: "Thus, the delicate balance between the promotion of foreign employment and the protection of national workers abroad is a continuous challenge."[48]

[48] Cited in ibid., 31.

Some countries' official emigration strategies make it clear that more labor emigration and remittances are given priority over the more effective protection of the rights of migrant workers. In Pakistan, say, the first-ever National Emigration Policy (enacted in 2009) identified fifteen priority areas, almost all of which were concerned with sending more workers abroad (especially to Saudi Arabia and the United Arab Emirates) and facilitating remittances rather than the protection of rights. Furthermore, migrant rights advocates have pointed out that "priority area 12" of the plan, which deals with protecting the right of emigrants, includes important measures such as predeparture training as well as more help lines and counseling at embassies abroad, but does not mention any formal engagements at the diplomatic level with receiving countries about the rights of migrant workers. A recent review of Pakistan's emigration policy concluded that it is "short of any state-to-state high-level dialogue initiative for emigrants' rights advocacy and for awareness raising and mobilization of migrants for their rights in the destination countries."[49]

Although there are some variations in different sending countries' labor emigration policy approaches and bargaining power vis-à-vis specific host countries, it is clear that all the major Asian countries sending workers to the Middle East and Southeast Asia are concerned that too much emphasis on migrant rights may come at the cost of reduced or, in the worst-case scenario, no access to the labor markets of these countries. The fear of losing access to markets and the consequent adverse impact on remittances has been found to be among the main reasons why some major sending countries in Asia have been reluctant to sign the CMW.[50] The Philippines, which has arguably been more active on rights protection than other countries in the region, was the first major Asian sending country to ratify the convention in 1995. Bangladesh signed the convention but did not ratify it until 2011. Indonesia signed in 2004 yet ratified the convention only in 2012. Pakistan has not ratified it. A UN review of the reasons for the nonratification of the CMW in 2003 (when Bangladesh and Indonesia had not ratified it yet) concluded that Bangladesh and Indonesia "are afraid of losing jobs abroad and of other sending countries picking up their workers' share if they ratify the ICMR [CMW]."[51]

The use of and experiences with labor export bans by the Philippines, Indonesia, and other countries are a good example of how major sending countries struggle to balance the twin objectives of sending more workers abroad and protecting their rights. The Philippines has a long history of labor emigration and is a major recipient of remittances. As such, promoting emigration has become a core part—and some argue the core feature—of the country's overall economic strategy. According to Walden Bello (2011), congressperson and chair of the Parliamentary Committee

---

[49] See http://www.nccr-pakistan.org/publications_pdf/Migration/Jan_EmigrationPolicyReview.pdf (accessed November 25, 2011), 16.

[50] Piper and Iredale 2003.

[51] Ibid., 2–3. See http://unesdoc.unesco.org/images/0013/001395/139529e.pdf (accessed November 28, 2011).

on Overseas Workers Affairs, "Our foreign policy has been reduced to one item: promoting the export of our workers and securing their welfare abroad."

The Philippine Overseas Employment Administration (POEA) has a dual mandate: to promote and develop the overseas employment program and protect the rights of migrant workers. Its legal mandate includes a requirement to restrict the official deployment of Filipino migrants to countries that provide adequate protection of the rights of migrant workers.

Section 4 of the Migrant Workers and Overseas Filipinos Act of 1995, as amended by the Republic Act No. 10022 in 2009, states that:

> the State shall allow the deployment of overseas Filipino workers only in countries where the rights of Filipino migrant workers are protected. The government recognizes any of the following as a guarantee on the part of the receiving country for the protection of the rights of overseas Filipino workers.

> (a) It has existing labor and social laws protecting the rights of workers, including migrant workers;
> (b) It is a signatory to and/or a ratifier of multilateral conventions, declarations or resolutions relating to the protection of workers, including migrant workers; and
> (c) It has concluded a bilateral agreement or arrangement with the government on the protection of the rights of overseas Filipino Workers:

> Provided, That the receiving country is taking positive, concrete measures to protect the rights of migrant workers in furtherance of any of the guarantees under subparagraphs (a), (b) and (c) hereof.

> In the absence of a clear showing that any of the aforementioned guarantees exists in the country of destination of the migrant workers, no permit for deployment shall be issued by the Philippine Overseas Employment Administration.[52]

The act further clarifies that the Philippines' Department of Foreign Affairs (DFA) issues "certification" to the POEA, "specifying therein the pertinent provisions of the receiving country's labor/social law, or the convention/declaration/resolution, or the bilateral agreement/arrangement which protect the rights of migrant workers."[53]

In May 2011, the POEA, based on advice from the DFA, approved seventy-six countries for the continuing deployment of Filipino migrant workers.[54] The POEA also asked the DFA to further review and reevaluate the countries not included on the list. In October 2011, after this re-

---

[52] See http://www1.umn.edu/humanrts/research/Philippines/RA%2010022-%20%20Migrant%20 Workers%20Act.pdf (accessed November 23, 2011).
[53] Ibid.
[54] POEA 2011a.

view, another forty-nine countries were added to the list of compliant countries, thus open for the deployment of Filipino migrants.[55] At the same time, the POEA announced a ban on the deployment of migrant workers to forty-one countries that the DFA found to be noncompliant with the guarantees stipulated in the Migrant Workers and Overseas Filipinos Act.

Some migrant rights advocates were critical of this ban as it only included countries that received only a small number of migrant workers from the Philippines.[56] Others—including the DFA itself—were concerned about potential adverse impacts on relations with these countries including a potential backlash toward Filipino workers currently employed in these countries.[57] Soon after the list of banned countries was published, the DFA asked the POEA for a ninety-day reprieve "to provide enough time to work on the possible bilateral agreements with the 41 countries, enabling them to comply with the requirements of the Migrant Workers and Overseas Filipinos Act." In early November 2011, the POEA recalled Resolution 7, which announced the ban, and granted the ninety-day reprieve.

Importantly, by late 2011 key destination countries in the Persian Gulf states (including Saudi Arabia, the United Arab Emirates, Qatar, Kuwait, and Bahrain) as well as Singapore had not been included on any of the published lists of eligible and banned countries. Instead, these countries were identified as "conditionally compliant" in late 2011, and the DFA continued to assess them. They were given a grace period of six months (i.e., longer than the three-month grace period offered to those countries on the noncompliant list), "giving some countries in the Middle East and other countries a chance to amend their laws to ensure the protection of our OFWs [Overseas Filipino Workers]."[58] According to an official at the DFA in October 2011, "We are not shutting the door to any host country but paving the way to reach a bilateral agreement and strengthening the diplomatic ties between the Philippines and the host countries. We do not want to antagonize them."[59] Congressperson Walden Bello made it clear in November 2011 that "we are trying to balance safety and livelihood."[60]

On May 22, 2012, the POEA issued a resolution that added thirty-one countries, including Singapore, to the list of compliant nations.[61] Through another resolution issued on June 28, 2012, the POEA deemed the previ-

---

[55] POEA 2011b.

[56] See http://blogs.wsj.com/searealtime/2011/11/07/manila-ban-has-no-bite/tab/print/ (accessed February 12, 2012). For a list of key destination countries for migrant workers from the Philipppines, see http://www.poea.gov.ph/stats/Stock%20Estmate%202009.pdf (accessed March 11, 2012)

[57] See http://gulfnews.com/news/world/philippines/philippines-to-defer-ban-on-labour-export-1.927136 (accessed February 17, 2012).

[58] Bello 2011.

[59] DFA ambassador Vic Lecaros, October 26, 2011, http://www.sunstar.com.ph/manila/local-news/2011/10/26/ofws-may-still-work-countries-without-laws-protect-them-187166 (accessed November 25, 2011).

[60] http://www.mb.com.ph/articles/339964/noncompliant-ofw-destinations-must-reform (accessed August 30, 2012).

[61] POEA 2012a.

ously partially compliant and noncompliant thirty-two countries as "compliant without prejudice to negotiations for the protection of the rights of household service workers and/or other categories of workers for the purpose of continuing deployment to these countries."[62] The resolution further noted that the "POEA may continue deployment to these countries and DFA will continue to negotiate for the better protection of household service workers even beyond 12 April 2012."[63] The new and expanded list of eligible, compliant countries (184 in total) now includes all the key Persian Gulf states (Saudi Arabia, Bahrain, Kuwait, Qatar, and the United Arab Emirates).

The Philippines' experience with labor bans shows that while the Philippines government is clearly concerned about the rights of its migrant workers abroad, there appears to be a strong policy view that the more effective protection of rights must not come at the cost of significantly reduced access to labor markets in the GCC and some Southeast Asian countries.

Indonesia's recent experience with labor bans has been similar to that of the Philippines. Indonesia has used temporary labor bans since 2009. Kuwait has been banned since 2009, Jordan since 2010, and Syria since 2011. Malaysia was banned in 2009, but the ban was lifted in 2011. Although the Indonesian government announced in March 2011 that it had no further plans to make additions to its list of banned countries, it decided to impose a moratorium on labor export to Saudi Arabia in June 2011.[64] This was in response to the continuing rights abuses of Indonesian migrants in Saudi Arabia, including the beheading of an Indonesian maid as punishment for killing her employer in Saudi Arabia in June 2011. The Indonesian government said that the moratorium would only be lifted after the signing of a memorandum of understanding between the two countries to help safeguard the basic rights of migrant workers in Saudi Arabia. The moratorium was going to become effective on August 1, 2011, but Saudi Arabia announced in late June 2011 that it was banning domestic workers from Indonesia and the Philippines, citing demands for better terms of employment by the two countries.[65] Saudi Arabia consequently stopped issuing work visas to domestic workers from both these countries, and announced that it would make greater efforts to bring domestic workers and other migrant workers from other countries.[66] In July 2011, Saudi Arabia lifted a two-year embargo on recruiting Bangladeshi workers.

In late 2011 and early 2012, both Indonesia and the Philippines were negotiating the possibility of memorandums of understanding and bilateral agreements with Saudi Arabia and other GCC countries. In both

---

[62] POEA 2012b.

[63] See http://www.poea.gov.ph/gbr/2012/gbr_8_2012.pdf (accessed August 23, 2012).

[64] See http://www.thejakartapost.com/news/2011/11/03/govt-will-not-add-nations-migrant-worker-blacklist.html (accessed December 15, 2011).

[65] The Philippines had asked for higher wages.

[66] See http://www.economist.com/node/21523188 (accessed August 30, 2012).

countries, many activists have been critical of the ban. For example, Dedeh Elah, an activist from the Cianjur Migrant Workers Union, said that "instead of imposing the moratorium, it would be better for the government to provide better protection for Indonesian workers abroad, and improve training standards."[67]

The making and unmaking of labor export bans make it clear that the trade-off between encouraging labor emigration and protecting migrant workers' rights is at the heart of the overall policy approach and strategies adopted by the Philippines, Indonesia, and other Asian sending countries. Some sending countries are obviously concerned about the rights of their nationals working abroad, but the overriding priority has remained the promotion of more labor emigration and remittances. As a result, despite public demands and government rhetoric emphasizing the importance of protecting rights, in the end most sending countries have continued to trade rights restrictions for continued access to labor markets in GCC and some Southeast Asian countries.

A key challenge for any individual sending country is that GCC and other migrant-receiving countries in the region can easily mitigate the effects of any unilateral policy decision by a sending country to stop sending workers by turning to other, often lower-income countries for recruiting more workers. So there is a collective action problem. If one country complains about rights violations there has—so far—always been another country that is happy to step in and send migrant workers. The Colombo Process, aimed at helping unite major sending countries in their negotiations with major receiving countries in Asia, has "yet to graduate from an information-sharing platform to a bloc that can develop a common bargaining position in negotiations with labor-receiving countries."[68]

Sending Low-Skilled Workers to the United States and Canada: Perspectives of Latin American Sending Countries

The tension between the policy goals of maintaining or increasing labor emigration, on the one hand, and protecting migrant rights, on the other, has also been one of the primary dilemmas for Latin American (and other) countries sending migrant workers to the United States and Canada. While the rights restrictions involved in these trade-offs are qualitatively different from those observed in the Middle East (i.e., liberal democracies are less likely to restrict basic civil rights), the limited research on sending countries' interests in this region demonstrates that there is a clear perception of competing objectives: promoting labor emigration versus the protection of rights. As is the case with Asian countries sending migrant workers to the Gulf, the available evidence suggests that for

---

[67] http://www.thejakartapost.com/news/2011/07/30/ban-leaves-migrant-workers-limbo.html (accessed December 18, 2011).

[68] http://www.hrw.org/news/2011/07/08/united-they-work-divided-they-don-t (accessed January 30, 2012).

Latin American countries, the perceived need to maintain or expand access to North American labor markets has frequently trumped the more effective protection of migrant rights, especially for low-skilled migrant workers.

Most of the eighty-eight respondents interviewed in Mark Rosenblum's (2004) study of the emigration policy preferences of policymakers in Mexico and other Central American countries, for example, described the impacts of emigration as involving a trade-off between political-economic benefits and sociopolitical costs for migrants as well as their countries of origin. In these interviews, policymakers identified remittances and jobs as the top two perceived benefits from emigration, while the top two perceived concerns were human rights/exploitation and "family/cultural issues." Rosenblum (ibid., 104) concluded that "the informants essentially saw emigration as a necessary evil: supplying needed short-term and economic benefits but also imposing immediate human and cultural costs and hindering long-term development."

Mexico's "policy of nonintervention" in labor emigration to the United States in the second half of the twentieth century—most of which was illegal—can be interpreted as another case of a major sending country giving more priority to continuing labor emigration over more effective protections of its migrant workers abroad.[69] The share of Mexican emigrants in the United States within the total Mexican population rose from less than 2 percent in the 1950s to over 10 percent in the 2000s.[70] Since the end of the Bracero program—a bilaterally negotiated guest worker program for sending Mexican farmworkers to the United States—in 1964, most labor migration from Mexico to the United States has been illegal. The estimated stock of the "US unauthorized immigrant population from Mexico" was 4.6 million in 2000 and 6.7 million in 2009.[71]

In the early 2000s, the Vicente Fox administration (2000–2006) attempted to negotiate a new guest worker program and legalization for undocumented Mexicans in the United States—negotiations that were abandoned after the September 11, 2001, attacks. These negotiations marked the first formal steps that the Mexican government took to proactively engage with labor emigration and emigrants in the United States since the end of the Bracero program.[72] For most of the second half of the twentieth century, the Mexican government tacitly acquiesced to a trade-off between continuing labor emigration to the United States at the cost of the restricted rights that are a natural consequence of illegal status. Alexandra Delano (2009, 770) explains this policy approach in the following way:

> Mexico has been highly dependent on the continuation of emigration—through formal or informal channels—as a "safety valve" for

[69] Delano 2009.
[70] Pew Hispanic Center 2009.
[71] Passel and Cohn 2010.
[72] Delano 2009; Fitzgerald 2009.

economic and political pressures and, more recently, as a key source of income for remittance recipients. . . . In general, [the] Mexican government has tried to maintain a relatively disadvantageous but stable status quo in order to guarantee the continuation of the flows. . . . Thus, despite continued abuses and discrimination against Mexican workers, violations of contacts, and the costs of emigration, particularly for some regions, the government generally maintained a "policy of no policy" that included limited reactions to US migration policies and legislation.

The tension between promoting labor emigration and protecting migrant rights has also been at the core of Mexico's and the Caribbean countries' engagement with Canada's Seasonal Agricultural Worker Program (SAWP), which started in 1966. SAWP provides Canadian farmers with temporary migrant workers during the planting and harvesting seasons.[73] While the program used to be dominated by Jamaican men, the majority of participants are now Mexican workers. Migrants' stay is limited to a maximum of eight months, after which workers need to return to their home countries. In practice the majority of SAWP workers participate in the program over many years. SAWP is based on bilateral agreements between Canada and participating sending countries, which are responsible for selecting and recruiting workers for participation in the program. As Canadian growers can specify their preferred supply country, they can engage in "country surfing" for the best workers.[74] Consequently, sending countries are in direct competition with each other for the number of places made available to their nationals under the program. According to Jenna Hennebry and Kerry Preibisch (2009, 9), sending countries are "eager to capture workers remittances and ease unemployment at home, invest significant resources in recruitment and selection of workers, as well as providing liaison staff in Canada."

Sending countries compete in terms of the skills, perceived quality, and reliability of their workers as well as in terms of the services made available to Canadian growers, such as delivering workers quickly and just in time for production.[75] For example, the Mexican Ministry of Labor asks Canadian growers to complete end-of-year evaluations for each worker, and the assessments are used to determine that worker's future eligibility for the program—a policy that is plainly aimed at promoting labor discipline.[76]

As is the case with Asian countries sending workers to the Gulf, there is also evidence that countries sending workers to Canada under SAWP are prioritizing continued or expanded access to the program over the effective protection of rights. The trade-off between access and rights is

[73] See http://www.hrsdc.gc.ca/eng/workplaceskills/foreign_workers/ei_tfw/sawp_tfw.shtml (accessed March 14, 2012).

[74] Preibisch and Binford 2007.

[75] Prebisch and Binford 2007; Preibisch 2007.

[76] Hennebry and Preibisch 2010.

played out and "personified" in the role of the government liaison officer of the source countries in Canada. According to the official website for SAWP, when a Canadian employer violates the contract's terms, "workers should first contact the government liaison officer of their source country in Canada." Yet in addition to helping resolve disputes with employers and assisting workers whose rights have been violated, the government liaison officer is supposed to maximize the access for workers from their country to Canadian growers. These dual objectives can create a conflict of interest:

> Employers state that their choice of supply country for workers is determined in large part by the level of service that a consular office will provide. The Government Agents understand that they are in competition for worker placements on farms and therefore, have to be responsive to employers, and they were all aware that if a dispute is not resolved, a grower may select workers from another country.[77]

Clearly, the competition between sending countries for access to Canada's SAWP means that government liason officers balance their efforts to maintain or improve access to growers with efforts to protect migrant rights. Much to the frustration of workers advocacy groups in Canada, sending countries thus have not always been among the most outspoken supporters of the rights of their workers employed under SAWP. As one liaison officer interviewed by Preibisch and Leigh Binford (2007, 24) suggested, "[Voicing rights] causes some employers to switch, because a lot of them don't want backchat or voicing of rights."

Access versus Equal Treatment in the EU Posted Workers Directive

Instituted in 1996, the EU Posted Workers Directive (Council Directive 96/71/EC) requires that workers "posted" by an employer in one EU member state to temporarily work on a project in another member state should be guaranteed the minimum employment conditions of that second country.[78] A posted worker is defined in the directive as "a worker who, for a limited period, carries out his work in the territory of a Member State other than the State in which he normally works." Posted workers exclude independent labor migrants, self-employed migrants, and seafarers. The directive thus applies only to workers who are temporarily posted abroad by their companies.

The directive has two primary objectives. The first is to promote the free provision of services across EU member states by removing uncer-

---

[77] Verma 2007.

[78] See http://eur-lex.europa.eu/LexUriServ/LexUriServ.do?uri=CELEX:31996L0071:EN:HTML (accessed December 12, 2011).

tainties about the applicable legal standards when posting workers abroad. The opening of the directive states that "the abolition, as between Member States, of obstacles to the free movement of persons and services constitutes one of the Objectives of the community." The second aim is to provide protection of minimum conditions of employment. The directive notes that "a 'hard core' of clearly defined protective rules should be observed by the provider of services." In the context of this book, these two goals can be interpreted as relating to promoting openness to migrant workers (in this case, the provisions of services by migrants) and the protection of minimum rights.

The two objectives are clearly competing, especially since 2004, when the European Union was expanded to include eight eastern European countries with substantially lower average wages than those prevailing in the "old" (i.e., pre-2004 enlargement) EU member states. The objective of the free provision of services across EU member states suggests that member states should be able to freely provide their services to other member states without having to comply with that country's labor standards. The spirit of this aim implies that member states with lower wages and labor costs should be able to make use of their comparative advantage and supply their services at "competitive prices" to other higher-wage member states. At the same time, the objective of protecting minimum employment conditions suggests a desire to protect workers in any EU member state from being undercut by cheaper workers with fewer rights who are posted by companies based in other EU member states. It essentially boils down to the well-known conflict between labor standards and free trade, which in the context of the European Union has frequently been discussed as a conflict between service liberalization versus the "European social model."[79]

Given these dual and competing objectives, the question of how to define the minimum terms of conditions of employment that posted workers should be subject to is at the core of the directive, and as mentioned below, has been at the center of recent disputes about the meaning and implications of the directive. Article 3(1) of the directive defines minimum conditions as laid out by the host country's "law, regulation or administrative provisions," and/or by "collective agreements and arbitration awards." These conditions may refer to: maximum work periods and minimum rest periods; minimum paid annual holidays; minimum rates of pay; the conditions of hiring out workers; health, safety, and hygiene at work; protective measures for the employment of pregnant women, women who have recently given birth, and children as well as young people; and equality of treatment between men and women.

The implications of these minimum conditions, and the Posted Workers Directive more generally, were at the heart of the "Laval dispute," which was eventually settled by a ruling of the European Court of Justice in 2008. As already discussed in chapter 5, this case involved a Latvian

[79] See, for example, Woolfson and Sommers 2006.

construction company (Laval) winning a public tender to renovate a primary school near Stockholm. Laval paid its posted workers almost double the going wage rates in Latvia, but less than the collectively agreed-on wage for the sector in Sweden. The Swedish trade union took collective action and blocked all Laval sites in Sweden. Laval initiated proceedings in the Swedish courts in an attempt to have the Swedish trade unions' actions declared unlawful. After the Swedish courts ruled in favor of the trade union, Laval took the case to the European Court of Justice, which eventually ruled in favor of Laval. The court ruled that the Swedish unions' boycott constituted a violation of the principle of the free movement of services as the unions' demands exceeded the minimal national employment protections under Swedish national laws. The judgment was a victory for supporters of greater liberalization of service provisions across EU member states, and a blow to supporters of the protection of the rights and labor market regulations prevailing in some of the old EU member states.

How did the Latvian government view and engage with this case? In a nutshell, it strongly supported Laval, and was engaging with the Swedish government, Swedish trade unions, European Court of Justice, and other relevant parties to the dispute at the highest diplomatic level. As a new EU member state with some of the most neoliberal policies, Latvia was keen on arguing the broader case that the insistence of labor standards in the old EU member states should not become a stumbling block to expanding the provision of services across EU member states.

A few days after the Laval disputed started, the Latvian deputy foreign minister met with the Swedish ambassador to discuss the case, maintaining that Sweden should be supporting and enforcing the free movement of services across the European Union.[80] Latvia's foreign minister made it clear that the Swedish response "goes against our understanding of why we joined the EU."[81] The Latvian government then set up an interministerial working group headed by the Ministry of Foreign Affairs, and involving representatives of the ministries of the economy, justice, and welfare. A few months later the Latvian prime minister talked about the issue with the Swedish prime minister at an EU summit in Brussels, and wrote a letter to the European Commission's president expressing his concern. The Latvian government also stated at that point that it might take the issue to the European Court of Justice.

Most of the other new EU member states—which shared an interest in prioritizing the liberalization of the service provisions across EU member states over the protection of labor standards in the old member states—strongly supported the Latvian government's position in the Laval dispute. When considering the Laval case in 2007, the European Court of Justice invited submissions from all EU member states. As analyzed by Nicole Lindstrom (2010), government submissions clustered around new

---

[80] Ibid.
[81] James 2006. See http://www.worldproutassembly.org/archives/2006/06/sweden_lessons.html (accessed December 11, 2012).

and old member states. The new member states (joined by the United Kingdom and Ireland) contended that the Swedish trade unions' actions were not compatible with the free movement of services (Article 49) or the Posted Workers Directive, while most of the old EU member states strongly defended the rights to take industrial action as well as enforce national wage agreements and social policies more generally. In other words, Latvia and most other new EU member states were pushing for better access to the labor markets of the old EU member states, which in contrast, were defending their labor standards, which effectively acted as a restriction on the employment of migrants at a lower cost. Lindstrom (ibid., 1307) concluded that "with the ECJ ultimately ruling with the employers and against the expressed preferences of most old Member States and unions, the rulings furthered the cause of liberalization in the enlarged EU, but also mobilized political opposition."

Wage Parity as a Stumbling Block within GATS Mode 4 Negotiations

The tension between openness and equality of rights is also at the heart of the negotiations within the WTO's GATS Mode 4 framework. The GATS negotiations aim to liberalize the international movement of service providers. Services move across borders in four major ways or modes. Mode 1 cross-border supply occurs when the service rather than the supplier or consumer crosses national borders. Call centers are an example. Mode 2 involves the consumption of a service abroad when the consumer travels to the supplier. For instance, a patient travels abroad for medical services. Mode 3 relates to a "commercial presence," which reflects the international movement of capital, such as when a bank or other global company sets up a subsidiary in another country. Finally, Mode 4 involves the movement of "natural persons." The provider of the services in this case temporarily moves to the consumer in another country.

Through a system of "commitments" by WTO member states, GATS aims to achieve greater liberalization of the provision of services across borders. This technically involves each of the 153 WTO member states making specific commitments with regard to reducing market access barriers for each of the four modes of service supply. It is possible and standard practice for member states to link their commitments to various conditions. One of the most commonly used condition and barrier in member states' scheduling practices is to tie Mode 4 commitments to Mode 3. The majority of all Mode 4 commitments are connected to Mode 3 investments—meaning that they require a commercial presence of a foreign service supplier. Another key barrier is the requirement of wage parity, which means that foreign service providers need to be paid the prevailing wages given to similar workers in the country where the service is provided. As is the case under the EU Posted Workers Directive, the purpose of the wage parity requirement—and other related, frequently used requirements such as minimum wages along with work and social security benefits—is to protect workers in high-income countries from declining wages and what is sometimes viewed as unfair competition from low-cost service providers.[82]

So far, GATS Mode 4 has had a limited impact in practice on the liberalization of service provision. Mode 4 accounts for only about 5 percent of all GATS commitments to date.[83] Many low- and middle-income countries are frustrated with the slow progress of liberalization, and would like to see more Mode 4 movements. In 2005, Argentina, Bolivia, Brazil, Chile, Colombia, India, Pakistan, Peru, Mexico, and the Philippines submitted a "plurilateral request" to the WTO calling for greater liberalization of service provision under Mode 4. A key demand of this WTO communication was that "wage parity will not be a pre-condition of entry" for contractual service providers and independent professionals.[84] India has been one of the most vocal critics of the wage parity requirement, which is widely seen as restricting access to the labor markets of higher-income countries. For example, Sumanta Chaudhuri, Aaditya Mattoo, and Richard Self (2004, 366) assert that equal wages would limit access: "Wage-parity . . . is intended to provide a non-discriminatory environment, [but] tends to erode the cost advantage of hiring foreigners and works like a de facto quota." Rupa Chanda (2001, 635) goes further, asserting that "while wage parity may be required from the perspective of home country workers and labor unions, it negates the very basis of cross-country labor flows which stems from endowment-based cost differentials between countries." A recent presentation by the Indian government on Mode 4 negotiations confirmed that the wage parity requirement continues to be viewed as one of the most important factors restricting the access of service suppliers to higher-income countries.[85]

Most trade economists would agree with India's and other low-income countries' complaints about wage parity acting as a barrier to trade. For example, according to Alan Winters (2004, 48), a well-known trade economist and expert on the WTO:

> Paying prevailing local wages on temporary foreign workers is a one-stone-two-birds measure. It is intended to protect local workers from wage erosion and, presumably, to sweeten the pill of foreign competition, while, at the same time, it serves to protect foreign workers from being "exploited." The problem of imposing a minimum wage/price is that it clearly reduces the potential volume of, and benefits from, trade. The principal losers are host-country con-

---

[82] See the discussion in Panizzon 2010.

[83] Ibid.

[84] http://commerce.nic.in/trade/sub_tns-w-31.pdf (accessed January 6, 2012).

[85] See http://www.unctad.org/sections/wcmu/docs/ciem4_S4_Bangar_en.pdf (accessed January 6, 2012).

sumers, but such regulations also prevent developing countries from exploiting their comparative advantage.

The ongoing debates about wage parity within the GATS Mode 4 negotiations highlight a conflict between international instruments and institutions, specifically between the WTO, which has a normative concern with free movement, and the ILO, which has a focus on equality of rights.[86] As migration economist and ILO expert Phil Martin (2006, v) has pointed out, there is an inherent tension between GATS Mode 4 liberalization within the WTO and equality of rights as stipulated by the norms and standards of the ILO, especially ILO conventions 97 and 143, which call for migrant and local workers to receive the same wages for the same work:

> GATS liberalization may run headlong into the ILO push for more decent work. Differences are the fundamental basis for both trade and migration, while ILO standards rest on equality of treatment. Proponents of more GATS Mode 4 migration sometimes make frontal assaults on laws and norms calling for equal treatment of workers. For example, instead of equal wages for migrant and local workers, they sometimes advocate allowing foreign-service providers to work for below minimum wages so that developing countries can exploit their comparative advantage.

Engaging with Trade-Offs

If you ask workers and governments in low-income countries how they would want the labor immigration policies of high-income countries to change, their answers are likely to involve two core elements: more open admission policies and more rights for migrant workers, especially for low-skilled workers, whose international movements and rights are currently the most restricted in high-income countries.

It is easy to see the rationales underlying each of these two objectives. Increased labor migration has the potential to generate large income and other gains for migrants as well as their countries of origin. Better access to rights in high-income countries can be expected to enhance the human development of migrants working abroad. So when considered in isolation, each of these two aims makes perfect sense from the point of view of migrants and their countries of origin.

The problem is that these two objectives—more openness and more rights—can be conflicting. As the discussions in chapters 4 and 5 have shown, high-income countries' labor immigration policies are often characterized by a trade-off between openness and the restriction of specific

---

[86] Betts and Nicolaides 2009, 9.

rights. While both greater openness and more rights are clearly "good things" for migrants and their countries of origin, the existence of a policy trade-off suggests that we cannot have more of both at the same time.

This chapter has demonstrated that migrant workers along with their countries of origin are acutely aware of and engaging with this trade-off in practice. Every day migrant workers are making choices about whether to stay at home or move and work abroad under restricted rights. Large numbers are currently choosing the latter—that is, they are tolerating restrictions of some of their rights in exchange for the opportunity to migrate and work abroad. This points to the importance of considering the agency, "voice," and overall interests of migrants when explaining existing migration flows and policies, and when thinking normatively about whether particular trade-offs should be tolerated. Given that the human development of people is multidimensional and includes more considerations than just access to legal rights, it is not surprising to see migrant workers making 'sacrifices' in some dimensions of development (e.g. limited access to some legal rights) in exchange for advancing others (e.g. opportunities to access employment at higher wages and raise the household incomes of their families).

Many low-income countries sending migrant workers abroad make a similar choice. To the extent that they can influence the labor immigration policies of high-income countries, most low-income countries are pursuing emigration policies that are, often very explicitly, based on a trade-off between access to labor markets in high-income countries and some migrant rights. Few countries are willing to insist on full and equal rights for fear of reduced access for their workers to the labor markets of higher-income countries. Given the realities of the trade-offs based on the national interests of high-income countries in practice, it is a policy choice that is currently being made by a wide range of low-income countries seeking to improve the development of their citizens and their countries as a whole.

What does the fact that migrant workers and their countries of origin are making active choices that involve trade-offs between some rights for better access to higher-income countries tell us about whether labor immigration policies that restrict migrant rights are morally acceptable and desirable? This crucial normative question is addressed in the next chapter.

Chapter 7

The Ethics of Labor Immigration Policy

Up to this point, the book has focused on exploring the characteristics and drivers of policies for regulating the admission and rights of migrant workers in high- and middle-income countries. The analysis has shown that labor immigration programs that target higher-skilled migrant workers are more open and grant migrants more rights than programs targeting lower-skilled migrant workers. It has also suggested that high-income countries' labor immigration policies are often characterized by a trade-off between openness and specific rights granted to migrant workers after admission. The rights that have been restricted in practice as part of this policy trade-off include selected social rights, the right to free choice of employment, family reunion, the right to permanent residence (and thus citizenship), and—in countries that are not liberal democracies—selected civil and political rights. I have demonstrated how these policies may be explained by the national interests and policy constraints of immigration countries, and how they can be supported and sustained by the interests as well as choices of sending countries and migrants themselves.

This chapter moves the discussion from a positive analysis of *what is* to the equally important normative question of *what should be*. Given what we know about labor immigration policies in practice, what can we say about how high-income countries should regulate the admission and rights of migrant workers? Are TMPs that restrict migrant rights inherently unethical? If high-income countries' labor immigration policies involve a trade-off between openness and some rights, as indicated in this book, what rights restrictions—if any—are acceptable in order to enable more workers to access labor markets in high-income countries? Is there a case for advocating new and/or expanded TMPs for lower-skilled migrant workers, whose access to labor markets is currently more restricted in high-income countries?

The chapter looks at these questions in four parts. The first examines the key ethical questions that arise in the design of any labor immigration program (again defined as involving policy decisions on how to regulate openness to along with the selection and rights of migrant workers).[1] The discussion proposes a two-dimensional matrix of "ethical space" that isolates a number of different ethical frameworks based on the degree of "consequentialism" they allow and the "moral standing" they accord to noncitizens (migrants and people in migrants' countries of origin). Different ethical frameworks have different implications for how to evaluate policies for regulating the admission and rights of migrant workers. As

---

[1] The discussion in this first part draws on Ruhs and Chang 2008.

my intention is to contribute to national and international policy debates, I will argue for a pragmatic approach that is both realistic—by taking account of existing realities in labor immigration policymaking—and idealistic—by giving more weight to the interests of migrants and their countries of origin than most high-income countries currently do when designing labor immigration policies. Based on this combination of realistic and idealistic approaches, I explain and defend the five principles—or building blocks—informing my own normative approach to evaluating labor immigration policy.

The second part of the chapter draws on my normative approach in order to critically assess the main normative arguments against and for TMPs that restrict migrant rights. My discussion of the "case against" centers on three critiques based on human rights, equal membership, and exploitation. While each of these critiques is important within the context of their own normative starting points, I do not find them convincing given my own approach. As many of the existing normative defenses of TMPs suggest, in the context of an analysis that aims to contribute to real-world policy debates where some first-best policies are unfeasible, appropriately designed TMPs can be defended as "second-best" policies, notwithstanding their restrictions on migrant rights.

Having accepted the possibility of an ethically defensible TMP, the third part of the chapter examines which specific rights restrictions can be defended, and for how long. I argue for the unconditional protection of civil and political rights (except for the right to vote), and concentrate on other rights that are in practice most commonly restricted, and that have been part of a policy trade-off between openness and rights in high-income countries: social rights, the right to free choice of employment, the right to permanent residence, and the right to family reunion. I contend that given certain conditions and supporting policies, some restrictions of these rights are justifiable in exchange for better access to high-income countries' labor markets. Key supporting policies include measures that protect migrant workers' agency, such as their ability to make informed choices, and act on their decisions to both join and exit a particular labor immigration program.

The fourth and final part of the chapter discusses whether and how temporary labor immigration programs, especially for low- and medium-skilled migrant workers, can be in the national interest of migrant-receiving countries—a crucial issue set aside in the discussion of normative issues in the first three parts of the chapter. I focus on two sets of policy measures that are necessary to make low-skilled temporary labor immigration benefit receiving countries: the need to manage employer demand for migrant labor, and measures that facilitate the return of migrant workers whose temporary work permits have expired.

The aim of this chapter is to engage existing ethical theories in order to develop a normative framework and advance an argument for how to evaluate labor immigration policy, including the policy trade-offs between openness and rights that have been identified in this book's em-

pirical analysis. It is essential to emphasize at the outset that there is no
one right answer in this normative debate; indeed, there are few obvious
or clear answers to any of the questions analyzed in this chapter. The
analysis below thus inevitably reflects my own personal and ongoing
struggle with what are exceedingly difficult dilemmas. I do develop my
own normative position and policy implications at the end of the chapter, but I hope that readers who disagree with my particular approach
will still be able to engage with the bulk of the chapter in a meaningful
way.

What Consequences Should National Policymakers Care about, and for Whom?

International labor migration generates a complex set of economic, social, political, cultural, and other consequences for individuals, communities, and countries as a whole. Table 7.1 categorizes the major types of
impact (each indicated by an x) on nonmigrants in the migrant-receiving
country, nonmigrants in the migrant-sending country, and migrants themselves. The categories and distinctions in the table are clearly crude and
in many ways unsatisfactory, but the table is useful as a device for a basic
conceptualization and discussion of different types of impacts on different groups.

The types of impact included in the table reflect the major objectives
of policymaking mentioned in earlier chapters of the book: economic ef-
ficiency/welfare; distribution; national identity/social cohesion; national
security and public order; and individuals' rights.[2] The distinction between migrants and nonmigrants in sending and receiving countries is
meant as a conceptual simplification that does not address the important,
interrelated questions of how to define migrants (e.g., all foreign-born
persons or only foreign nationals?), and whether and how to distinguish
between different groups of migrants (e.g., short- and long-term migrants). For clarity and simplicity—and not for normative reasons—the
discussion below will assume that the groups of nonmigrants in receiving
countries are restricted to citizens of the receiving country. The term *non-
citizen* in the exploration below thus refers to migrants and their countries of origin.[3]

The design of national labor immigration policy requires national policymakers to define the policy objectives (the "social objective function"),

[2] Individuals' rights were included under "national identity/social cohesion" in the discussion in
chapter 3, and given the focus on normative questions, are highlighted as a separate type of impact in
table 7.1. In the table, the "x" linking "economic efficiency" and "migrants" is meant to stand for the
economic outcomes/welfare of migrants.

[3] Changing this assumption, such as by including permanent residents without citizenship in the
group of nonmigrants in the receiving country, does not affect the substance of the discussion. The question of when the status of a migrant changes from an outsider to insider (or from "nonmember" or
"semi-member" to "full member") is an important normative question not examined in this chapter.

TABLE 7.1. Types of impacts of international labor migration

	RC	SC	M
Economic efficiency	x	x	x
Distribution	x	x	
National identity/social cohesion	x	x	
National security and public order	x	x	
RC citizens' rights	x		
SC citizens' rights		x	
Migrants' rights			x

Notes: RC = migrant-receiving country; SC = migrant-sending country; M = migrants.

in a process that can be conceptualized as assigning weights to the different types of impacts listed in table 7.1. What impacts and whose interests should labor immigration policy serve?[4]

To identify and disentangle the key ethical issues in this inherently normative exercise, it is useful to distinguish between two main questions: To what extent, if at all, should the outcomes for collectives (such as economic efficiency or distribution) and the economic welfare of individuals be given priority over individuals' rights? And to what extent, if at all, should the interests of citizens of receiving countries be given priority over those of noncitizens (migrants and people in the migrants' countries of origin)? In order to scrutinize the ethical bases for making these decisions, it is necessary to address the more general (and much-debated) questions of what degree of consequentialism should be employed in the evaluation of alternative policy designs and what moral standing national policymaking should accord to noncitizens.

What Degree of Consequentialism?

An action (including policy) may be described by its consequences (or outcomes) and the means (or processes) by which the consequences are generated. Accordingly, the ethical evaluation of an action may concern itself with either consequences or processes, or with both. Different ethical theories disagree on the extent to which assessments of consequences and processes should enter into the overall ethical evaluation of an action. The degree to which the ethical evaluation is made in terms of outcomes (ends) rather than processes (means) may be used to locate moral theories along a spectrum bound by a minimally consequentialist position at the lower end and a strictly consequentialist position at the upper end.[5]

[4] One could argue that the process of assigning weights to the various outcome parameters in table 7.1 defines the national interest. This framework for defining the national interest would be in line with Joseph Nye (2002, 236), who suggests that "global interests can be incorporated into a broad and far-sighted concept of the national interest."

[5] This implies that I assume that even those arguments commonly known as rights-based ones have

The theory that probably comes the closest to being "minimally consequentialist" is Robert Nozick's (1974) version of libertarianism. In Nozick's world, rights are simply "side constraints" on the actions of individuals who may otherwise do as they wish.[6] The policy imperative for the "minimal state" that Nozick (ibid., 26) advocates thus is to protect individuals' rights by protecting all its citizens against violence, theft, and fraud, and ensure the enforcement of contracts. It follows that policies are to be evaluated only in terms of their consequences for individuals' rights, with little or no regard for their consequences for individuals' well-being or collective interest as a community.[7] The main difficulty with this approach is that there is no universal hierarchy among conflicting rights, such that the policymaker needs to decide which rights should be given priority.[8]

At the other end of the spectrum, strict consequentialism is defined as the extreme proposition that an action is to be evaluated in terms of its consequences alone, and therefore that an action is permissible if there is no alternative with "better" consequences, however measured.[9] Classical utilitarianism is an example of a strictly consequentialist position, in which the objective of a just society is to achieve the greatest net balance of satisfaction summed over all its members.[10] It is implied that the consequences justify the means of private action and public policy. Importantly, consequentialism is silent on the crucial question of how to weigh consequences for different groups within society.

To be sure, if all ethical theories were to be situated along a one-dimensional spectrum of consequentialism, most of them would be found somewhere in between the two extremes. It may be plausibly argued, for instance, that of the two Rawlsian principles of justice, the "priority of liberty principle" is a nonconsequentialist principle, while the "difference principle" is consequentialist in nature (as it makes the consequence for the distribution of welfare an ethically permissible standard for policy evaluation).[11] Similarly, by considering freedom as the end and primary

some minimal concern for consequences. For a discussion of this point, see Chang and Rowthorn 1995. Note that the terms *rights based* and *consequentialist* in this section, and the terms *nationalism* and *cosmopolitanism* in the following section, are simply used for linguistic convenience, indicating the underlying degree of consequentialism (rights based versus consequentialist) and moral standing extended to noncitizens (nationalism versus cosmopolitanism). The usage of these terms in this chapter does not necessarily reflect or correspond with the meaning given to these concepts in the broader literature.

[6] The idea of rights as side constraints holds that the rights of others determine the constraints on an individual's actions. In Nozick's theory, an individual's rights must not be violated for the sake of protecting someone else's rights or some greater social good.

[7] To avoid confusion, it is worth spelling out that a minimally consequentialist position *is* concerned with consequences, but only with consequences for individuals' rights (as means of actions), and not so much with consequences for the outcomes (or ends) for individuals or communities.

[8] For a discussion, see H.-J. Chang 2002.

[9] Compare Hausman and McPherson 1993. Of course, the operationalization of this principle requires that consequences be defined, and if there are potentially competing objectives (such as, in some cases, economic efficiency and income distribution), suitably weighed.

[10] See, for example, Sidgwick 1908.

[11] John Rawls's concept of "justice as fairness" is encapsulated in his two famous principles of justice. For one, each person has an equal right to a fully adequate scheme of equal basic rights and liberties; this

means of development, Sen (1999, 86) advocates a partly consequentialist theory that "can take note of, inter alia, utilitarianism's interest in human well-being, libertarianism's involvement with processes of choice and the freedom to act and Rawlsian theory's focus on individual liberty and on the resources needed for substantive freedoms."

The desirable degree of consequentialism in the ethical evaluation of public policies (or moral judgment of private action) has been a much-debated problem in moral philosophy.[12] It is not my intention to take a specific position in this debate, or discuss critically some of the arguments in favor of or against any particular degree of consequentialism. I merely want to point out that the design of labor immigration policy, or more generally any argument on labor immigration, is necessarily based—either explicitly or, as has been the case more often, implicitly—on an underlying ethical framework that is characterized by a specific degree of consequentialism, as derived from a particular stance in the rights versus consequences debate.

What Moral Standing for Migrants and Their Countries of Origin?

Having decided on the degree to which consequences should inform the design of a labor immigration program, the policymaker needs to determine for whom consequences should be taken into account. In other words, should national policymaking only consider the consequences of immigration for citizens in the receiving country, or should it also consider the consequences for noncitizens (migrants and people in migrants' countries of origin)? Furthermore, if the policymaker factors in the consequences for noncitizens, should the consequences for all citizens and noncitizens be given equal weights? If not, what should determine the degree to which the policymaker lets the consequences for migrants and their countries of origin influence the design of the labor immigration program?

The answers to these questions depend on the degree of moral standing that the national policymaker accords to noncitizens. Most discussions of immigration policy and indeed most contributions to moral philosophy tacitly assume that the national policymaker accords full moral standing to citizens only. Conversations about the moral standing of noncitizens are scarce and frequently avoided. I maintain, however, that a comprehensive assessment of how consequences should affect labor immigration policy must include an explicit look at the moral standing of noncitizens.

---

scheme should be compatible with a similar scheme for all (the priority of liberty principle). Second, social and economic inequalities are to satisfy two conditions: they must be attached to offices and positions open to all under conditions of fair equality of opportunity; and they must be to the greatest benefit of the least advantaged members of society (the difference principle). See Rawls 1985, 227.

[12] See, for example, Scheffler, 1988.

As a first step in that direction, it is necessary to acknowledge that as with degrees of consequentialism in moral theories, there is a spectrum of degrees of moral standing that the national policymaker may extend to noncitizens. This spectrum is bound by minimal moral standing, on the one end, and maximal (almost-full) moral standing, on the other. I exclude the cases of no (or zero) and full moral standing for noncitizens as unrealistic and untenable positions. The former would imply that the country does not treat noncitizens as human beings, while the second makes the concept of citizenship meaningless.

Advocates of a minimal moral standing for noncitizens usually employ what Simon Caney (1998, 32) calls the "negative arguments from anarchy." This approach comes in three versions, suggesting that due to the absence of an international community that defines as well as enforces rights and duties; the lack of significant cooperation among nation-states; or the lack of international cooperation motivated by cosmopolitan ideals, nation-states are under no obligation to include ethical considerations in their dealings with foreigners. A more positive claim for according a low moral standing to noncitizens proposes that it is a moral duty for a nation to follow the national interest (narrowly understood as the promotion of the interests of citizens only) in its dealings with other nations.[13]

In contrast, many of those who believe in maximal (almost-full) moral standing for noncitizens hold that there is a set of (comprehensive) universal rights to which everybody is entitled, regardless of their citizenship status. One of the most prominent examples of a position that comes close to this "ethical cosmopolitanism" is the Universal Declaration of Human Rights. As discussed in chapter 2, while still allowing nation-states to regulate who and how many migrants to admit, the CMW and other human rights treaties emphasize that human rights are universal (that is, they apply everywhere), indivisible (political and civil rights cannot be separated from social and cultural rights), and inalienable (they cannot be denied to any human being, and should not be transferable or salable).

Advocates of ethical standpoints that lie between the described extremes of nationalism and cosmopolitanism contend that just because certain moral principles are not completely enforceable at the international level, or are not embraced by other countries, a state cannot deny all ethical duties toward noncitizens. They argue that a strict ethical cosmopolitanism (for example, the Universal Declaration of Human Rights) is equally problematic because it clashes with anticosmopolitan institutions such as states in the real world.[14] In other words, where nation-states are the guarantors of cosmopolitan rights, there is a natural tendency toward friction and conflict between the rights of citizens and noncitizens. For these and many other reasons, few people subscribe to any of the two extreme views (just as few people advocate a strictly or minimally consequentialist position), but support a position of what may

---

[13] See, for example, Morgenthau 1951.
[14] O'Neill 2000.

be called moderate cosmopolitanism, which incorporates elements of both nationalism and cosmopolitanism. For example, Charles Beitz (1983) suggests that a moderately strong cosmopolitan view would include the duty to pursue cosmopolitan goals with an upper boundary on the associated cost, with the upper boundary defining the degree of priority that a government accords to its citizens' interests.

Just as it is difficult to identify and ethically justify the appropriate degree of consequentialism, it is no easy task to justify a specific degree of moral standing for noncitizens.[15] Again, I do not want to argue in favor of a particular moral standing but rather point out that the way in which consequentialism should influence the design of a labor immigration program critically depends on what degree of moral standing the policymaker extends to noncitizens.

It is useful to conclude this section by summarizing the main arguments with the help of figure 7.1.[16] The figure makes it clear that the role of consequences in the design of labor immigration policy depends on the degrees of consequentialism and the moral standing extended to noncitizens. Together, they constitute an ethical framework for the evaluation of labor immigration policy.

Different ethical frameworks have different implications for the objectives and design of desirable labor immigration policy. By way of illustration, it is useful to briefly think through some of the basic implications of the four frameworks that make up the corners of the ethical space in figure 7.1. Under consequentialist nationalism—the framework that, arguably, comes closest to the reality we currently observe in most countries– openness, selection, and rights are determined based on an assessment of the consequences for economic efficiency, distribution, national identity, and security in the receiving countries—with little to no importance given to the outcomes or rights of migrants and people in their countries of origin. For instance, points-based systems that aim to "optimally select" migrants in terms of their skills and other characteristics in order to maximize the benefits and minimize the costs of immigration for the receiving country can be justified by a normative framework of consequentialist nationalism. Guest worker programs that restrict the employment of migrants to specific sectors of the labor market that suffer from labor shortages and that limit migrants' access to the welfare state are another example. This normative approach is typically associated with two major challenges. First, it inevitably leads to controversies and debates about the methods as well as conclusions of impact assessments. Second, consequentialist nationalism is silent on the question of which of the four objectives—economic efficiency, distribution, national identity,

---

[15] For discussions, see Beitz 1983; Goodin 1988; Shue 1988; Nussbaum et al. 1996; Caney 1998; O'Neill 2000.

[16] To avoid confusion between table 7.1 and figure 7.1, it is worth recalling that an ethical framework serves to assign weights to the various types of impacts in table 7.1. There is, however, no direct correspondence between the dimensions of table 7.1 and figure 7.1, as the axes in table 7.1 are not meant to capture a spectrum of a single dimension (as in figure 7.1) but instead are simply used to organize the list of types of impacts.

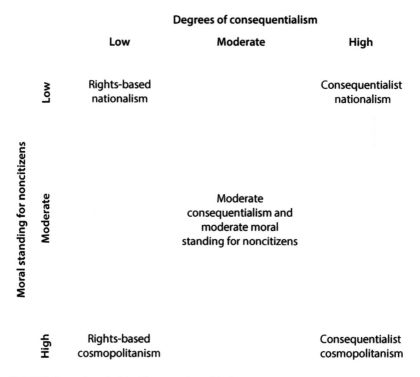

FIGURE 7.1. Examples of ethical frameworks (ethical space)

and security—should be given the most weight and how trade-offs should be evaluated.

Consequentialist cosmopolitanism requires labor immigration policies to be informed by the outcomes (rather than the rights of) all people, such as migrants as well as nonmigrants in receiving and sending countries. As migration can create large benefits for migrants and their countries of origin, the number of admitted foreign workers under a cosmopolitan position is likely to be higher than that under a position with a low degree of moral standing for noncitizens. In fact, it could be claimed that if economic efficiency and distribution were the only outcome parameters, consequentialist cosmopolitanism would require open borders, as the free flow of labor increases world welfare and decreases global inequality.[17] Importantly, consequentialist cosmopolitanism would tolerate a restriction of migrant rights as long as the consequences of more migration create net benefits for migrants' welfare or other measures of well-being. Consequentialist cosmopolitanism thus can and has been used to justify and advocate new, expanded guest worker programs that combine better access to global labor markets with restrictions of rights—especially for lower-skilled migrants.[18]

[17] See, for example, Hamilton and Whalley 1984.
[18] See, for example, Winters et al. 2003.

Under rights-based cosmopolitanism, the policy imperative is to protect to an equal degree the individual rights of all people, that is, migrants as well as nonmigrants. It can be argued that the policy principles of the CMW—universality, inalienability, and indivisibility—are based on an ethical framework for rights-based cosmopolitanism. While this normative framework does not provide ready-made answers to the question of what to do if there are competing rights between different groups, it is clear on the implications for labor immigration policy and guest worker programs: policies that involve restrictions of rights are morally unacceptable even if they create "good consequences" for other outcomes, such as countries' economies or individual's economic welfare.

Finally, rights-based nationalism requires that immigration policy be driven by a concern for protecting the rights of citizens in the receiving country. As is the case with rights-based cosmopolitanism, a key question within this approach is how to evaluate the rights of different groups like employers and workers. If employers' rights to contract are given priority, immigration policy would need to be much more open to admitting migrants than would be the case if workers' rights were prioritized.

While not everybody might agree with the particular way in which I have drawn implications for labor immigration policy from each of these four ethical frameworks, I hope that the brief discussion has at least shown how different normative starting points can lead to sometimes radically different policy implications.

Struggling for a Normative Framework: Building Blocks of My Approach

Given the multitude of competing ethical theories and frameworks, how should we choose and justify one over the others? There is no single most correct starting point for theoretical reflection in the ethical discourse on immigration.[19] As normative discussions are critically informed by values rather than just "facts," people with different values may reasonably disagree about the most desirable degrees of cosmopolitanism and consequentialism in the evaluation of public policies. Any considered argument for a particular normative approach necessarily reflects the current outcome of an ongoing struggle with what are exceedingly difficult normative issues as opposed to firm conclusions of a "scientific" exercise. The perhaps obvious but often overlooked implication is that any case for a particular normative starting point needs to be clearly justified and argued, and made with some humility.

With these caveats, the discussion below develops five core considerations (or building blocks) of my own normative approach to labor immigration policy, including questions about how to respond to trade-offs between openness and rights.

[19] Carens 1996.

My argument begins with the distinction between what Joseph Carens (1996) calls the "realistic" and "idealistic" approaches to morality. The realistic approach is firmly based on existing realities, and stresses the importance of avoiding overly large discrepancies between the *ought* and the *can*. In contrast, the idealistic approach is less constrained by considerations of practicality and focuses only on what *ought to be*, regardless of whether or not the implied policies are currently feasible. Carens (ibid., 169) makes the important point that "the assumptions we adopt should depend in part on the purposes of our inquiry." If the objective of the ethical discourse is to yield practical policy implications—as it is in this chapter—there is a strong argument to be made for adopting a combination of both approaches. On the one hand, idealistic considerations are needed to "break new ground" in thinking about ethics and public policies. On the other hand, if the discussion is to yield any practical policy implications, there must be a significant realistic component. Timothy King (1983, 533) makes the eminently sensible point along this line that "to ask people to accept policies which threaten to lower their own well-being sharply in the name of some abstract moral principle is clearly impracticable."

My own interpretation of what it means to combine a realistic and idealistic approach to the ethics of labor immigration policy leads me to advocate an "enlightened national interest" approach, which is based on the following two considerations:

1. *Acceptance of the need for national labor immigration policy to prioritize the interests of citizens.* In a world of sovereign nation-states, national policymakers must prioritize—at least to some extent—the interests of citizens over those of migrants and their countries of origin. This means that whenever there are trade-offs between impacts on citizens and noncitizens, policy can legitimately prioritize the former over the latter.

2. *Recognition of the duty to actively promote the interests of migrants and their countries of origin.* International labor migration has significant impacts, and can generate considerable benefits for migrants and their countries of origin. Yet most national labor immigration policymaking is based on near-exclusive concerns with the interests of citizens of receiving countries. Given global poverty and inequality, there is an ethical mandate to look for ways in which opportunities for international migration—especially for low-skilled workers in lower-income countries—to access labor markets in high-income countries can be expanded.

The first of these considerations reflects the need to be realistic about current policymaking and what can be expected of national policymakers. The second consideration is based on my personal concern, undoubtedly shaped by my own experiences as a migrant in different countries and cultures, with the cosmopolitan goals of reducing global poverty and inequalities while promoting global justice. I am attracted to arguments for a national interest approach that include—as, for example, Beitz (1983) has suggested—a duty to pursue cosmopolitan goals, but with a constraint that is based on a limit to the costs imposed on citizens.

With regard to rights, my normative approach combines a fundamental recognition and respect for some of the basic principles of human rights with the avoidance of "rights fetishism," and an active consideration of the agency of and choices currently made by migrants and their countries of origin:[20]

3. *Recognition of the moral weight of human rights principles.* The principles enshrined in international human rights treaties, such as dignity and equality, carry important moral weight and have become widely accepted reference points in public debates in liberal democracies. Any restriction of migrant rights along with the derogation of the principle of equality is, in some fundamental sense, morally problematic and needs to be justified by strong arguments.

4. *Rejection of rights fetishism.* As rights are not the only dimension of human development (or human well-being), they should not be used as the sole criterion for evaluating the moral desirability of immigration policies. The agency, choices, and interests of migrants and their countries of origin need to be considered when evaluating immigration policies that involve restrictions of migrant rights.

In terms of figure 7.1, I am making the case for a normative approach that is located in the "ethical subspace" of moderate degrees of both cosmopolitanism and consequentialism, where moderate does not imply a perfect balance but instead simply the exclusion of extreme ethical framework along the borders of figure 7.1. Cynics might maintain that this constitutes a cheap "centrist cop-out."[21] It does not. For the reasons given above, I strongly believe that to have any chance of success in the real world, an approach that aims to pursue cosmopolitan policy goals needs to balance the legitimate self-interest of nation-states with the interests of migrants and their countries of origin. At the same time, any approach that purports to consider the overall interest and human development of migrants needs to reject rights fetishism while taking seriously any restriction of migrants' rights. My approach implies that there are no easy choices in labor immigration policy. All morally desirable labor immigration policies, I contend, must involve at least some balancing of rights and consequences as well as the interests of citizens and noncitizens.

[20] The term *rights fetishism* is commonly used to indicate and criticize an overemphasis on rights. See, for example, Posner 2002, 156.

[21] Paul Krugman used the term *centrist cop-out* in the context of a discussion of US media reporting of competing arguments made by political parties; see http://www.nytimes.com/2011/07/29/opinion/krugman-the-centrist-cop-out.html (accessed December 12, 2011).

This brings me to the fifth and final core consideration of my normative approach:

5. *No presumption in favor of a one-size-fits-all approach.* The ethics of labor immigration policy of sovereign nation-states may, at least to some extent, be specific to country and time.

This consideration is based on the recognition that there are significant contextual differences between different countries. These differences are manifested, for example, in differences of economic development, cultural and social values, international relations with specific migrant-sending countries and the world community as a whole, the role and power of the judiciary, and perhaps most important in the context of a normative debate, the actual capacity of the state to act and implement certain policies (compare this to the discussion in chapter 3 about variations in institutions and constraints of immigration policymaking across different countries).[22] Given the sovereignty and self-determination of nation-states, these contextual differences suggest that there is unlikely to be a single ethical framework and corresponding labor immigration policy that can be identified as the most desirable one for all countries at all times. Rather than looking for a one-size-fits-all ethical framework and labor immigration policy, we need to allow for ethical valuations that may, at least to some extent, vary across countries and over time. This does not equate to an argument for ethical relativism, implying that morality is relative to prevailing social norms and culture. It does suggest, however, that while we may identify some universal principles and features of an ethical labor immigration policy, there may be some morally defensible variations of specific policy aspects.

The five building blocks discussed above indicate the broad features of my normative approach. While outlining some important starting points, as a whole they still leave room for a wide range of different evaluations and associated policy implications. In the next section, I use these five considerations as a basis for critically examining some of the main normative arguments in favor of and against restricting migrant rights under TMPs.

The Ethics of Temporary Labor Immigration Programs

All temporary labor migration programs restrict at least some of the rights of migrant workers. The empirical analysis in chapters 4 and 5 has shown that labor immigration programs that target lower-skilled migrants restrict more rights than those targeting higher-skilled migrants. It has also found evidence of a trade-off between openness and some rights:

---

[22] For a discussion of the ethical obligations of weak states, see, for example, O'Neill 2000, 2002.

programs that are more open to admitting migrant workers are often more restrictive in terms of the rights they accord to migrant workers. As shown in chapter 6, migrants and sending countries are acutely aware of and actively engage with these trade-offs, frequently tolerating rights restrictions in exchange for better access to the labor markets of higher-income countries.

Are temporary labor migration programs that restrict the rights of migrant workers fundamentally objectionable from a moral point of view?

Three Critiques: Human Rights, Equal Membership, and Exploitation

One of the most common normative critiques of TMPs, especially of programs for admitting low-skilled migrant workers, is based on the argument that they violate fundamental principles of human rights. There is debate about the exact interpretation of the rights and protections stipulated in international legal instruments. Not all human rights are absolute, and it is clear that these instruments do allow for some distinction between the rights and entitlements of citizens and noncitizens.[23] It is equally clear, however, that many (although not necessarily all) of the temporary labor migration programs and associated rights restrictions in high-income countries are not compatible with the human rights principles of universality, indivisibility, and inalienability, and the specific rights stipulated in the CMW in particular. Universalistic rights-based theories oppose the active promotion of new policies that are based on an explicit distinction between the rights and entitlements of different categories of residents (such as temporary residents, permanent residents, and citizens).

A quite different but equally powerful critique of TMPs is based on the assertion that a democratic national community must provide all its members with equal "terms of membership" and access to citizenship rights. This argument has been made, for example, by Michael Walzer, a communitarian who suggests that the political community can be thought of as a "club" or "family." He contends that if migrant workers are admitted into the political community, they must be given equal rights and opportunities to be set on the road to citizenship. Any other arrangements would constitute a "family with live-in servants." Walzer (1983, 61) summarizes the issue of guest workers as follows:

> Democratic citizens, then, have a choice: if they want to bring in new workers, they must be prepared to enlarge their own membership; if they are unwilling to accept new members, they must find ways within the limits of the domestic labor market to get socially

---

[23] See, for example, Weissbrodt 2008.

necessary work done. And those are their only choices. Their right to choose derives from the existence in this particular territory of a community of citizens; and it is not compatible with the destruction of the community or its transformation into yet another local tyranny.

A strong defender of the national community's right to limit immigration, Walzer makes it clear that not admitting migrant workers at all is better than admitting migrants under restricted rights—not because it is better for migrant workers, but because it is better for the national community. David Miller (2008, 376) makes a similar argument, acknowledging that the requirement of equality of citizenship rights will often result in the admission of fewer migrant workers:

These are the reasons, I believe, why admitting immigrants poses greater problems for contemporary states than it did for liberal states a century ago: they have to be admitted as equal citizens, and they have to be admitted on the basis that they will be integrated into the cultural nation. These are both potential obstacles to admission, insofar as they impose costs and constraints on the receiving state.

A third argument against TMPs is that they are inevitably exploitative—a slippery concept, as I explain below. While this claim frequently builds on egalitarianism (universal as in human rights, or within the national community as in Walzer's case), it has also been made based on neoclassical theories of economics. Daniel Attas (2000), for example, maintains that the source of exploitation in guest worker programs is not political—the source is not the denial of political rights and access to citizenship (as Walzer argues) but rather the denial of equal economic rights. Attas holds that because of the restriction of specific labor rights—especially the right to free choice of employment—guest workers receive a wage that is lower than their marginal product of labor in equilibrium (i.e., lower than the wage they could obtain if they were free to take up employment that pays the highest wage for their labor in the economy). This constitutes an "unequal exchange" (i.e., an exchange where one party does not receive their fair or just share), which under most definitions is a key characteristic of exploitation. Attas (ibid., 88) puts forth that the removal of the restriction of economic rights could eliminate exploitation in guest worker programs.

Thus, although there may not be sufficient grounds to require the admission of guest workers to full political citizenship, full economic membership seems justified. This might be all that is needed to expel the spectre of exploitation. Were guest workers to enjoy the same economic rights as local workers, and particularly the freedom of occupational choice, then the cause of unequal exchange would be removed.

These three arguments constitute important, powerful critiques of TMPs based on specific normative starting points. Within my own normative framework, though, I do not find any of these fundamental critiques convincing. I have three interrelated concerns about the three assertions: the critiques are concerned with a set of interests that I consider too narrow; they give insufficient weight to alternatives, such as to the consequences of rejecting guest worker programs for migrants and sending countries; and they do not place sufficient emphasis on the agency, interests, and actions/policies of migrants and their countries of origin.

As I will argue in more detail in the concluding chapter, human rights critiques often (but not always) fail to consider the potential consequences, such as greater economic welfare and human development, that TMPs may generate for migrants and others. While I am not claiming that consequences should always trump rights, I find it hard to see how a strictly rights-based argument that does not give any weight to the impacts of migration for the welfare or well-being of rights holders can be in the best interest of migrants, especially if migrants are currently making choices that suggest that they value rights *and* improvements in economic welfare along with other dimensions of human development (see the discussion in chapter 6).

Communitarian rationales such as Walzer's are primarily (and in some cases only) concerned with the collective interests of the national community in the receiving country, with little to no consideration for the interests of individual potential migrants (still in the sending country and seeking employment abroad), or those of the sending country in general. Within my normative approach, the argument that temporary labor migration programs are objectionable because they change the nature of the community in the receiving country and therefore are, in some sense, "bad for us" is not sufficient for opposing such programs. A realistic approach has to accept, of course, that immigration countries may not want immigration to radically change the nature of their community, but this does not exclude a consideration of policies that involve relatively small adjustments (e.g., the acceptance of a temporary presence of migrant workers who enjoy most yet not all the rights of citizens) in exchange for large benefits for migrants and their countries of origin.

My objection to the exploitation proposition is not that I disagree with the assessment that TMPs are exploitative based on the most commonly used definitions of exploitation. Rather, my concern is that such arguments often do not give a convincing account of why guest worker programs that exploit are ethically inferior to what would happen under realistic alternative policy scenarios. I consider and develop this notion more fully after reviewing some of the main points in defense of TMPs.

No Escaping from "Second Best" and "Dirty Hands":
The Normative Defense of TMPs

Most normative defenses of TMPs begin with the observation that such policies inevitably constitute second-best policies that lead to dirty-hands solutions. Howard Chang, for example, defends and advocates for the use of guest worker programs for low-skilled workers as second-best policies. Chang suggests that from the perspective of liberal principles of global social justice, first-best migration policies would involve more open borders as well as legal permanent residence with access to all citizenship rights. He considers this first-best policy as politically unfeasible as it would create fiscal burdens that residents of the receiving country would be unwilling to accept. Given this political feasibility constraint, Chang proposes TMPs that selectively restrict migrants' access to the welfare state while at the same time "seeking the broadest rights possible for aliens within the constraints of political feasibility." Chang (2002, 15) draws attention to the need to consider the alternatives along with the agency and choices of migrant workers themselves: "If guest worker programs make us uneasy, then exclusion should only make us more so, because it keeps alien workers in a state of poverty that they would prefer to escape as guest workers."

Daniel Bell (2006) makes a similar argument in the context of labor immigration policies in East Asia. His analysis of foreign domestic worker programs in Singapore and Hong Kong led him to conclude that there is no realistic prospect of foreign domestic workers obtaining equal access to citizenship rights. In other words, equal rights are politically infeasible. Bell (ibid., 297) states that "the fact that the door is closed to equal rights does have one practical benefit—it means that there are more doors open to temporary contract workers." Comparing foreign domestic workers programs in Hong Kong, Singapore, and Canada, Bell notes that while the programs in Hong Kong and Singapore are much more restrictive in terms of rights than the Canadian program (Canada's Live-in Caregiver Program grants migrants access to permanent residence after two years working in Canada), Singapore and Hong Kong admit many more foreign domestic workers relative to their population size than Canada. Bell (ibid., 297–98) thus observes: "The choice, in reality, is between few legal openings for migrant workers with the promise of equal citizenship and many openings for migrant workers without the promise of equal citizenship."[24]

Emphasizing the importance of migrant agency and considering alternatives to guest worker programs, Bell (ibid., 304) proposes three conditions that may justify unequal rights for migrant workers: if "(1) this arrangement works to the benefit of migrant workers (as decided by migrant

---

[24] In 2010, following a landmark legal judgment, domestic workers in Hong Kong *did* get access to permanent residence. The Hong Kong government is currently appealing this judgment. This points to the inherent difficulties with deciding what is politically feasible and what is not. But some judgments are easier than others.

workers themselves); (2) it creates opportunities for people in relatively impoverished societies to improve their lives; and (3) there are no feasible alternatives to serve the ends of (1) and (2)." In an interesting twist, Bell suggests that these conditions can justify unequal rights for temporary migrant workers in East Asia, but not necessarily in Western liberal democracies that do not share the values and cultural peculiarities underpinning East Asian societies. Bell explicitly warns against the "exportability" of his analysis.

A third and related line in defense of TMPs addresses the critique that such programs are inevitably exploitative. In an important article on guest workers and exploitation, Robert Mayer (2005) contends that the fact that guest worker programs are exploitative (he argues that this is not always the case) does not necessarily imply that they should not be tolerated. Like Bell, Mayer defends TMPs, even when they are exploitative, under certain conditions. Mayer's criteria are not too dissimilar from the conditions offered by Bell. In contrast to Bell, however, Mayer (ibid., 311) does not limit the applicability of his analysis to specific national or cultural contexts: "Even when guestworker programs are exploitative, it is argued that the unfairness should be tolerated if the exploitation is modest, not severe, and if the most likely nonexploitative alternative worsens the plight of the disadvantaged."

The implementation of this approach in practice requires a definition and measure of exploitation in general and modest exploitation in particular. Different people disagree on how to define and measure exploitation. Mayer (ibid., 317) is critical of egalitarian and neoclassical theories of exploitation, as they are "too sweeping and indiscriminate in their judgements." In developing his own theory and argument, Mayer starts with the example of highly skilled and highly paid migrants working abroad on temporary employment contracts. Mayer claims that such "privileged guests" do not seem to be exploited even when they work under restricted rights (e.g., no free choice of employment and no access to citizenship). He suggests that this instance points to the need for a more sensitive standard of exploitation. Mayer proposes a "sufficiency theory of exploitation," suggesting that only people who are below a threshold of sufficiency can be exploited. In other words, guest workers who "have enough" in their home countries before considering migration (i.e., who start from a position of financial sufficiency) cannot be exploited. A job offer under a guest worker program is exploitative only if migrants who do not have "enough" in their home countries would be the only ones to accept the job offer. The assessment of whether exploitation is happening in practice then hinges on our assessment of what constitutes enough in any given case. Mayer asserts that the German Gastarbeiter program was less exploitative than the US Barcero program because the wages and conditions on offer under the German program (which were similar to those provided to German workers) would have encouraged workers who have enough in Turkey to participate in the program,, whereas the tough working conditions and low take-home pay (after deducting various migration costs) of Braceros would have been unacceptable to Mexicans who start from a position of sufficiency in Mexico.

All three arguments in favor of TMPs are very much grounded in a realistic approach to the ethics of migration that requires us to engage with second-best and dirty-hands policies as well as the agency and choices that migrants make. I very much share this approach. I disagree with arguments that reject TMPs—and the inherent trade-offs between openness and rights—outright without offering realistic alternative policy scenarios that will provide better outcomes than the guest worker option.

The key question is whether there are any "clean-hands" alternatives to TMPs that lead to better outcomes. I am skeptical, especially when it comes to the migration of low- and medium-skilled migrant workers. As shown in chapters 4 and 5, permanent labor immigration programs that grant close to equal rights are generally reserved for highly skilled migrants. My empirical analysis of labor immigration programs strongly suggests that expecting countries to both admit more low- and medium-skilled migrants *and* grant them equal rights is not a realistic scenario in the short to medium term. The most likely clean-hands alternative to guest worker programs for low- and medium-skilled workers is exclusion. Based on my analysis of the interests and choices of migrants along with their countries of origin (see chapter 6), I do not see any evidence to indicate that exclusion leads to better outcomes for migrants and sending countries than participation in a guest worker program.

My own normative approach thus leads me to reject the three fundamental critiques of TMPs provided by human rights, communitarianism, and arguments about exploitation. There is, in my view, a strong case for considering—as Chang, Bell, and Mayer each do in slightly different ways—the expansion of temporary labor migration programs that selectively restrict migrant rights, but at the same time provide many more workers access to the labor markets of higher-income countries.

What Rights Restrictions Are Justifiable, and for How Long?

If we accept the possibility of an ethically defensible temporary labor migration program, two other important normative questions arise: What specific rights of migrant workers should we allow to be restricted under such programs, and for how long?

Given my particular normative approach, my starting point for addressing this question is that no labor immigration policy should restrict migrants' basic civil and political rights, with the crucial and widely accepted exception of the right to vote in national elections. Any normative approach that purports to be concerned about human rights, including my own, at a minimum must surely call for the protection of civil and political rights. So I advocate a "firewall" around civil and political rights in all policy debates on temporary labor migration programs.[25] If restric-

[25] The term *firewall* is adopted from Carens (2008, 441), who argues that in the context of debates

tions of civil and political rights are part of a policy trade-off that facilitates greater openness to admitting migrant workers than would otherwise be the case—as is currently true in some countries in the Middle East and Southeast Asia—the significance of protecting basic civil and political rights is, in my view, worth the "cost" of reduced access for potential migrants to labor market in these countries.

With regard to other rights, rights restrictions under temporary labor migration should be limited to those rights that demonstrably can be shown to create net costs for the receiving country, and hence may be part of a policy trade-off between openness and rights that high-income countries are likely to make in practice. The specific rights this applies to will, to some extent, vary from one country to another (e.g., depending on the characteristics of the welfare state). The empirical analysis of labor immigration programs in chapters 4 and 5 of this book suggests that the trade-offs that we observe in practice in liberal, democratic high-income countries have involved a few specific rights, including selected social rights, the right to free choice of employment, the right to family reunion, and the right to access to permanent residence. Based on the discussion above, there is a strong normative case for limiting any potential rights restrictions to these rights and calling for the equality of all other citizenship rights (except, as mentioned above, the right to vote in national elections).

Social Rights

As discussed earlier in the book, the legal access that migrant workers have to the welfare state is a critical determinant of their net fiscal contribution—the difference between the taxes they pay and the public services and benefits they receive. In countries with progressive taxation systems and welfare states that redistribute from the rich to the poor, low-paid workers can be expected to make a smaller tax contribution and greater use of welfare benefits than higher-paid workers. The net-fiscal effects of low-skilled immigration are often negative. Consequently, the extent to which low-skilled labor immigration benefits the host country is partly dependent on the degree to which low-skilled migrant workers' access to the welfare state can be restricted —hence the trade-off between openness and selected social rights in practice (see the discussion in chapters 3, 4, and 5).

Which social rights can justifiably be restricted under a temporary labor migration programs? My answer comes in two parts. The first repeats the general point made above: any restriction of social rights is only defensible if there is demonstrable evidence—not just a perception—that granting the rights would indeed create a net fiscal loss for the receiving country, and because of this, lead to reduced openness to admitting migrant workers.

---

about the rights of irregular migrant workers, "it is morally required to create a firewall between the enforcement of immigration rules and the enforcement of other laws, so that irregular migrants could exercise their rights without risking deportation."

Second, when thinking about the specific social rights that may be restricted under temporary labor migration programs, I agree with Carens's basic distinction between social benefits that are based on prior employment and tax contributions (contributory benefits) and those that are based on low income, such as means-tested benefits aimed at helping the poor. The moral argument for restricting access to contributory benefits is much weaker than that for limiting access to means-tested benefits (such as social housing, low-income support, education grants for low-income earners, etc.). As Carens (2008, 430) argues, "Since the goal of the programs is to support needy members of the community and since the claim to full membership is something that is only gradually acquired, exclusion of recent arrivals does not seem unjust (although it may be ungenerous)."

The distinction between contributory and means-tested benefits also can be justified in terms of costs and benefits for the receiving country. The net costs of providing access to means-tested benefits to low-paid workers is likely to be significantly greater than that of providing access to contributory benefits. In most countries, nobody (regardless of citizenship) can receive contributory benefits unless they have been employed and paid taxes for a minimum period, so access to contributory benefits is always restricted in that fundamental sense.

Restrictions to access to health services are, in my view, hard to justify given that the denial of health care often will create more costs than benefits for the receiving country (e.g., if migrants with infectious diseases cannot attend medical services). As regards education, a case can be made for restricting temporary migrant workers' access to public education, since the primary purpose of admitting migrant workers is employment and not study. I do not, however, support restrictions on the access to public education for the children of migrant workers (if they are admitted as discussed below).

The Right to Free Choice of Employment

As noted earlier in the book, restrictions of the right to free choice of employment are necessary to enable migrant-receiving countries to use temporary labor migration programs as a tool for responding to labor shortages in specific sectors and/or occupations of the labor market. Without this restriction, much of the receiving country's rationale for establishing temporary labor migration programs in the first place is significantly reduced. It is important to emphasize that the necessary constraint on free choice of employment is one that restricts migrants to work in specific sectors and/or occupations, not with specific employers, as is currently the case under many programs. One of the primary sources of migrants' vulnerability while employed under a TMP is the requirement that they work solely for the employer specified on their work permit. Migrants may then find it difficult or impossible to escape unsatisfactory working conditions (unless they are willing and financially able to return home). This problem may be exacerbated by some employers' illegal practices of retaining migrant workers' passports and providing "tied accommodation"—accommodation provided by the employer on the condition that, and as long as, the migrant keeps working for that employer.

The effective protection of migrants' rights thus requires at least some portability of temporary work permits, enabling migrants to change employers whenever necessary. As mentioned above, however, it is important to recognize that immediate, complete, and unlimited portability—across all occupations and sectors of the host country's labor market—would undermine the alignment of the size and composition of economic immigration with what is likely to be a sector-specific demand for migrant labor. In addition, this may substantially reduce the propensity of local employers to recruit migrant workers because the latter would be free to leave the employer who recruited them before at least part of that employer's recruitment costs have been recovered.

A more realistic policy objective would be to facilitate the portability of temporary work permits *within a defined job category* and *after a certain period of time*. The duration of the period after which permits become portable requires a realistic assessment of the time needed for employers to cover at least part of their basic migrant worker recruitment costs. Arguably, this period is unlikely to exceed six months. In this connection, it is crucial to note that it may not be desirable for employers to receive a guarantee that they can recover *all* their migrant worker recruitment costs. Such a policy could significantly reduce the risks associated with hiring migrant workers relative to those associated with recruiting local workers (who may leave the employer anytime, also before the employer's investment in the workers has been recovered). This, in turn, could encourage employers to recruit migrant workers over local workers.

The Right to Family Reunion

Although migrants do not have an unrestricted right to family reunion under the CMW, the protection of the family is covered by the International Covenant on Civil and Political Rights (Article 23). So any restriction of this right needs to be based on strong arguments. I believe that the trade-off between openness and this particular right in temporary labor immigration programs, especially in those targeting low- and medium-skilled migrant workers, does provide justification for some restrictions—but within limits.

It is important to distinguish between two types of restrictions on the rights to family reunion: an absolute restriction that does not allow family reunion under any circumstances, and a conditional restriction that grants the right to family reunion to those labor migrants who can provide proof that their incomes are sufficient to ensure that the family member or dependent will not become a fiscal burden on the state—that is, will not create net fiscal costs for the host country's welfare state. The latter conditional right raises the difficult and in practice highly contested question of how to define "fiscal burden on the state," and thus where to set the minimum income threshold required of the labor migrants to be eligible for bringing in a family member or dependent.[26]

As demonstrated in earlier chapters, the extent to which the right to family reunion can be restricted is likely to be a key consideration in how open a particular country is to admitting labor migrants, especially low- and medium-skilled workers. Insisting on an unrestricted right to family reunion, particularly, for low- and medium-skilled migrants, is likely to result in fewer opportunities for workers to access the labor markets of higher-income countries. As chapter 6 has shown, there are a large number of people—some with and others without families in their home countries—who currently choose to work abroad without the right to family reunion. It is also relevant to consider that there are many citizens who choose to take up jobs that in practice take them away from their families for extended periods of time.

The main principles of my normative approach require a balancing of rights with consequences along with a consideration of the agency and choices of migrant workers that we currently observe in practice. For these reasons, I believe that a limited restriction on the right to family reunion can be morally justified. I am opposed to a complete denial of the right to family reunion (apart from seasonal programs that recruit migrants for a few months only), but support policies that impose restrictions based on a minimum earnings threshold that the labor migrant must meet in order to be eligible for bringing in a family member or dependent. At what level this income threshold should be set will vary across countries and hence needs to be debated in a transparent way.[27] The costs arising from family members' likely use of welfare benefits and public services, including the costs of education for children, are in my view legitimate considerations when deciding on this minimum income threshold. In some countries, this conditional restriction of family reunion will exclude many but not all low-skilled (and thus low-paid) guest workers from family reunion.

Time-Limited Restrictions of Rights and Access to Permanent Citizenship

Is there a limit to the period of time for which restrictions on the rights discussed above can be morally justified? I agree with Carens (2008) and many others who have argued that the passage of time increases the strength of migrants' moral claims to equality of rights. While my normative approach can be used to justify the selective restrictions of migrant workers' rights for a limited period of time, it does not support policies

---

[26] For example, on a recent debate in the United Kingdom, see MAC 2011.

[27] For a discussion of alternative approaches, see ibid.

that create a group of second-class residents who are permanently excluded from equal access to citizenship rights. So a key question is: How long can migrants' rights justifiably be restricted? As Carens (ibid., 422) suggests, philosophical reflection cannot provide a clear answer. I consider four years a reasonable time period, although I recognize that it is hard to justify why it should not be three or five years. Anything less than three years seems to me "too short" to ensure that the policy generates the intended benefits for receiving countries as well as migrants and their countries of origin, while restrictions that last longer than five years seem to come close to "long term" or "permanent exclusion" from equal citizenship rights—something that I reject.

Let's suppose we agree on an acceptable period of time for which the rights of migrant workers admitted under a TMP can be restricted. What should happen at the end of this period? Should migrant workers be granted access to permanent residence (and thus, eventually, citizenship)? In important recent contributions to the ethics of immigration policy, Carens (ibid.), Alex Reilly (2011), and Patti Tamara Lenard and Christine Straehle (2011) have all maintained that migrants admitted under TMPs should be granted eventual access to permanent residence status and therefore citizenship. While I can see how this conclusion can be defended as a logical extension of the assertion about moral claims to equal citizenship rights increasing over time, I am concerned—within my normative approach—that the requirement to grant eventually all temporary migrants access to permanent residence and citizenship would significantly lower receiving countries' incentives to admit some migrant workers—especially low- and medium-skilled workers—in the first place. The requirement to grant eventual access to equal rights means that all the net costs that the temporary restrictions are aimed at minimizing might eventually have to be borne by the receiving country. While some receiving countries may consider it in their national interests to ultimately grant permanent residence to migrant workers admitted under TMPs, this is unlikely to be the case for all countries.

Given these concerns, I argue that there must be a time limit (four years, for instance, as I have proposed above) after which receiving countries need to decide whether to grant temporary migrant workers access to permanent residence or require them to leave. A policy option that I reject is the renewal of temporary work permits with restricted rights for longer than that limit. One way of implementing such a policy would be to operate a points-based system that uses transparent criteria for regulating the transfer of migrant workers from temporary residence status with restricted rights to permanent residence status with almost equal rights.

Enabling Workers to Make Considered Choices
before and after Migration

Respecting the agency and choices of prospective and current migrant workers is a core consideration that underlies as well as informs my normative approach in general, and the justifications of the rights restrictions discussed above in particular. For rights restrictions to be acceptable, it is critical to have policies in place that protect agency and enable migrants to make informed, rational choices about both participating in and—equally important—exiting from a temporary labor immigration program. This requires at least three types of policies in migrant-receiving countries.

First, migrants' legal rights, including the limits of any rights restrictions, must be effectively protected and enforced. This requires strict penalties against employers, recruitment agencies, and any other agents in the migration process who violate laws and regulations setting out rights for migrant workers in immigration, employment, recruitment, and other areas. The protection of migrant rights also requires effective mechanisms of redress for migrant workers who feel that they are denied their legal rights.

Second, to make considered choices, workers considering becoming temporary labor migrants must be provided with good information about the conditions of employment and residence while working under a TMP abroad, including clarity about any restrictions of their rights. In practice, workers obtain information from a wide range of sources including networks of friends, families, and other workers who are already working abroad. While governments are clearly not the only supplier of information about the conditions of employment and life for temporary migrant workers, the fact that their temporary migration policies restrict some of the rights of migrant workers does, in my view, create a special obligation to ensure that the "terms of the deal" are transparent, easily accessible, and made clear to workers before they join the program. There must be "truth in advertising."

Third, receiving countries' policies must effectively protect migrant workers' "exit options"—meaning migrant workers' ability to leave their employers and exit from the TMP altogether. This requires policies that ensure that migrant workers do not become trapped in the host country because, for example, they were charged excessive recruitment fees that need to be repaid and prevent them from considering a return to their home countries.

Making Temporary Migration Programs Work

To complete my normative assessment of TMPs that selectively restrict the rights of migrant workers, I need to address a question that many people consider to be at the heart of the debate in migrant-receiving countries, especially when it comes to policies for admitting low- and medium-skilled migrant workers: Is it possible to design and implement new and/ or expanded temporary labor migration programs for low- and medium-skilled migrant workers in a way that delivers the intended benefits for the migrant-receiving country yet avoids the adverse consequences that such programs have often generated in the past?

There is no doubt that many of the past large-scale temporary labor migration programs, most notably the Bracero program in the United States (1942–64) and Gastarbeiter program in Germany (1955–73), failed to meet their stated policy objectives and instead generated a number of adverse, unintended consequences. From the perspective of the receiving countries, the two most important adverse impacts included: the emergence of labor market distortions along with the growth of a structural dependence by certain industries on the continued employment of migrant workers, and the nonreturn and eventual settlement of many guest workers. The slogan "there is nothing more permanent than temporary foreign workers" has been a popular summary of the perceived failure of past guest worker programs.[28]

Managing Employer Demand for Migrant Labor

The key to addressing the issue of unintended labor market distortion is to recognize that, if the goal is to generate net benefits for the economy and country as a whole, temporary labor immigration programs, especially those for admitting low- and medium-skilled migrant workers, cannot be designed based on the needs and interests of employers alone.

Employer-led labor immigration policies often become special interest policies that give significant influence to recruitment agencies and the "migration industry." Employers, migrants, and intermediaries clearly benefit from increased migration, but the admission of more migrant workers may not always be in the best interest of domestic workers as well as the economy and society as a whole. To be sustainable, labor immigration policies need to be based on the national interest, which, I contend, involves balancing the interests of all affected parties, including those of domestic workers.

The practical implication is that employer demand for migrant labor needs to be critically evaluated, and then actively managed and regulated by the state. An argument that employers commonly make when asking for new or expanded temporary labor immigration programs is that migrant workers are needed to fill "labor and skills shortages," and "to do the jobs that domestic workers will not or cannot do." It is an important task for governments to critically assess this claim and design policies that create the right incentives for employers. There are three issues that need to be scrutinized and debated: the definition of labor shortages; the feasibility and desirability of the alternatives to immigration as a way of responding to shortages; and the incentives that employers face when recruiting migrant workers.[29]

Labor shortage is a highly slippery concept. The existence of unfilled job vacancies does not, by itself, indicate that there are labor shortages

---

[28] There is a plethora of studies providing empirical evidence for the so-called policy failures of past guest worker programs. For overview, see, for example, Castles 1986; Martin and Teitelbaum 2001.

[29] For detailed conceptual and empirical analyses of these issues, see Ruhs and Anderson 2010b.

that would justify the admission of migrant workers. There are several reasons, including the fact that there is no universally accepted definition of a labor shortage. Employers may claim there is a shortage if they cannot find local workers at the prevailing wages and employment conditions, and most media reports of shortages are based on surveys that ask employers to report hard-to-fill jobs at current wages and employment conditions.

In contrast, a basic economic approach emphasizes the role of the price mechanism in bringing markets that are characterized by excess demand or excess supply into equilibrium. In a simple textbook model of a competitive labor market, where supply and demand are crucially determined by the price of labor, most shortages are temporary, and eventually eliminated by rising wages that increase supply and reduce demand. Of course, in practice labor markets do not always work as the simple textbook model suggests. Prices can be "sticky," and whether and how quickly prices clear labor markets both depend on the reasons for labor shortages, which can include sudden increases in demand and/or inflexible supply. Nevertheless, the fundamental point of the economic approach remains that the existence and size of shortages depend on the price of labor.[30] Most of the industries and occupations reporting labor shortages should have rising relative real wages, faster-than-average employment growth, and relatively low and declining unemployment rates.

If there are labor shortages, is immigration a sensible response? Answering this question requires an assessment of the feasibility and desirability of alternatives to migrants. In theory, at an individual level, employers may respond to perceived staff shortages in different ways. These include: increasing wages and/or improving working conditions to attract more residents who are either inactive, unemployed, or employed in other sectors, and/or to increase the working hours of the existing workforce, which in turn may require a change in recruitment processes and greater investment in training as well as increasing skills; changing the production process to make it less labor intensive by, for example, increasing the capital and/or technology intensity; relocating to countries where the labor costs are lower; switching to the production (provision) of less labor-intensive commodities and services; and employing migrant workers.

Of course, not all these options will be available to all employers at all times. For instance, most construction, health, social care, and hospitality work cannot be offshored. An employer's decision about how to respond to a perceived labor shortage naturally will depend in part on the relative cost of each of the feasible alternatives. If there is ready access to cheap migrant labor, employers may not consider the alternatives to immigration as a way of reducing staff shortages. Although migrants are often a cost-attractive option for employers, they may not be a sensible choice for the overall economy. There is clearly the danger that the recruitment of migrants to fill perceived labor and skills needs in the short run exacerbates shortages, and thus entrenches certain low-cost and migrant-intensive production systems in the long run, potentially reducing their competitiveness over time.

There is no one right answer to the question of whether immigration, higher wages, or other responses are best in terms of labor shortages. Choosing among these alternatives is an inherently normative concern that requires a balancing of different interests. The implication for the design of temporary labor immigration programs is that there needs to be transparency and debate about the feasibility as well as consequences of the various responses to labor shortages in different sectors and occupations. This debate may sometimes lead to the conclusion that labor immigration, including that of low-skilled workers, is a sensible policy, while at other times the alternatives may be more attractive. There can be no one-size-fits-all answer for all countries and all times—but as noted above, there is a process that one can propose so that any introduction or expansion of a temporary labor immigration program is based on analysis and debate aimed at ensuring that the policy does serve the national interest of the receiving country.

The key policy implication of this discussion is that to make the admission of low-skilled migrant workers benefit the national interest of the migrant-receiving countries, governments need to implement policies aimed at linking the admission of new migrant workers to the needs of the domestic labor market, where these needs are defined in terms of labor shortages and a debate about sensible responses. While there are no best practices for such policies, there are at least three different yet overlapping policy approaches to achieving this goal: labor market tests; expert committees and shortage occupation lists; and economically oriented work permit fees.

Labor Market Tests

Labor market tests are mechanisms that aim to ensure that migrant workers are only admitted after employers have seriously and unsuccessfully searched for local workers to fill the existing vacancies. In theory, labor market tests serve an important function because they are meant to prevent employers from recruiting migrant workers over available and suitable local workers. In practice, however, such tests have proved notoriously difficult to implement, not least because employers have shown considerable ingenuity in ensuring that no local workers are found to fill their vacancies when it suits them.[31] In the worst-case scenario, both employers and local workers are actually not interested in engaging in employment relationships. This could happen, for example, when employers have a predetermined preference for employing migrant workers and

[31] Martin 2003.

local workers prefer to live off unemployment benefits rather than accept low-wage jobs. Certainly, without the right incentives and enforcement, any labor market test simply becomes a bureaucratic obstacle that serves neither employers nor local workers.

The weakest form of labor market test involves employers attesting that they have unsuccessfully searched for local workers and will pay migrant workers the prevailing (rather than legal minimum) wages in the given occupation (as is the case, for example, under Tier 2 of the United Kingdom's points-based system). Labor market tests that rely on employer attestation typically do not involve any preadmission checks (i.e., to see whether or not the employer has actually made efforts to recruit local workers) but instead rely on postadmission enforcement. It is unlikely that attestation-based policies are strong enough to ensure that employers do not use migrant workers to bypass domestic workers.

A stronger type of labor market test, which I argue is necessary for low-skilled labor immigration programs, involves some sort of preadmission certification of employers' claims that no local workers are available to do the job. For example, in Ireland, employers need to advertise their vacancies with FÁS, a public employment and training agency, for a minimum of eight weeks. FÁS contributes to the efforts to identify available local workers. If no match can be found after eight weeks, FÁS issues a letter to the employer certifying that a labor market test has taken place and that no local workers could be found for the job. This letter enables the employer to proceed with a work permit application for a non-EEA national. Other European countries operate similar systems. In Germany, application for a work permit requires approval from the Federal Employment Agency. Although some of these certification-based tests have worked better than others, effective implementation has proved challenging in a wide range of contexts and different countries, partly because employers in certain sectors, especially though not only involving low-waged work, often have a preference for recruiting migrant over domestic workers.[32] Still, to make low-skilled immigration benefit the national interest of migrant-receiving countries, it is critical that the government is serious in its efforts to implement effective labor market test.

Expert Committees and Shortage Occupation Lists

A second and potentially complementary policy approach is to use expert committees for drawing up shortage occupation lists. Australia, Canada, and Spain have special government units or independent advisory bodies to analyze labor shortage complaints. The United Kingdom went further, establishing Migration Advisory Committee (MAC), a body of independent labour market experts tasked to advise the government if there are skilled labor shortages that can be sensibly remedied by migrant workers

[32] See Anderson and Ruhs 2010.

from outside the EEA. MAC was created to develop objective analyses of labor shortages and appropriate policy responses. It recommends a list of shortage occupations. For an occupation to be included on MAC's shortage occupation list, it needs to meet three hurdles: the job needs to be skilled; there needs to be a shortage; and it must be sensible to address the shortage by recruiting migrants from outside the EEA. To analyze each of these questions, MAC uses a combination of top-down indicators (e.g., changes in relative wages and unemployment rates in different occupations) along with bottom-up evidence from employers, unions, government departments, civil society, and experts.

Economically Oriented Work Permit Fees

In order to create the right incentive structure for them, employers could be required to pay a fee for each migrant worker recruited and employed. The rationale would be to encourage employers to search for and recruit local workers who can be employed without paying a fee, and seriously consider alternative responses to perceived labor shortages. The revenues collected from this tax could then be used to fund enforcement and/or integration assistance, cover social costs, and/or compensate resident workers for their income losses. The key difficulty of such a fee/tax is the evaluation of the various public costs and benefits associated with the employment of migrants. Another practical challenge is the need to ensure that employers do not illegally deduct the tax from migrant workers' wages. To prevent this, work permit fees need to be effectively enforced with credible and significant penalties for employers who pass the fees on to their workers, or who employ migrants illegally so as to avoid paying the fees.

As noted in chapter 4, Singapore has been among the few countries to use economically oriented fees to "micromanage" the inflow and employment of temporary migrant workers. Singapore's so-called foreign-worker levies are payable by the employer per migrant employed. The levies are flexible (i.e., regularly revised), specific to the migrant's skill level and sector of employment, and rise with the share of migrants employed at a company.

Measures to Facilitate Return

It is apparent that any temporary labor immigration policy needs to include a number of policies to facilitate and maintain the general expectation of the temporariness of stay. First, policies need to be in place to prevent a situation in which a foreign worker decides to overstay a temporary work permit because his or her savings target could not be achieved within the work permit's period of validity. This requires strict enforcement against employers and recruiters who provide foreign workers with misleading information about employment conditions and living costs in the receiving country, and against employers who engage in contract substitution. As mentioned earlier, this refers to the illegal practice whereby the migrant worker is issued with a new contract specifying lower conditions of work and/or pay on arrival in the country of employment despite having signed an authorized contract prior to departure.[33]

Second, temporary work permits must be issued for a period that allows migrant workers—especially those in low-wage occupations—to generate the net financial gains necessary to make migration financially worthwhile. For example, in 2003 the United Kingdom introduced a low-skilled guest worker program (the Sector-Based Scheme) that issued one-year work permits for employing migrants in low-wage occupations in the hospitality and food-processing sectors. It is highly questionable whether it makes any financial sense to expect Bangladeshi workers—the leading recipients of these permits—to work in a low-wage job in the United Kingdom for one year only. Unsurprisingly, the Sector-Based Scheme was closed after a few years partly because of concerns about overstaying.

Third, migrant workers with a valid work permit need to be given the right as well as opportunity to travel freely—or at the least without excessive restrictions—between the sending and receiving countries. This will help migrants maintain networks in their home country, thereby increasing the probability of their return.

Fourth, financial return incentives could include the transfer of migrant workers' social security payments to their countries of origin. A study of the portability of pension and health care benefits for international migrants concludes that only 20 percent of migrants worldwide currently work in host countries where the full portability of pension benefits (but not necessarily health care benefits) to their home countries is assured. Indeed, the lack of portability of long-term social security benefits in many countries may hinder return migration and probably contributes to the informal employment of migrants in host countries.[34]

Fifth, host countries could also open special savings accounts offering migrant workers the opportunity to save part of their wages at special, high interest rates on the condition that the savings would only be released to migrant workers on their return to their home countries. Such financial incentives have been tried before, with mixed success. The most infamous example is the Bracero program, which required a portion of migrants' earnings in the United States to be deducted for retirement in Mexico. This policy ultimately failed because migrants never received the money, and their claims for deferred wages have been under investigation for decades.

Finally, there is a need for clear and effective procedures for punishing employers who employ migrant workers without valid work permits as

[33] ILO 1999.
[34] Holzmann, Koettl, and Chernetsky 2005.

well as for removing migrant workers who illegally overstay their temporary work visas. The latter is likely to require the cooperation of sending countries, which could, for example, take measures to regulate their migrant worker recruitment industries and assist in the return of migrant workers deported by the authorities of the receiving country.

Summary: The Case for Tolerating Some Trade-Offs between Openness and Rights

All temporary labor immigration programs restrict at least some rights of migrant workers. Selective rights restrictions can be part of a policy trade-off between openness to immigration, on the one hand, and rights for migrant workers, on the other. Insisting on equal rights therefore may encourage high-income countries to admit fewer migrant workers than would be the case if some rights could be restricted. Thus, there is an important normative question about whether and to what extent we should tolerate restrictions of migrant rights in exchange for more opportunities for migrant workers to access the labor markets of higher-income countries. Depending on one's preferred ethical framework for evaluating public policies, different people will disagree about how to address this question, which does not have one right answer.

Taking a pragmatic approach that combines realistic and idealistic considerations, I have argued in this chapter that there is a case for accepting some selective restrictions of the rights of migrant workers as long as the following conditions are met:

- There should be a firewall around the civil and political rights of migrant workers—with the exception of the right to vote in national elections, which can be reasonably restricted
- Any rights restriction needs to be based on evidence about its net benefits for the receiving country and should lead to greater openness toward admitting migrant workers
- Rights restrictions should be limited to selected social rights, free choice of employment, the right to family reunion, and the right to permanent residence
- Migrants' rights to free choice of employment need to be restricted in a way that limits migrants' employment to specific sectors and occupations, not to specific employers (except for a short initial period)
- Restrictions on social rights need to be limited to restricted access to means-tested benefits and not include contributory benefits
- Restrictions on the right to family reunion should be regulated by an evidence-based threshold for the income required to ensure that family members/dependents do not create net fiscal costs for the receiving state

- Any rights restrictions under TMPs need to be time limited—for example, to four years—and after this period, migrants need to be granted access to permanent residence (and thus eventually also to citizenship) or required to leave

To protect prospective and actual migrant workers' agency and capacity to make well-informed decisions, I have maintained that any temporary labor immigration program needs to be accompanied by the following policies:

- Effective enforcement of immigration laws and protection of the legal rights of migrant workers, with effective punishment for employers, recruitment agencies, or any other agents in the migration process that do not respect migrants' legal rights
- Transparency about the terms of the deal, including clear information about migrant workers' wages and employment conditions, living costs and conditions, and rights restrictions
- Effective protection of migrant workers' exit options for leaving the TMP whenever they wish to do so

To make temporary labor immigration policies benefit the national interest (rather than just employers' interests) of receiving countries, the following policies are necessary:

- Active management of employer demand for migrant labor through effective labor market tests, shortage occupations lists, and/or the use of economic fees aimed at incentivizing employers to consider the range of alternative responses to labor shortages
- Measures to facilitate the return of migrants whose temporary work permits have expired

As long as these conditions are met, I conclude that there is a strong normative case for supporting the introduction of new, improved temporary labor immigration programs for low- and medium-skilled workers in high-income countries.

Chapter 8

The Price of Rights

What Next for Human Rights–Based Approaches to International Labor Migration?

In most high-income countries, the majority of migrant workers are admitted and employed under TMPs that in one way or another restrict migrants' rights. The rights of migrant workers that are most frequently restricted include the right to free choice of employment, social rights (i.e., equal access to public services and welfare benefits), the right to permanent residence and citizenship, and the right to family reunion. In countries that are not liberal democracies, such as the GCC countries and Singapore, some migrant workers employed under temporary labor immigration programs are also denied some basic civil and political rights.

This book explores the characteristics and drivers of these rights restrictions in practice. The analytic starting point and key theme developed in the book is that in addition to their intrinsic value as human rights, the rights of migrant workers play an important instrumental role in shaping the effects of international labor migration for receiving countries along with migrants and their countries of origin. Different types of restrictions on the rights of migrant workers can be associated with different costs and benefits for all parties. This is why any analysis of the characteristics and determinants of restrictions on migrant rights must look at the relationship between these restrictions and the national interests of migrant-receiving and migrant-sending-countries as well as the interests of migrants themselves.

Because rights shape the effects of labor immigration, migrant rights are in practice a core component of nation-states' labor immigration policies. The design of any labor immigration policy involves simultaneous policy decisions on how to regulate the *number* and *skills* of migrant workers to be admitted as well as the *rights* to be granted to migrants after admission. Consequently, migrant rights cannot be studied in isolation of admission policies. To understand how, when, and why nation-states restrict the rights of migrant workers—and discuss what rights migrant workers should have—we need to examine how particular rights restrictions are related to policies that regulate the admission (i.e., numbers and selection) of migrant workers.

My empirical analysis of these issues and interrelationships in high-income countries shows that labor immigration programs that target the admission of higher-skilled workers are more open and grant migrants more rights than programs targeting lower-skilled workers. There is also evidence that labor immigration programs can be characterized by trade-offs between openness and some migrant rights—that is, programs that are more open to admitting migrant workers are also more restrictive with regard to specific rights. It is crucial to emphasize that the trade-off between openness and rights affects only a few specific rights rather than all rights, and that they most commonly include selected social and economic rights as well as rights relating to residency and family reunion. My empirical analysis suggests that trade-offs between openness and migrant rights can be found in policies that target a range of skills, but are generally not present in labor immigration programs specifically designed for admitting the most highly skilled workers for whom there is intense international competition.

In principle, the empirical findings of this book may be compatible with a range of different explanations and conceptualizations of policy-making processes. My approach conceptualized the design of labor immigration policy in high-income countries as a process of choice under constraints. Nation-states decide how to regulate the number, selection, and rights of migrant workers admitted in order to achieve a common set of potential national policy objectives (economic efficiency; distribution; social cohesion and national identity; and national security and public order) given a common set of potential constraints and institutional factors that limit and mediate the ways in which these policy objectives are translated into actual policies. The constraints are domestic and international legal constraints as well as a limited capacity to control immigration, while institutional factors include the prevailing political system, welfare state, and labor market structures.

If migrant rights are instruments and the result of a policy choice, it is plausible to expect high-income countries to selectively and strategically restrict some of the rights of migrant workers to maximize their net benefits for the receiving country. All rights—for migrants and nonmigrants—create multifaceted costs and benefits that vary across different types of rights, between the short and long run, and—critically –between workers with different skills. For most rights, high-income countries can be expected to perceive equality of rights with citizens as best for the national interest. The equality of labor rights, for example, can play an important role in ensuring that migrant workers are not preferred to domestic workers because they can be employed at a lower cost due to reduced rights. Some other rights, however, can create net costs for the receiving country, at least in the short run. For instance, granting low-skilled migrants in low-paid jobs equal access to the welfare state may create net fiscal costs for the receiving country that may not be offset by other types of benefits that employing low-skilled migrants may create. Where rights create net costs for the receiving country, openness to labor immigration can be expected to critically depend on the extent to which costly rights can be restricted and hence the trade-off between openness and rights. These are not just theoretical hypotheses but instead key considerations that have clearly influenced policy decisions in practice. As my discussion of the drivers of labor immigration policies has shown, the costs that specific rights are perceived to create are typically the primary explanation for many of the rights restrictions that we observe in practice.

Migrant workers and their countries of origin are acutely aware of and engaging with the trade-off between admission and rights in practice. Large numbers of migrant workers have migrated to countries where their rights are (sometimes severely) restricted, and few low-income migrant-sending countries are willing to insist on full and equal rights for their nationals working abroad for fear of reduced access to the labor markets of higher-income countries. This is not surprising as international labor migration can generate large human development gains for migrants and create significant benefits for migrants' countries of origin. The presence of large numbers of migrant workers in countries that severely restrict migrants' rights does not mean that these countries' labor immigration policies are morally acceptable. Yet the agency, choices, and interests of migrants and their countries of origin should, in my view, be a crucial part of any normative conversation about the desirability of tolerating restrictions on specific migrant rights in order to facilitate more international labor migration.

In the remainder of this concluding chapter, I return to a discussion of the human rights of migrants. The book's analysis of the roles and interests of nation-states in restricting migrant rights was in part motivated by the reluctance of most high-income countries to sign international migrant workers conventions by the United Nations and ILO. What are the implications of this book's conclusions for human rights debates along with the rights-based approaches to migration advocated by many international organizations and NGOs concerned with protecting as well as promoting the interests of migrant workers?

Blind Spots and Unintended Consequences of Human Rights

Many UN agencies and migration NGOs call for more countries to "respect the human rights of migrants" by ratifying and implementing the rights stipulated in the CMW and other international legal instruments. As discussed in chapter 2, the CMW stipulates a wide range of rights for migrant workers including equal access to most economic and social rights. Although fewer than fifty countries have ratified the CMW since it was adopted in 1990, the convention has become a common reference point in arguments for a human rights–based approach to migration, which the OHCHR has recently defined as follows:

The human rights–based approach:

Is based on the international framework of human rights law as provided in the international bill of rights and the core human rights instruments

> Establishes accountability between duty-bearers and rights-holders
>
> Focuses on vulnerability, marginalisation and exclusion
>
> Emphasises participation and empowerment
>
> A human rights–based approach emphasises that human rights are interdependent and inalienable, and that there is no hierarchy between different sets of rights.[1]

As noted earlier, the analysis in this book highlights the danger of a blind spot in this type of human rights–based approach to migration (as I will argue in the next section, not all human rights approaches are inherently characterized by this blind spot). Human rights–based arguments are often focused on protecting and promoting the rights of *existing* migrants without considering the consequences for the admission of new migrant workers—that is, without considering the interests of the large number of *potential future migrants* who are still in their countries of origin and seeking to access the labor markets of higher-income countries. The trade-off between openness and specific migrant rights in high-income countries' labor immigration policies means that insisting on equality of rights for migrant workers can come at the price of more restrictive admission policies and, therefore, discourage the further liberalization of international labor migration, especially for lower-skilled workers whose international movement is currently most restricted, and where more migration could lead to large income and human development gains.

Put differently, from a global justice point of view, more migration and more rights for migrants are both "good things."[2] Yet the trade-off between openness and rights in high-income countries' labor immigration policies means that for some specific rights and some groups of migrants, it is not possible to have more of both, so a choice needs to be made. Human rights approaches to migration that demand all the rights stipulated in the existing international labor standards run the danger of doing good in one area (i.e., in promoting the rights of existing migrants) while doing harm in another (i.e., by making it more difficult to increase opportunities for workers to migrate and legally work in higher-income countries).

It is of course possible to argue that rights should always trump access—that it can never be morally justified to restrict the rights of migrant workers in order to encourage/facilitate more migration. This is, implicitly or explicitly, the normative view underlying arguments for equality of rights within many human rights–based approaches to migration. It is not a perspective that I share. As mentioned in chapter 7, a strong normative case can be made for the *selective* and *temporary* restriction of a few specific rights of migrant workers admitted under TMPs in order to give

---

[1] Ndiaye 2011.
[2] See Ruhs and Martin 2008.

more workers in low-income countries the opportunities to migrate legally and take up employment in higher-income countries. Under my normative approach, the temporary rights restrictions that I would find acceptable in exchange for more open admission policies relate to the right to free choice of employment, equal access to selected social rights, the right to family reunion, and the right to permanent residence and citizenship. In other words, I endorse a pragmatic approach that includes a temporary, limited, and evidence-based trade-off between the two goods of more migration and more rights to promote the interests of both current and potential future migrants.

UN Agencies' Reluctant Engagement with the Price of Rights

Halfway through writing this book—when I had published a few articles and working papers that began to develop my theoretical approach and arguments—I was invited to speak about my research concerning the rights of migrant workers at an international conference organized by the OHCHR in Geneva.[3] The purpose of this conference was to prepare for high-level discussions about the human rights of migrant workers at the annual meeting of the Global Forum on Migration and Development (GFMD) in 2009 in Athens. The GFMD is an "initiative of the United Nations Member States to address the migration and development interconnections in practical and action-oriented ways."[4] The rights of migrant workers were a key theme of the GFMD conference in Athens.

I considered the invitation to speak at the OHCHR with mixed feelings. I was keen to engage the United Nations' major human rights agency in a dialogue about the idea that some rights for migrant workers can create net costs for receiving countries, at least in the short term, which may lead to a trade-off between openness and rights in labor immigration policy. At the same time, I was aware that this argument might be misinterpreted to imply a rejection of all human rights–based approaches to migration (it does not, as I discuss in the final section below). After some reflection, plus a phone call with an OHCHR official who sounded increasingly alarmed as I explained what I wanted to say in my fifteen minutes, but who in the end did not "dis-invite" me, I accepted the invitation.

A few minutes before the start of the panel I was on, the panel chair, a senior official at the OHCHR, asked me to confirm the title of my presentation. I told him that the title of my talk was "The Costs and Benefits of Migrant Rights." He raised an eyebrow and made a note. A few minutes later, he introduced me: "We are very pleased to welcome Dr. Martin Ruhs from Oxford University. He will talk about the benefits of migrant

---

[3] See ibid.; Ruhs 2010a, 20010b.
[4] http://www.gfmd.org (accessed February 24, 2012).

rights." I gave my talk as planned, looking at the potential benefits and costs of migrant rights. It turned out to be an interesting session. An OHCHR staffer presented a paper from their agency that explored the benefits of migrant rights for the development of migrant-sending countries (with no mention of any potential costs).[5] As I left and was saying good-bye to the two OHCHR officials organizing the conference, I commented, "Well, that was a good session. I think I got away with talking about the costs of rights and the potential trade-off with openness in high-income countries' admission policies." They smiled nervously and responded: "Just about, just about."

I am recalling this anecdote because it reflects a general reluctance of many (but not all) UN agencies and other international and national organizations concerned with migration and human rights to explicitly consider and engage in a debate about the costs and benefits of rights along with the consequent potential for a policy trade-off between some rights and countries' openness to admitting migrant workers. While some UN and other international organizations simply refuse to talk about the issue, others have dismissed it as a "nonissue" (i.e., as something that is not real outside academic debates), while still others recognize the potential policy trade-off, but without—at least so far—explicitly engaging with it.

For example, the Global Migration Group (2008, 59)—an interagency group bringing together the heads of over fifteen UN agencies plus the International Organization for Migration (IOM, a UN-affiliated organization, but not formally part of the United Nations) and the World Bank to discuss migration—recently published a report on international migration and human rights that made it clear that all TMPs should strictly adhere to all the international human rights instruments:

> The proliferation of temporary migration schemes should not lead to the curtailment of the rights of migrant workers in the work place, especially regarding the principles of equality of treatment with national workers and non-discrimination. The view that such programmes necessarily involve a trade-off of migrant numbers with their rights undermines the framework of migrant protection and rights elaborated in international instruments. . . . It is extremely important that those programmes [of temporary and circular migration] are in strict compliance with the relevant international human rights instruments, in particular to ensure non-discrimination with regard to remuneration and other conditions of work.

The ILO—the UN agency responsible for drawing up and overseeing international labor standards—also explicitly rejects the "discourse" of a trade-off between openness and migrant rights. Its 2010 position paper

<hr>

[5] OHCHR 2009.

on a rights-based approach to migration argues that "the current promotion of temporary migration programmes is often associated with a misplaced discourse of trading off rights in exchange for increased access to job opportunities in destination countries." At the same time, however, the organization argues that there are acceptable restrictions of the rights of migrant workers under TMPs.

> Special efforts should be made to prevent temporary migration schemes from resulting in limitations on equal access to labour and human rights for migrant workers vis-à-vis native workers. This relates in particular to the principles of equality of opportunity and treatment and non-discrimination, including the right to equal pay for equal work, to decent and safe conditions of work, and to the right of association. Of particular concern is the all-too-common practice of employers withholding migrant workers' passports in complete breach of internationally recognized human rights standards. Some limitations on the enjoyment of rights may be reasonable, at least for a limited period of time, such as the right to family reunification and the immediate enjoyment of social security and social protection benefits. However, there are others that should never be compromised, such as the fundamental labour rights of freedom of association and collective bargaining.[6]

In 2006, the ILO published a multilateral framework on labor migration. The ILO describes the framework as a "comprehensive collection of principles, guidelines and best practises on labour migration policy, derived from relevant international instruments and a global review of labour migration policies and practices of ILO constituents."[7] It highlights that the framework "takes account of national labour market needs," and more generally, constitutes a "non-binding framework which clearly recognises the sovereign right of all nations to determine their own migration policies."[8]

Although the ILO's multilateral framework gives no sense of a hierarchy of rights for migrant workers, or a potential trade-off between some rights and migrant worker admission policies, the framework has in practice been used by some other organizations to promote a rights-based approach, but without at the same time calling on nation-states to ratify the CMW or other international legal instruments.

For example, the final report of the Global Commission on International Migration (2005)—a body encouraged by Kofi Annan in 2003, with a mandate to "provide the framework for the formulation of a coherent, comprehensive and global response to the issue of international migration" (ibid., vii)—advocates a liberalization of international labor

---

[6] ILO 2010, 212, 169.
[7] Ibid., 246.
[8] Ibid., 250, 247.

migration through more TMPs.[9] It also supports a rights-based approach to migration with reference to the ILO multilateral framework, but the commission report does not explicitly call for ratification of the CMW. It notes that "given the decision of many states not to ratify the 1990 Convention, the Commission considers that there is a particular need for complementary approaches to the issue of migrant rights" (ibid., 57).

This particular wording can be interpreted to suggest an underlying recognition of the potential tension between calling for more migration through TMPs, on the one hand, and ratification of the CMW, on the other.

Ambiguity about the relationship between promoting more migration and better protection of the rights of migrant workers is also a feature of the work and official policy documents of the IOM. Unlike UN agencies, the IOM is primarily an agency that serves the interests of its member states without a specific normative mandate on protecting human rights. Traditionally, the IOM has primarily been a service agency whose work facilitates and promotes migration (the IOM's tagline is "Migration for the benefit of all"). More recently, the IOM has begun to formally express views on human rights. These views are not particularly specific, yet they make it clear that human rights are considered alongside and in the context of efforts to facilitate and promote migration as well as help countries manage their borders. In its 2009 position paper on the human rights of migrants, the IOM does not explicitly call on states to ratify the CMW or other human rights treaties. It also does not mention the ILO's multilateral framework. The IOM's (2009, 5) paper concludes that

> a prime objective of the Organisation is to enhance the humane and orderly management of migration and the effective respect for the human rights of migrants in accordance with international law. Traditionally providing migration assistance, IOM is now taking measures and implementing projects to actively promote respect for the human rights of migrants. The Organisation has assumed a more dynamic role in this realm without transforming itself into a supervisory or monitoring agency in terms of the application of international norms. Respect for the human rights of migrants is essential to ensure their dignity and well-being, an objective that is central to the spirit and philosophy of IOM.[10]

Among the UN agencies, the UNDP has gone the furthest to identify a core set of basic rights for migrant workers that must never be violated. The UNDP's Human Development Report 2009 dedicated to international migration and human development, concluded that migration can create large benefits for human development. It called on high-income

---

[9] The Global Commission on International Migration (2005, 16) recommended that "states and the private sector should consider the option of introducing carefully designed temporary migration programmes as a means of addressing the economic needs of both countries of origin and destination."

[10] IOM 2009, 5.

countries to open their doors to more migrant workers (especially those with low skills) to maximize the benefits of migration for human development. With regard to the rights of migrant workers, the UNDP (ibid., 101) report did not call for the ratification of the CMW but instead referred to the ILO's multilateral framework as a "'soft law' type of approach [that] accommodates the inherent differences between states and allows for gradual implementation," and offered the following recommendations concerning migrant workers' rights:

> Even if there is no appetite to sign up to formal conventions, there is no sound reason for any government to deny such basic migrant rights as the right to:
>
> - Equal remuneration for equal work, decent working conditions and protection of health and safety;
> - Organize and bargain collectively;
> - Not be subject to arbitrary detention, and be subject to due process in the event of deportation;
> - Not be subject to cruel, inhumane or degrading treatment; and
> - Return to countries of origin.
>
> These should exist alongside basic human rights of liberty, security of person, freedom of belief and protection against forced labor and trafficking.

The UNDP report explicitly rejects the desirability of a trade-off between more migration and restriction of these basic rights, but remains silent on the desirability of any policy trade-offs that involve selective restrictions of other rights such as equal access to social rights.[11] Given its focus on promoting development and recommendation for more migration, it is perhaps not surprising that it is UNDP rather than the OHCHR or ILO that has gone the furthest in distinguishing between basic rights and other rights for migrant workers, and in analyzing potential trade-offs between access to high-income countries and rights after admission.

Clearly, all official policy documents and statements need to be read and interpreted with caution, as they do not necessarily always reflect the more nuanced conversations and analyses that may be happening behind the scenes and/or within specific units of these large international organizations. The statements explored above do not necessarily reflect the unitary views of these organizations as well as all the officials and analysts working for them. Nevertheless, taken as a whole, the speeches, position

---

[11] The UNDP report also contains empirical analysis that, the report argues, provides evidence that there is no trade-off between openness and rights (see also Cummins and Rodriguez 2010). As I have explained in detail elsewhere (see Ruhs 20010b), the UNDP's analysis is limited in many ways. Most important, it does not analyze the relationship between policy openness to labor immigration and the rights of migrant workers under TMPs (as discussed in this book; Ruhs 2010a; Ruhs and Martin 2008) but rather the relationship between the number of all migrants in high-income countries and selected indicators of integration.

papers, and policy documents on the rights of migrant workers do make it clear that there has, with few exceptions, been a great reluctance among the major UN agencies to explicitly consider and engage with the relationships between migrant rights, national interests, and nation-states' policies for admitting migrant workers.

One could argue that the reluctance to engage with the trade-off between openness and rights is not surprising, and indeed is "required" of standard-setting organizations with the primary aim of advocating and promoting the better protection of human rights, such as the OHCHR and ILO. If the only goal were to encourage policies that lead to more respect for human rights in the long run, an exclusive focus on rights could be justified on the grounds that arguments about trade-offs arising from interests of nation-states can be made by other organizations that are concerned with international labor migration more broadly, not just rights. In practice, however, the ILO and to a lesser extent the OHCHR are not only concerned with rights but also aspire to influence countries' policies toward admitting migrant workers "here and now." For example, the ILO is routinely engaged in technical cooperation projects that provide advice to national governments about how to regulate labor immigration and migrant rights. But if informing debates and policymaking on labor immigration is indeed a major objective for the ILO and other right-based organizations (and I agree that it should be), there is a strong case for the need to more actively engage with the kinds of issues analyzed in this book—that is, the costs that some rights create for receiving countries as well as the consequent policy trade-offs between admitting more migrant workers and extending more rights to them. Such an engagement does not need to reject human rights altogether. Yet it does need to involve a reframing of the human rights–based approach to migration as currently advocated by most UN agencies.

Reframing the Human Rights–Based Approach to Migration

I conclude that there is a strong case for advocating a rights-based approach to international labor migration that is premised on the protection of a universal set of core rights, and that takes the interests of nation-states into account by explicitly tolerating temporary restrictions of a few specific rights that can be shown to create net costs for receiving countries, and that are, as a consequence, part of a policy trade-off between openness and rights. Allowing such rights to be restricted should encourage the further liberalization of international labor migration.

The decision about how to distinguish between core and other rights needs to be based on analysis and discussion of the two questions addressed in this book. Which rights create net costs for the receiving country and therefore are part of a potential policy trade-off with openness to admitting migrant workers? And from a normative point of view, which rights must never be restricted regardless of the consequences for nation-states' admission policies?

In response to the first question (analyzed theoretically and empirically in chapters 3–6), I found that the specific rights that have been implicated in trade-offs in high-income countries' labor immigration policies are selected social rights, the right to free choice of employment, the right to permanent residence and citizenship, rights relating to family reunion, and in countries that are not liberal democracies, some civil and political rights. My response to the second question (analyzed in chapter 7) is that the core rights that must never be violated should include all civil and political rights (except for the right to vote in national elections), and that restrictions should be temporary and limited to the right to free choice of employment, equal access to means-tested public benefits, the right to family reunion, and the right to permanent residence and citizenship.[12] I have looked at a number of supporting policies, such as the transparency of policies and the effective protection of opportunities for migrant workers to exit TMPs, which are required to make these restrictions acceptable from a moral point of view. This means that I advocate a rights-based approach to migration that includes as core rights most of the rights enshrined in UN and ILO conventions.

For the sake of clarity, it is important to underscore that I do not reject human rights. The approach that I advocate can be interpreted as a *reframing* of the human rights–based approach as currently advocated by most UN agencies. Identifying core rights that must never be violated regardless of the consequences, and having more explicit debate about the desirability of temporary restrictions on other migrant rights can be consistent with human rights. First, at a conceptual level, as Amy Gutmann (2001) and many other human rights scholars have pointed out, there can be multiple foundations of human rights. The approach I advocate puts more emphasis on the importance of individuals' agency rather than on using human rights to insist on automatic equal treatment between citizens and migrant workers.

Second, it can be argued that the approach I propose *could*—under some interpretations—be consistent with human rights jurisprudence in practice. International human rights jurisprudence generally distinguishes between rights that are absolute, in the sense that there can be no justification for restricting them. Examples include the right to life, and the right not to be tortured or treated in an inhuman or degrading way. Most human rights are not absolute, which means that they can be limited and restricted under certain conditions. Most nonabsolute rights can be restricted based on the proportionality principle, which requires that the aim of the restriction is legitimate (e.g., to protect the rights of others or wider society), and that the restriction is reasonable and proportionate.[13]

---

[12] The right to permanent residence and citizenship is not a right enshrined in international legal instruments but rather a right frequently discussed in public debates about migration and the rights of migrant workers.

[13] The application of the proportionality principle in human rights adjudication necessarily raises

This was recently emphasized, for instance, in a 2011 speech on migration by the director of the Human Rights Council and Special Procedures Division at the OHCHR: "Where differential treatment is contemplated, between citizens and non-citizens or between different groups of non-citizens, this must be undertaken for a legitimate objective, and the course of action taken to achieve this objective must be proportionate and reasonable."[14]

Within the human rights framework, the approach I advocate thus can be interpreted as a call for more explicit debate about legitimate objectives, reasonableness, and the proportionality of restricting migrant rights in order to increase nation-states' openness to admitting migrant workers, and about the implications for the core rights that should be included in a reframed rights-based approach to international labor migration.[15]

Finally, there is a precedent within the UN system for stressing the fundamental importance of specific rights from a larger list of rights. In 1998, the ILO passed the Declaration on Fundamental Principles and Rights at Work, commonly known as core labor standards.[16] The declaration "commits Member States to respect and promote principles and rights in four categories, whether or not they have ratified the relevant Conventions. These categories are: freedom of association and the effective recognition of the right to collective bargaining, the elimination of forced or compulsory labour, the abolition of child labour and the elimination of discrimination in respect of employment and occupation."[17]

The ILO declaration therefore identified a short list of fundamental rights that are given preeminence over other ILO conventions. Its rationale was partly to "reconcile the globalisation of the economy and the defence of workers' fundamental rights."[18] The core labor standards were adopted in the context of dwindling numbers of ratifications of ILO conventions and a general criticism that the ILO's labor standards were not effective enough at protecting workers' rights in a rapidly globalizing economy. According to Jan Martin Witte (2008, 17),

> Under the circumstances, business as usual was not a viable option for the ILO. A bold move was needed for the organization to regain its relevance and credibility; new instruments were required to demonstrate that the organization and its stakeholders were serious about addressing the issue of labor standards in the globalized

---

complex and contested issues, including the "balancing" of things that are hard to balance. For a recent discussion of the challenges and pathologies of proportionality reasoning, see Endicott 2012.

[14] Ndiaye 2011.

[15] Different human rights experts are likely to disagree about whether restrictions of rights in order to allow more labor immigration can ever be justified based on the proportionality principle. It is, to the best of my knowledge, an untested case. For a recent discussion of the challenges related to applying the proportionality principle, including a number of incommensurabilities and pathologies, see Endicott 2012.

[16] My brief discussion of the ILO's core labor standards below draws from Ruhs 2013.

[17] http://www.ilo.org/declaration/thedeclaration/lang--en/index.htm (accessed March 12, 2012).

[18] Michelotti and Nyland 2000, 1.

economy. The Declaration on Fundamental Principles and Rights at Work, passed in 1998, was part of these efforts to reposition the ILO. Rather than taking the approach to promoting the ILO's entire body of labor standards, the Declaration focuses on a number of essential conventions, labelled "core labour standards."

The adoption of the core labor standards naturally generated significant debate. Some critics voiced concerns that the standards would detract from the importance of the wider set of ILO conventions, and that it was a mistake to separate out and concentrate on a small set of core rights.[19] Others, though, praised the core labor standards as a critical and "pragmatic" step toward more effective protection of workers' rights in the global economy.[20]

Open Debate

This book contributes to an underresearched and underdebated set of issues in international labor migration. As such, my empirical findings and normative arguments cannot and should not settle the positive and normative questions raised. The measurement and analysis of the effects of different type of rights for different groups is in its infancy, and much more research is needed to advance our understanding of the multifaceted costs and benefits of different rights as well as the existence and dynamics of trade-offs between specific rights and admission policies.

Equally crucial, there needs to be much more open debate about which rights restrictions, if any, should be tolerated given the interests, politics, and policy trade-offs made by migrant-receiving countries in practice. A key potential pitfall of many of the existing human rights–based approaches to migration is that they exclude or minimize the space for politics about issues that are fundamentally and inherently conflictual, and therefore require open debate. As Michael Ignatieff (2001a, 20) has contended: "When political demands are turned into rights claims, there is a real risk that the issue at stake will become irreconcilable, since to call a claim a right is to call it non-negotiable, at least in popular parlance."

The rights-based approach to international labor migration that I propose would be based on Ignatieff's (2001b, 95) argument that "we need to stop thinking of human rights as trumps and begin thinking of them as a language that creates the basis for deliberation." Bringing the state and politics back into right-based approaches to international labor migration would open up a space for legitimate and important debates and deliberation about the desirability or otherwise of restricting specific rights, for how long, under what circumstances, and so on. This would enable a reasoned debate between organizations that advocate more migration,

---

[19] See especially Alston 2004; Alston and Heenan 2004.
[20] See, for example, Maupain 2005; Langille 2005.

such as the World Bank and the UNDP, and those primarily concerned with the protection and equality of rights, such as the OHCHR and the ILO. Rather than shying away from these issues (as has sometimes been the case), UN agencies and other international organizations should, in my view, play a leading role in promoting this type of research and debate.

Appendix 1

Tables A.1–A.10

TABLE A.1. Countries by income classification and targeted skill levels of labor immigration programs, 2009

	GNI class.	GNI pc08	only LS	LS	MS	HS1	HS2	only HS2	# programs
Norway	U-HIC	87,070	1	1	1	1	1	0	2
Switzerland	U-HIC	65,330	0	0	0	1	1	0	1
Denmark	U-HIC	59,130	0	0	0	2	3	1	3
Sweden	U-HIC	50,940	0	1	1	1	1	0	1
Netherlands	U-HIC	50,150	0	1	1	1	1	0	2
Ireland	U-HIC	49,590	0	0	1	2	1	0	2
Finland	U-HIC	48,120	0	1	1	2	2	0	2
United States	U-HIC	47,580	1	2	1	1	4	3	6
Austria	U-HIC	46,260	1	1	1	1	1	1	3
United Kingdom	U-HIC	45,390	0	0	1	1	1	1	2
Belgium	U-HIC	44,330	0	0	1	1	1	0	1
Germany	U-HIC	42,440	0	0	0	1	1	1	2
France	U-HIC	42,250	1	2	2	0	1	1	4
Canada	U-HIC	41,730	1	2	2	3	3	0	5
Australia	U-HIC	40,350	0	0	1	4	2	0	4
Kuwait	U-HIC	38,420	0	1	1	1	1	0	1
Japan	U-HIC	38,210	1	1	0	1	1	0	2
Italy	U-HIC	35,240	1	2	1	1	1	0	2
Singapore	U-HIC	34,760	0	1	2	2	1	0	3
Spain	U-HIC	31,960	1	2	1	2	2	0	3
Hong Kong	U-HIC	31,420	0	1	1	1	2	1	3
Greece	U-HIC	28,650	0	2	2	1	1	1	3
New Zealand	U-HIC	27,940	1	2	1	2	1	0	3
Israel	U-HIC	24,700	0	1	1	1	1	0	2
Slovenia	U-HIC	24,010	1	2	1	1	1	0	2
Republic of Korea	U-HIC	21,530	1	1	0	1	1	0	2
Portugal	U-HIC	20,560	0	1	1	2	2	0	2
Taiwan	U-HIC		0	1	1	1	1	0	2
United Arab Emirates	U-HIC		0	1	1	1	1	0	1
Czech Republic	L-HIC	16,600	2	2	0	1	1	0	3
Saudi Arabia	L-HIC	15,500	0	1	1	1	1	0	1
Slovak Republic	L-HIC	14,540	1	1	1	1	1	0	2
Hungary	L-HIC	12,810	1	2	1	1	1	0	2
Oman	L-HIC	12,270	0	1	1	1	1	0	1
Poland	U-MIC	11,880	0	1	1	1	1	0	2
Mexico	U-MIC	9,980	0	0	1	2	3	2	4
Turkey	U-MIC	9,340	0	1	1	1	1	0	1
Venezuela	U-MIC	9,230	0	1	1	1	1	0	1
Brazil	U-MIC	7,350	0	1	1	1	2	2	3
Argentina	U-MIC	7,200	1	2	1	2	2	0	3
Malaysia	U-MIC	6,970	0	1	2	1	1	1	3
Colombia	U-MIC	4,660	0	1	1	1	1	0	1

TABLE A.1. (*Continued*)

	GNI class.	GNI pc08	only LS	LS	MS	HS1	HS2	only HS2	# programs
Dominican Republic	U-MIC	4,390	1	1	2	2	2	0	3
China	L-MIC	2,940	0	0	0	1	1	0	1
Thailand	L-MIC	2,840	0	0	0	1	1	0	1
Indonesia	L-MIC	2,010	0	0	0	1	1	0	1
U-HICs (30 countries)			11	30	28	40	41	10	71
L-HICs (4 countries)			4	7	4	5	5	0	9
U-MICs (9 countries)			2	9	11	12	14	5	21
L-MICS (3 countries)			0	0	0	3	3	0	3
Europe (18 countries)			6	17	17	22	23	6	39
Eastern Europe (3 countries)			4	5	2	3	3	0	7
North America (2 countries)			2	4	3	4	7	3	11
Latin America (6 countries)			2	6	7	9	11	4	15
East Asia (3 countries)			1	2	1	3	4	1	6
Southeast Asia (6 countries)			1	4	5	7	6	1	12
Western Asia (6 countries)			0	6	6	6	6	0	7
Australia and New Zealand (2 countries)			1	2	2	6	3	0	7
Total (46 countries)			17	46	43	60	63	15	104

U-HICs: upper-high-income countries with GNI per capita exceeding US$20,000 in 2008 (based on World Bank data).
L-HICs: lower-high-income countries with GNI per capita less than US$20,000 in 2008 (based on World Bank data).
U-MICs: upper-middle-income countries.
L-MICs: lower-middle-income countries.
only LS: programs that target only low-skilled workers.
LS: programs that target low-skilled workers and possibly others.
MS: programs that target medium-skilled workers and possibly others.
HS1: programs that target high-skilled workers and possibly others.
HS2: programs that target high-skilled workers and possibly others.
onlyHS2: programs that target high-skilled workers only.

TABLE A.2. Basic descriptive statistics of aggregate openness index, 2009

	obs	mean	sd	min	max
All programs, all countries	104	0.67	0.10	0.47	0.92
Temporary migration programs, all countries	91	0.67	0.10	0.47	0.92
All programs, upper-high-income countries	80	0.65	0.08	0.47	0.86

TABLE A.3. Aggregate openness scores of labor immigration programs analyzed, by country, 2009

Country	Program	Openness
Argentina	Temporary migrant workers	0.736
	Employed workers	0.917
	Scientific and specialized personnel	0.917
Australia	Employer nomination scheme	0.556
	Skilled regional sponsored	0.611
	Skilled independent	0.653
	Skilled Australian sponsored	0.653
Austria	Settlement permit key worker migrant program	0.556
	Seasonal migrant program	0.569
	Researchers and specific cases of gainful employment	0.639
Belgium	Work permit type B	0.694
Brazil	Program NR 63/05	0.708
	Program NR 64/05	0.736
	Program NR 62/04	0.833
Canada	Quebec selected skilled workers	0.500
	Seasonal agricultural worker program	0.500
	Provincial nominees	0.569
	Federal skilled worker progam	0.625
	Low-skilled pilot project	0.639
China	Work visa	0.750
Colombia	Visa TT: General program	0.889
Czech Republic	Green card A and B	0.667
	Green card C	0.694
	Short-term seasonal work permit	0.750
Denmark	Positive list	0.542
	The green card scheme	0.708
	The pay limit scheme	0.778
Dominican Republic	Permanent residents	0.583
	Temporary residents	0.611
	Nonresidents	0.611
Finland	Residence permit for an employed person	0.625
	Ordinary residence permit	0.639
France	Temporary permit for temporary work (3–12 months)	0.667
	Temporary permit for temporary employment (at least twelve months)	0.667
	Seasonal workers	0.667
	Skills and talent program	0.694
Germany	Residence permit (skilled)	0.472
	Settlement permit	0.722

TABLE A.3. (*Continued*)

Country	Program	Openness
Greece	Residence permit for regular staff	0.667
	Residence permit for executives	0.667
	Seasonal work permit	0.667
Hong Kong	Imported workers	0.569
	Professionals program	0.625
	Quality migrants program	0.639
Hungary	Seasonal employment visa	0.750
	A long-term visa for the purpose of gainful employment	0.750
Indonesia	Expatriate work-IKTA and stay permit	0.625
Ireland	Work permit scheme	0.569
	Green card permit	0.653
Israel	B-1 visa (migrant worker)	0.639
	B-1 visa (foreign experts)	0.653
Italy	Nonseasonal	0.569
	Seasonal	0.569
Japan	Trainee visa	0.528
	Working visa	0.583
Kuwait	General program (private sector workers)	0.708
Malaysia	Professional visit pass	0.528
	Employment pass (EP)	0.569
	Visit pass (temporary employment)	0.667
Mexico	Immigrants for technical work	0.694
	Immigrants for scientific work	0.722
	Immigrants for managerial positions	0.722
	Professional immigrant program	0.806
Netherlands	General labor scheme	0.639
	Highly skilled migrants	0.667
New Zealand	Seasonal workers	0.639
	Essential skills visa	0.667
	Skilled	0.681
Norway	Skilled workers/specialists	0.667
	Seasonal worker	0.667
Oman	Employment visa	0.722
Poland	Short-term (seasonal) work permit	0.806
	Work permit	0.833
Portugal	Residency visa	0.583
	Residency visa for research/highly qualified assignment (visa type II)	0.750
Republic of Korea	Employment visa (nonprofessional employment)	0.542
	Employment visa (special occupations, professional employment)	0.736
Saudi Arabia	General program (labor and worker law and related regulations)	0.722
Singapore	Work permit (foreign worker)	0.583
	S pass	0.667
	Employment pass	0.806
Slovak Republic	Short-term (seasonal) work permit	0.750
	Work permit	0.750
Slovenia	Residence permit (seasonal work)	0.556
	Residence permit (for employment and work)	0.583
Spain	Contingente	0.500
	General regime	0.625
	High skill	0.764

TABLE A.3. (*Continued*)

Country	Program	Openness
Sweden	General work permit program	0.722
Switzerland	Work permits "B"	0.542
Taiwan	Work permit (blue-collar workers)	0.542
	Work permit (white-collar workers)	0.861
Thailand	Work permit	0.569
Turkey	Work permit	0.806
United Arab Emirates	Residence permit for employment issued for an employee	0.806
United Kingdom	Tier 2 skilled workers (general) (points-based system)	0.653
	Tier 1 general highly skilled workers (points-based system)	0.750
United States	EB2 advanced degree holders	0.653
	H1B	0.653
	H-2A	0.708
	H-2B	0.708
	EB1 priority workers	0.833
	O1	0.833
Venezuela	Labor transient visa (VT-L)	0.861

Notes: The names of labor immigration programs in the table above are abbreviations (often translated) that may not always correspond with the exact formal name of the program.

TABLE A.4. Correlations between openness indicators, 2009

	Quota	Job offer	LMT	Sector/ occupation	Fees	Conditions	Trade union	Nationality/ age	Gender/ marital status	Skills	Language	Self-sufficiency
All programs in all countries												
Quota	1											
Job offer		1										
LMT		0.35**	1									
Sector/occupation				1								
Fees					1							
Conditions		0.17*				1						
Trade union			0.27**				1					
Nationality/age		-0.22**			0.22**			1				
Gender/marital status		-0.22**				-0.17*			1			
Skills		-0.54**	-0.45**							1		
Language		-0.59**	-0.27**	0.22**				0.28**	0.24**	0.38**	1	
Self-sufficiency				0.22**		0.24**						1
Temporary migration programs in all countries												
Quota	1											
Job offer		1										
LMT		0.31**	1									
Sector/occupation				1								

	Fees	Conditions	Trade union	Nationality/age	Gender/marital status	Skills	Language	Self-sufficiency
Fees	1							
Conditions		1						
Trade union	-0.19*	0.26*	1					
Nationality/age		0.25**		1				
Gender/marital status					1			
Skills	-0.41**	-0.48**				1		
Language	-0.56**	-0.23**				0.29**	1	
Self-sufficiency		0.22**				-0.28**		1

All programs in upper-high-income countries

	Quota	Job offer	LMT	Sector/occupation	Fees	Conditions	Trade union	Nationality/age	Gender/marital status	Skills	Language	Self-sufficiency
Quota	1											
Job offer		1										
LMT		0.40**	1									
Sector/occupation				1								
Fees	-0.21*				1							
Conditions	0.30**	0.21*			-0.21*	1						
Trade union	-0.24**	0.36**					1					
Nationality/age	-0.31**				-0.25**	-0.20*		1				
Gender/marital status						-0.21*			1			
Skills	-0.53**	-0.50**							0.34**	1		
Language	-0.56**	-0.29**						-0.26**	0.32**		1	
Self-sufficiency										0.23*	-0.23*	1

Notes: **p < 0.05; *p < 0.10; correlation with p > 0.10 not shown. For an explanation of openness indicators in this table, see appendix 2.

TABLE A.5. Openness indicators and targeted skills: Pairwise correlation coefficients, 2009

	Quotas	Job offer	LMT	Sector/ occupation	Fees	Conditions	Trade union	Nationality/ age	Gender/ marital status	Skills	Language	Self-sufficiency
All programs in all countries												
onlylowskill			-0.31**				-0.21**			0.32**		
lowskill		-0.29**	-0.40**				-0.34**	-0.17*		0.55**	0.25**	
lowmedskilled	-0.17*	-0.33**	-0.49**				-0.24**	-0.16*		0.57**	0.20**	
onlylowmedskilled	-0.16*	-0.20**	-0.41**				-0.20**	-0.24**		0.35**	0.18*	
All programs in upper-high-income countries												
onlylowskill	-0.20*		-0.26**				-0.21*			0.37**		
lowskill		-0.34**	-0.52**	-0.25**			-0.41**	-0.22*		0.65**	0.30**	
lowmedskilled		-0.39**	-0.54**				-0.30**	-0.22*		0.66**	0.22*	
onlylowmedskilled		-0.26**	-0.40**	-0.23*	-0.20*			-0.24**		0.43**	0.24**	
Temporary migration programs in all countries												
onlylowskill	-0.17*				0.19*		-0.19*			0.30**		
lowskill	-0.21**	-0.21**	-0.36**				-0.31**	-0.23**		0.53**		
lowmedskilled	-0.23**	-0.27**	-0.46**				-0.23**			0.55**	0.17*	
onlylowmedskilled	-0.20*		-0.40**				-0.18*	-0.29**		0.31**		
Temporary migration programs in upper-high-income countries												
onlylowskill	-0.25*		-0.24*	-0.31**				-0.24*		0.35**		
lowskill		-0.25**	-0.50**				-0.38**	-0.33**		0.62**		
lowmedskilled	-0.26**	-0.32**	-0.55**				-0.29**	-0.24**		0.62**		
onlylowmedskilled			-0.38**	-0.30**		0.23*		-0.32**		0.38**		

Notes: **p < 0.05; *p < 0.10; correlation with p > 0.10 not shown. lowmedskilled: programs targeting low- and/or medium-skilled migrants. onlylowmedskilled: programs targeting low- and/or medium-skilled migrants only (programs targeting medium and high skills are excluded). For explanation of the openness indicators in this table, see appendix 2.

TABLE A.6. Regression of migrant rights on targeted skills, country income group, type of migration program (temporary or permanent), and region, 2009

	Aggregate rights (equ)	Political rights	Economic rights	Social rights (equ)	Residence rights	Family rights
onlylowmedskill	-0.185*	-0.045	-0.094*	-0.24*	-0.19*	-0.467*
	(0.022)	0.028	(0.027)	(0.047)	(0.029)	(0.058)
u-hic	0.014	0.008	0.084	-0.122	0.033	0.106
	(0.037)	(0.048)	(0.046)	(0.081)	(0.049)	(0.098)
Tmp	-0.194*	-0.035	-0.067	-0.283*	-0.338*	-0.282*
	(0.035)	(0.047)	(0.044)	(0.077)	(0.047)	(0.094)
Europe (ref.)						
North America	-0.06	-0.019	-0.053	-0.147*	-0.015	-0.067
	(0.0333)	(0.044)	(0.041)	(0.072)	(0.044)	(0.088)
Latin America and	0.041	0.012	0.045	-0.059	0.028	0.27*
the Caribbean	(0.048)	(0.064)	(0.061)	(0.106)	(0.064)	(0.128)
East Asia	-0.077*	0.043	-0.097*	-0.106	-0.102*	-0.155
	(0.038)	(0.049)	(0.047)	(0.082)	(0.05)	(0.1)
Southeast Asia	-0.126*	-0.202*	-0.093*	-0.076	-0.13*	-0.129
	(0.033)	(0.044)	(0.041)	(0.072)	(0.044)	(0.087)
Western Asia	-0.133*	0.049	-0.007	-0.124	-0.348*	-0.308
	(0.061)	(0.08)	(0.076)	(0.133)	(0.081)	(0.162)
Australia and	-0.04	-0.005	0.004	-0.245*	0.032	0.049
New Zealand	(0.045)	(0.059)	(0.056)	(0.097)	(0.059)	(0.119)
Eastern Europe	0.001	-0.028	0.078	-0.053	-0.171*	0.294*
	(0.054)	(0.071)	(0.062)	(0.118)	(0.072)	(0.144)
Constant	0.891*	0.6*	0.904*	1.182*	0.914*	0.829*
	(0.05)	(0.066)	(0.063)	(0.109)	(0.067)	(0.133)
N	73	73	73	73	73	73
Adj. R2	0.73	0.28	0.291	0.53	0.78	0.64

Notes: Standard errors in parentheses; * indicates statistical significance at $p < 0.05$.
onlylowmedskill: programs targeting low- and/or medium-skilled migrants only (programs targeting medium and high skills are excluded from the sample).
u-hic: upper-high-income country (reference: all other countries in the sample).
tmp: temporary migration program (reference: permanent migration programs).

TABLE A.7. Pairwise correlation coefficients between rights and targeted skills, 2009

	All programs in all countries			Temporary migration programs in all countries		
	onlylowskill	lowskill	onlylowmed	onlylowskill	lowskill	onlylowmed
Vote						
Stand for election						
Associate						
Identity documents						
Protection of criminal courts						
Free choice of employment	-0.40	-0.45	-0.48	-0.41	-0.37	-0.47
Equal pay						
Equal conditions						
Join unions						
Redress (employment)	-0.33	-0.26	-0.24	-0.30		-0.22
Unemployment benefits (abs)	-0.39	-0.40	-0.42	-0.36		-0.37
Public retirement pension schemes (abs)		-0.21	-0.40		-0.35	-0.37
Public education and training (abs)		-0.33	-0.24			-0.23
Public including social housing (abs)	-0.29		-0.45	-0.26	-0.24	-0.40
Public health services (abs)						
Unemployment benefits (equ)	-0.39	-0.36	-0.45	-0.36	-0.25	-0.40
Public retirement pension schemes (equ)	-0.44	-0.43	-0.41	-0.42	-0.39	-0.38
Public education and training (equ)		-0.21	-0.24			-0.23
Public including social housing (equ)	-0.36	-0.36	-0.44	-0.33	-0.29	-0.40
Public health services (equ)						
Time limit on residence	-0.51	-0.60	-0.62	-0.57	-0.56	-0.68
Security of residence: Employment	-0.20	-0.34	-0.39			-0.32
Security of residence: Criminal convictions						
Direct access to citizenship	-0.45	-0.60	-0.60	-0.44	-0.55	-0.59
Redress (residence)		-0.21				
Family reunion	-0.30	-0.34	-0.50	-0.27	-0.24	-0.47
Spouse's rights to work	-0.36	-0.48	-0.45	-0.32	-0.38	-0.40
Redress (family reunion)	-0.32	-0.51	-0.48	-0.30	-0.49	-0.46

Notes: $p < 0.05$ for all coefficients shown; coefficients with $p > 0.05$ not shown.
onlylowskill: programs targeting low-skilled migrants only.
lowskill: programs targeting low-skilled migrants and others.
Onlylowmed: programs targeting low and/or medium-skilled migrants only.
equ: social rights measured in terms of equality of access; see discussion in chapter 4.
abs: social rights measured in absolute terms; see discussion in chapter 4.
For an explanation of rights in this table, see appendix 3.

TABLE A.8. Correlations between rights (aggregate and subindexes) and openness, 2009

Targeted skill level	Openness					
	onlyLS	LS	MS	HS1	HS2	onlyHS2
Temporary migration programs in upper-high-income countries						
Observations	11	30	26	33	32	7
Aggregate rights (equ)				−0.39**	−0.38**	
Aggregate rights (abs)				−0.43**	−0.42**	
Political rights				−0.31*	−0.36**	
Economic rights				−0.28*		
Social rights (equ)				−0.31*	−0.38**	
Social rights (abs)				−0.42**	−0.48**	
Residence rights				−0.31*		
Family rights						
Temporary migration programs in upper-high-income countries, excluding GCC countries						
Observations:	11	28	24	31	30	7
Aggregate rights (equ)					−0.32*	
Aggregate rights (abs)				−0.33*	−0.37**	
Political rights					−0.33*	
Economic rights						
Social rights (equ)					−0.32*	
Social rights (abs)				−0.33*	−0.44**	
Residence rights						
Family rights						
All programs in upper-high-income countries, excluding GCC countries						
Observations	11	28	26	38	39	10
Aggregate rights (equ)				−0.30*	−0.28*	
Aggregate rights (abs)				−0.34**	−0.32*	
Political rights						
Economic rights						
Social rights (equ)					−0.27*	
Social rights (abs)				−0.34**	−0.36**	
Residence rights						
Family rights						

Notes: **p < 0.05; *p < 0.10; corr. with p > 0.10 not shown.
equ: social rights measured in terms of equality of access; see discussion in chapter 4.
abs: social rights measured in absolute terms; see discussion in chapter 4.

TABLE A.9. Correlations between individual rights and openness, programs in upper-high-income countries, 2009

	Openness											
	All programs in upper-high-income countries (N = 71)						Temporary migration programs in upper-high-income countries (N = 61)					
Targeted skill level	onlyLS	LS	MS	HS1	HS2	onlyHS2	onlyLS	LS	MS	HS1	HS2	onlyHS2
Observations	11	30	28	40	41	10	11	30	26	33	32	7
Vote												
Stand for election												
Associate	-0.61**			-0.45**	-0.32**					-0.45**	-0.35*	
Identity documents							-0.62**					
Protection of criminal courts				-0.42**	-0.33**					-0.43**	-0.37**	
Free choice of employment		0.31*						0.31*				
Equal pay												
Equal conditions												
Join unions		-0.51**	-0.53**	-0.31*				-0.51**	-0.53**	-0.31*		
Redress (employment)												
Unemployment benefits (abs)			-0.33*	-0.32**	-0.38**						-0.42**	
Public retirement pension (abs)				-0.56**	-0.44**					-0.56**	-0.49**	
Public education and training (abs)		-0.38**	-0.37*	-0.29*				-0.38**	-0.37*	-0.35*	-0.33*	

Public incl. social housing (abs)					
Public health services (abs)					
Unemployment benefits (equ)	−0.32*	−0.30*			
Public retirement pension (equ)	−0.32*	−0.47**	−0.36**		
Public education and training (equ)	−0.38**	−0.37**	−0.29*	−0.38**	−0.37*
Public including social housing (equ)				−0.46**	−0.36**
Public health services (equ)				−0.38**	−0.33*
Time limit on residence					
Security of residence: Employment	−0.32**				
Security of residence: Criminal convictions	−0.28*				
Direct access to citizenship	−0.42**	−0.45**	−0.42**	−0.45*	
Redress (residence)					
Family reunion					
Spouse's right to work	−0.37**	−0.30*	−0.35*	−0.33*	
Redress (family reunion)	−0.27*	−0.7*			

Notes: ** p < 0.05; * p < 0.10; correlation with p > 0.10 not shown. For an explanation of rights in this table, see appendix 3.

TABLE A.10. Correlations between individual rights and openness, programs in upper-high-income countries excluding GCC countries, 2009

	Openness											
	All programs in upper-high-income countries excluding GCC countries (N = 69)						Temporary migration programs in upper upper-high-income countries excluding GCC countries (N = 59)					
Targeted skill level	onlyLS	LS	MS	HS1	HS2	onlyHS2	onlyLS	LS	MS	HS1	HS2	onlyHS2
Observations	11	28	26	38	39	10	11	28	24	31	30	7
Vote												
Stand for election												
Associate				−0.37**						−0.36**		
Identity documents	−0.61**	−0.42**					−0.61**	−0.42**				
Protection of criminal courts				−0.47**	−0.36**					−0.48**	−0.4**	
Free choice of employment												
Equal pay												
Equal conditions				−0.28*								
Join unions												
Redress (employment)												
Unemployment benefits (abs)					−0.35**						−0.38**	
Public retirement pension schemes (abs)				−0.5**	−0.41					−0.49**	−0.45**	
Public education and training (abs)												

Public incl. social housing (abs)	0.38**							
Public health services (abs)				0.39**				
Unemployment benefits (equ)								
Public retirement pension schemes (equ)		–0.3*	–0.38**			–0.37**	–0.32*	
Public education and training (equ)								
Public including social housing (equ)	0.35*							
Public health services (equ)				0.35*				
Time limit on residence					0.41*			
Security of residence: Employment		–0.33*						
Security of residence: Criminal convictions								
Direct access to citizenship								
Redress (residence)								
Family reunion								
Spouse's right to work		–0.32*				–0.3*		
Redress (family reunion)								–0.7*

Notes: **p < 0.05; *p < 0.10; correlation with p > 0.10 not shown. For an explanation of rights in this table, see appendix 3.

Appendix 2

Overview of Openness Indicators

P1 [Quota] Is there a numerical quota or other limit on the annual number of migrant workers admitted under this program, or on the stock of migrant workers?

    0 = hard quota that is relatively small
    1 = hard quota that is relatively large
    2 = soft quota/limit
    3 = no quota or any other numerical limit

P2 [Job offer] Does admission under the program require migrants to have a job offer in the host country?

    0 = yes, migrants without a job offer are not admitted
    1 = job offer not strictly required, but it is one of the criteria influencing admission
    2= no, job offer does not influence admission

P3 [Labor market test] Do the regulations for admitting migrant workers under this program include a labor market test?

    0 = very strong labor market test in all sectors/occupations covered by the program
    1 = strong labor market test, but some occupations/sectors exempted
    2 = weak labor market test
    3 = No labor market test

P4 [Sector/occupation] Is the labor immigration program restricted to specific sectors or a defined list of occupations?

    0 = yes
    1= no

P5 [Fees] Does the program require employers to pay a fee/levy for employing migrant workers (other than administrative fees to do with the work permit application process)?

    0 = yes
    1= no

P6 [Conditions] Does the program require employers to pay a certain wage and/or meet employment conditions that exceed the minimum standards required by the country's labor laws and regulations?

0 = yes, strong wage restrictions (e.g., collectively agreed wage)
1= yes, weak wage restrictions (e.g., prevailing wages in absence of collective wage agreements)
2= no

P7 [Trade union] Do trade unions have a role in individual work permit application processes?

0 = yes, trade unions play a strong role
1 = yes, trade unions play some/weak role
2 = no, no role for trade unions

P8 [Nationality/age] To what extent, if at all, is the admission of migrant workers restricted to or influenced by the applicant's nationality and/or age (range)?

0 = admission restricted to migrants with specified nationality *and* age
1 = admission restricted to migrants with specified nationality *or* age
2 = admission influenced by nationality and/or age (e.g., through points systems)
3 = nationality and age do not matter for admission

P9 [Gender/marital status] To what extent, if at all, is the admission of migrant workers restricted to or influenced by the applicant's gender and/or marital status?

0 = admission restricted to migrants with specified gender *and* marital status
1 = admission restricted to migrants with specified gender *or* marital status
2 = admission influenced by gender and/or marital status (e.g., through points systems)
3 = gender and marital status do not matter for admission

P10 [Skills] Is the admission of migrant workers restricted to or influenced by (migrants with) specified professional skills and/or qualifications?

0 = yes, very specific skills and/or qualifications required
1 = yes, specific skills required
2 = yes, generic minimum skills/qualifications threshold

3 = no, specified skills and/or qualifications are not among criteria/ factors for admission

P11 [Language] To what extent, if at all, is the admission of migrant workers influenced by the applicant's host country language skills?

0 = host country language skills required
1 = language skills not absolutely required, but they influence admission
2 = language skills are not a criterion for admission

P12 [Self-sufficient] Is admission limited to migrant workers who can prove that they can be self-sufficient (i.e., that they will not require public funds/assistance) in the host country?

0 = yes
1 = no

Appendix 3
Overview of Migrant Rights Indicators

Civil and Political Rights

R1 [Vote] Does admission under this program create a legal right for migrants to vote in local and/or regional elections?

> 0 = no right to vote in any elections
> 1 = right to vote in local/regional elections *after some time*
> 2 = immediate right to vote in local/regional elections

R2 [Stand for election] Does admission under this program create a legal right for migrants to stand for election?

> 0 = no right to stand for elections
> 1 = right to stand for election *after some time*
> 2 = immediate right to stand for election

R3 [Associate] Do migrant workers have the right to form trade unions and other associations?

> 0 = no right to form any associations
> 1 = right to form some associations
> 2 = same rights to form associations as citizens

R4 [Identity documents] Do migrant workers have the right not to have identity documents confiscated by anyone, other than a public official duly authorized by the law?

> 0 = no, no such right specified or implied in any law
> 1 = yes, right implied by existing laws (e.g., constitutional laws)
> 2 = yes, right for migrants explicitly specified

R5 [Protection of criminal courts] Do migrant workers have the right to equal treatment and protections (with citizens) before criminal courts and tribunals?

> 0 = no, migrants enjoy significantly fewer protections than citizens
> 1 = no, migrants enjoy some protection but fewer than citizens
> 2 = yes, equality of treatment with citizens

Economic Rights (Focus on Selected Rights at Work)

R6 [Free choice of employment] What restrictions, if any, are there on migrant workers' right to free choice of employment?

>0 = employment tied to specific employer and no change of employer possible
>1 = employment tied to specific employer; change of employer possible, but requires new work permit application
>2 = workers can freely change employers within a specific sector/occupation/region
>3 = migrant workers have completely free choice of employment

R7 [Equal pay] Do migrant workers have the right to equal pay to that received by local workers doing the same work?

>0 = no
>1 = yes

R8 [Equal conditions] Beyond the issue of equal pay, do migrant workers have the same rights to equal employment conditions and protections (e.g., overtime, hours of work, weekly rest, paid holidays, sick pay, health and safety at work, protection against dismissal) as local workers?

>0 = no, migrant workers have significantly fewer legal rights
>1 = migrants have right to most of the employment conditions and protections for citizens
>2 = yes, right to same employment conditions and protections

R9 [Join unions] Do migrant workers have the right to join trade unions?

>0 = no
>1 = yes

R10 [Redress employment] Do migrant workers have the right to redress if the terms of their employment contract have been violated by their employer?

>0 = no
>1 = yes, but limited
>2 = yes, same as citizens

Social Rights (Focus on Equal Access to Selected Social Security Benefits and Public Services)

R11 [Unemployment benefits] Do migrant workers have the right to equal access to unemployment benefits?

0 = no access to any unemployment benefits
1 = access to *some, but not all* types of unemployment benefit; no equal access under this program
2 = equal access to all types of unemployment benefits *after some time*
3 = yes, immediate equal access to all types of unemployment benefits

R12 [Public retirement pension schemes] Do migrants have the right to equal access to public retirement pension schemes?

0 = no access to any public retirement pension schemes
1 = access to *some, but not all* types of public retirement pension schemes; no equal access under this program
2 = equal access to all types of public retirement pension schemes *after some time*
3 = yes, immediate equal access to all types of public retirement pension schemes

R13 [Public education and training] Do adult migrant workers have the right to equal access to public educational institutions and services (degree-level courses and vocational training)?

0 = no access to any public educational institutions and services
1 = access to *some, but not all* public educational institutions and services; no equal access under this program
2 = equal access to all types of public educational institutions and services *after some time*
3 = yes, immediate equal access to all public educational institutions and services

R14 [Public including social housing] Do migrant workers have the right to equal access to public housing including social housing schemes?

0 = no access to any public/social housing schemes
1 = access to *some, but not all* public/social housing schemes; no equal access under this program
2 = equal access to all types of public/social housing schemes *after some time*
3 = yes, immediate equal access to all public/social housing schemes

R15 [Public health services] Do migrant workers have the right to equal access to public health services?

> 0 = no access to any public health services
> 1 = access to *some, but not all* public health services; no equal access under this program
> 2 = equal access to all types of public health services *after some time*
> 3 = yes, immediate equal access to all public health services

Residency Rights and Access to Citizenship

R16 [Time limit on residence] Do migrant workers have temporary or permanent residence status?

> 0 = strictly temporary residence permit, with no opportunity to acquire permanent residence status
> 1 = temporary status, but with opportunity to switch to permanent status after five years or more
> 2 = temporary status, but with opportunity to switch to permanent status in fewer than five years
> 3 = permanent residence status

R17 [Security of employment: residence] How, if at all, does loss of employment affect residence status?

> 0 = loss of employment automatically implies loss of residence permit
> 1 = loss of employment implies loss of residence status unless new job found within specified time period
> 2 = loss of employment does not affect residence status

R18 [Security of residence: criminal convictions] How, if at all, do criminal and other convictions affect residence status?

> 0 = minor convictions (administrative offenses) can lead to loss of residence status
> 1 = only major convictions (criminal offenses) can lead to loss of residence status
> 2 = convictions do not affect residence status

R19 [Direct access to citizenship] Do migrant workers have direct access to citizenship?

> 0 = no direct access to citizenship
> 1 = Can naturalize after five years or more
> 2 = Can naturalize in fewer than five years

R20 [Redress residence] Do migrant workers admitted under this program have the right to legal remedies/redress in case of withdrawal or nonrenewal of residence permit, or in case of a deportation order?

    0 = no
    1 = yes, but relatively limited
    2 = yes

Family Reunion for Migrant Workers and Employment Rights of Family Members/Dependents

R21 [Family reunion] Do migrant workers have the right to family reunion?

    0 = no right for family reunion with any family members or dependents
    1 = family reunion limited to migrants' spouse/partner and minor children
    2 = family reunion for migrants' spouse/partner, minor children, and adult children
    3 = family reunion for migrants' spouse, partner, children, and other family members

R22 [Spouse's right to work] Does the spouse/partner of the principal migrant have the right to work (without having to apply for permission)?

    0 = no
    1 = yes, but limited (e.g., by sector or occupation)
    2 = yes, unrestricted right to work

R23 [Redress family reunion] Is there a judicial remedy to challenge the refusal by the authorities to allow family formation/reunification?

    0 = no
    1 = yes, but relatively limited
    2 = yes

References

Abella, M. 2008. "Migration, Development, and Human Rights: An Overview of the Issues." A paper prepared for the Global Forum on Migration and Development 2008, Manila.

Adamrah, M. 2011. 'Govt Will Not Add Nations to Migrant Workers Blacklist." *Jakarta Post*, November 3. http://www.thejakartapost.com/news/2011/11/03/govt-will-not -add-nations-migrant-worker-blacklist.html (accessed August 31, 2012).

Adamson, F. B. 2006. "Crossing Borders: International Migration and National Security." *International Security* 31 (1): 165–99.

Agustin, L. 2003. "Forget Victimization: Granting Agency to Migrants." *Development* 46 (3): 30–36.

Alkire, S. 2002. "Dimensions of Human Development." *World Development* 30 (2): 181–205.

Alston, P. 2004. "Core Labour Standards and the Transformation of the International Labour Rights Regime." *European Journal of International Law* 15 (3) 457–521.

Alston, P., and J. Heenan. 2004. "Shrinking the International Labor Code: An Unintended Consequence of the 1998 ILO Declaration on Fundamental Principles and Rights at Work." *New York University Journal of International Law and Politics* 36:221–64.

Anderson, B., and M. Ruhs. 2010. "Migrant Workers: Who Needs Them? A Framework for the Analysis of Shortages, Immigration, and Public Policy." In *Who Needs Migrant Workers? Labour Shortages, Immigration, and Public Policy*, ed. M. Ruhs and B. Anderson, 15–52. Oxford: Oxford University Press.

Anderson, B., M. Ruhs, B. Rogaly, and S. Spencer. 2006. *Fair Enough? Central and East European Migrants in Low-Wage Employment in the UK*. York, UK: Joseph Rowntree Foundation. http://www.jrf.org.uk/system/files/1617-migrants-low-wage-employment .pdf (accessed December 25, 2011).

Archer, M. 2000. *Being Human: The Problem of Agency*. Cambridge: Cambridge University Press.

Attas, D. 2000. "The Case of Guest Workers: Exploitation, Citizenship, and Economic Rights." *Res Publica* 6 (1): 73–92.

Australian Government. 2009. "Factsheet: What Will the Australian Government Do to Prevent Overstaying by Pacific Seasonal Workers?" Canberra: Department of Education, Employment, and Workplace Relations.

Awad, I. 2009. "International Labour Migration and Employment in the Arab Region: Origins, Consequences, and the Way Forward." Paper presented at the ILO's Employment Forum, Beirut, October 19–21.

Baldwin-Edwards, M. 2005. *Migration in the Middle East and Mediterranean: A Regional Study Prepared for the Global Commission on International Migration*. Greece: Mediterranean Migration Observatory. http://aei.pitt.edu/7046/1/Migration_in_the_Middle _East_and_Mediterranean.pdf (accessed December 23, 2011).

———. 2011. *Labour Immigration, Labour Markets, and Demographics in the GCC Countries: National Patterns and Trends*. Athens: Mediterranean Migration Observatory. http://www2.lse.ac.uk/government/research/resgroups/kuwait/documents/Baldwin -Edwards,Martin.pdf (accessed January 22, 2012).

Barrett, A., and Y. McCarthy. 2008. "Immigrants and Welfare Programmes: Exploring the

Interactions between Immigrant Characteristics, Immigrants Welfare Dependence, and Welfare Policy." *Oxford Review of Economic Policy* 24 (3): 543–60.

Bauböck, R. 1994. *Transnational Citizenship*. Aldershot, UK: Edward Elgar.

———. 2001. "Recombinant Citizenship." In *Inclusions and Exclusions in European Societies*, ed. M. Kohli and A. Woodward, 38–58. London: Routledge.

Beitz, C. 1983. "Cosmopolitan Ideals and National Sentiment." *Journal of Philosophy* 80 (10): 591–600.

Bell, D. A. 2006. *Beyond Liberal Democracy: Political Thinking for an East Asian Context*. Princeton, NJ: Princeton University Press.

Bell, D. A., and N. Piper. 2005. "Justice for Migrant Workers? The Case of Foreign Domestic Workers in Hong Kong and Singapore. In *Multiculturalism in Asia*, ed. W. Kymlicka and H. Baogang, 196–222. Oxford: Oxford University Press.

Bello, W. 2011. "Our Failed Labor Export Policy. *Philippine Daily Inquirer*, April 4. http://opinion.inquirer.net/viewpoints/columns/view/20110404-329240/Our-Failed-Labor-Export-Policy (accessed August 31, 2012).

Betts, A., and K. Nicolaides. 2009. "The Trade-Migration Linkage: GATS Mode IV." Paper presented at the Global Trade Ethics Conference, Princeton University, February 19. http://www.princeton.edu/~pcglobal/conferences/wtoreform/Betts_Nicolaides_memo.pdf (accessed December 25, 2011).

Bhagwati, J. 2008. Introduction to *Skilled Immigration Today: Prospects, Problems, and Policies*, ed. J. Bhagwati and G. Hanson. Oxford: Oxford University Press.

Billstrom, T. 2008. *Speech at the Federation of Indian Chambers of Commerce and Industry (FICCI)*. New Delhi. http://www.regeringen.se/sb/d/8065/a/115666 (accessed December 23, 2011).

———. 2009. *Towards Responsive, Effective, and Fair Migration Policies*. Paris. http://www.oecd.org/dataoecd/6/45/43284110.pdf (accessed December 23, 2011).

Boeri, T., and H. Brücker. 2005. "Why Are Europeans So Tough on Migrants?" *Economic Policy* 44:629–703.

Böhning, R. 1991. "The ILO and the New UN Convention on Migrant Workers: The Past and the Future." *International Migration Review* 25 (4): 698–709.

Borang, F. 2007. "Labor Market Structures, Labor Market Actors, and Immigration Policy." Paper presented at the General Conference of the European Consortium on Political Research, Pisa, September 6–8.

Borjas, G. J. 1995. "The Economic Benefits from Immigration." *Journal of Economic Perspectives* 9 (2): 3–22.

———. 1999. *Heaven's Door: Immigration Policy and the American Economy*. Princeton, NJ: Princeton University Press.

Bosniak, L. 2006. *The Citizen and the Alien: Dilemmas of Contemporary Membership*. Princeton, NJ: Princeton University Press.

Boswell, C. 2007. "Theorizing Migration Policy: Is There a Third Way?" *International Migration Review* 41 (1): 75–100.

Boyer, G., T. Hatton, and K. O'Rourke. 1994. "Impact of Emigration on Real Wages in Ireland, 1850–1914." In *Migration and the International Labor Market, 1850–1939*, ed. T. J. Hatton and J. G. Williamson, 221–39. London: Routledge.

British Council and Migration Policy Group. 2011. *Migrant Integration Policy Index III*. Brussels: British Council. http://www.integrationindex.eu (accessed February 2, 2012).

Bucken-Knapp, G. 2009. *Defending the Swedish Model: Social Democrats, Trade Unions, and Labor Migration Policy Reform*. Lanham, MD: Lexington Books.

Bundesministerium des Inneren. 2008. *Aktionsprogramm der Bundesregierung: Beitrag der Arbeitsmigration zur Sicherung der Fachkraeftebasis in Deutschland*. Press release, July

16. http://www.bmi.bund.de/SharedDocs/Pressemitteilungen/DE/2008/mitMarginal spalte/07/aktionsprogramm_arbeitsmigration.html?nn=109632 (accessed December 23, 2011).

Buonanno, P., and D. Montolio. 2008. "Identifying the Socioeconomic and Demographic Determinants of Crime across Spanish Provinces." *International Review of Law and Economics* 28 (2): 89–97.

Bush, G. W. 2007. *Immigration Reform: Address in Georgia*. http://www.presidentialrheto ric.com/speeches/05.29.07.html (accessed December 23, 2011).

Calavita, K. 1992. *Inside the State*. New York: Routledge, Chapman and Hall.

Caney, S. 1998. "Cosmopolitanism, Realism, and the National Interest." In *The Legal and Moral Aspects of International Trade*, ed. G. Parry, A. Querishi, and H. Steiner, 26–40. London: Routledge.

Carens, J. 1996. "Realistic and Idealistic Approaches to the Ethics of Migration." *International Migration Review* 30 (1): 156–70.

———. 2008. "Live-in Domestics, Seasonal Workers, and Others Hard to Locate on the Map of Democracy." *Journal of Political Philosophy* 16 (4): 371–496.

Carling, J. 2008. "The Determinants of Migrants' Remittances." *Oxford Review of Economic Policy* 24 (3): 582–99.

Carr Center for Human Rights. 2005. *Measurement and Human Rights: Tracking Progress, Assessing Impact*. Carr Center for Human Rights Policy project report. Cambridge, MA: Harvard University. http://www.hks.harvard.edu/cchrp/pdf/Measurement_2005 Report.pdf (accessed February 2, 2012).

Castles, S. 1986. "The Guest-Worker in Western Europe: An Obituary." *International Migration Review* 20 (4): 761–78.

———. 2004. "Why Migration Policies Fail." *Ethnic and Racial Studies* 27 (2): 205–27.

Castles, S., and A. Davidson. 2000. *Citizenship and Migration: Globalization and the Politics of Belonging*. New York: Routledge.

Castles, S., and E. Vasta. 2004. "Australia: New Conflicts around Old Dilemmas." In *Controlling Immigration: A Global Perspective*, ed. W. Cornelius, P. Martin, and T. Tsuda, 141–73. Stanford, CA: Stanford University Press.

Center for Global Development. 2010. *Commitment to Development Index 2010*. Washington, DC: Center for Global Development. http://www.cgdev.org/files/1424561_file _CDI_2010_FINAL_Web.pdf (accessed February 2, 2012).

Cerna, L. 2008. *Towards an EU Blue Card: The Proposed Delegation of National Immigration Policies to the EU Level*. Working paper 08-65. Oxford: Center on Migration, Policy, and Society.

Chanda, R. 2001. "Movement of Natural Persons and the GATS." *World Economy* 24 (5): 631–54.

Chang, H. F. 2002. "Liberal Ideals and Political Feasibility: Guest-Worker Programs as Second-Best Policies." *North Carolina Journal of International Law and Commercial Regulation* 27 (3).

Chang, H.-J. 2002. "Breaking the Mould: An Institutionalist Political Economy Alternative to the Neoliberal Theory of the Market and the State." *Cambridge Journal of Economics* 26 (5): 539–59.

Chang, H.-J., and R. Rowthorn. 1995. Introduction to *The Role of the State in Economic Change*, ed. H.-J. Chang and R. Rowthorn, 1–27. Oxford: Clarendon.

Chaudhuri, S., A. Mattoo, and R. Self. 2004. "Moving People to Deliver Services: How Can the WTO Help?" *Journal of World Trade* 38 (3): 363–94.

Cheng, S. 2010. *On the Move for Love: Migrant Entertainers and the US Military in South Korea*. Philadelphia: University of Pennsylvania Press.

Chiswick, B. 1984. "Illegal Aliens in the United States Labor Market: An Analysis of Occupational Attainment and Earnings." *International Migration Review* 18 (3): 714–32.

Cholewinski, R. 1997. *Migrant Workers in International Human Rights Law: Their Protection in Countries of Employment.* Oxford: Clarendon Press.

CIC (Citizenship and Immigration Canada). 2010a. *Annual Report to Parliament on Immigration, 2010.* http://www.cic.gc.ca/english/pdf/pub/immigration2010_e.pdf (accessed December 23, 2011).

———. 2010b. *Fact and Figures 2010—Immigration Overview: Permanent and Temporary Residents.* http://www.cic.gc.ca/english/resources/statistics/facts2010/index.asp (accessed December 23, 2011).

Clemens, M., C. E. Montenegro, and L. Pritchett. 2009. *The Place Premium: Wage Differences for Identical Workers across the U.S. Border.* Washington, DC: Center for Global Development. http://www.cgdev.org/files/16352_file_CMP_place_premium_148.pdf (accessed December 25, 2011).

Commission on Integration and Cohesion. 2006. *Our Shared Future.* http://www.integrationandcohesion.org.uk (accessed March 16, 2012).

Cornelius, W. A., and M. R. Rosenblum. 2005. "Immigration and Politics." *Annual Review of Political Science* 8 (1): 99–119.

Cornelius, W. A., T. Tsuda, P. Martin, and J. F. Hollifield, eds. 2004. *Controlling Immigration: A Global Perspective.* Palo Alto, CA: Stanford University Press.

Cox, A., and E. Posner. 2009. "The Rights of Migrants." *New York University Law Review* 84 (6): 1403–63.

Crook, C. 2011. "Fixing America's Immigration Mess." *Financial Times*, May 15. http://www.ft.com/cms/s/0/559e3700-7f1e-11e0-b239-00144feabdc0.html#axzz1hOmAQPa7 (accessed December 23, 2011).

Cummins, M., and F. Rodriguez. 2010. "Is There a Numbers versus Rights Trade-off in Immigration Policy? What the Data Say." *Journal of Human Development and Capabilities* 11 (2): 281–303.

De Genova, N. 2002. "Migrant 'Illegality' and Deportability in Everyday Life." *Annual Review of Anthropology* 31:419–47.

Delano, A. 2009. "From Limited to Active Engagement: Mexico's Emigration Policies from a Foreign Policy Perspective." *International Migration Review* 43 (4): 764–814.

Dell'Olio, F. 2002. "Supranational Undertakings and the Determination of Social Rights." *Journal of European Public Policy* 9 (2): 292–310.

Desai, M., D. Kapur, J. McHale, and K. Rogers. 2009. "The Fiscal Impact of High-Skilled Emigration: Flows of Indians to the US." *Journal of Development Economics* 88 (1): 32–44.

Devitt, C. 2010. "Varieties of Capitalism, Variation in Labor Immigration." *Journal of Ethnic and Migration Studies* 37 (4): 579–96.

DeVoretz, D. 2008. "An Auction Model of Canadian Temporary Immigration for the 21st Century." *International Migration* 46 (1): 3–17.

Diaz, G., and G. Kuhner. 2009. "Mexico's Role in Promoting and Implementing the ICRMW." In *Migration and Human Rights: The United Nations Convention on Migrant Workers' Rights*, ed. P. de Guchteneire, A. Pécoud, and R. Cholewinski, 219–46. Cambridge: Cambridge University Press.

Dito, M. E. 2008. "GCC Labour Migration Governance." Paper presented at the United Nations Expert Group Meeting on International Migration and Development in Asia and the Pacific, Bangkok, September 20–21.

Dolmas, J., and G. Huffman. 2004. "On the Political Economy of Immigration and Income Redistribution." *International Economic Review* 45 (5): 1129–68.

Drinkwater, S., and K. Clark. 2008. "The Labour Market Performance of Recent Migrants." *Oxford Review of Economic Policy* 24 (3): 495–516.

Drinkwater, S., P. Levine, E. Lotti, and J. Pearlman. 2007. "The Immigration Surplus Revisited in a General Equilibrium Model with Endogenous Growth." *Journal of Regional Science* 47 (3): 569–601.

Dustmann, C., A. Glitz, and T. Frattini. 2008. "The Labor Market Impact of Immigration." *Oxford Review of Economic Policy* 24 (3): 478–95.

Economic Strategies Committee, Singapore. 2010. *Report of the Economic Strategies Committee.* http://app.mof.gov.sg/data/cmsresource/ESC%20Report/ESC%20Full%20 Report.pdf (accessed December 23, 2011).

Economist Intelligence Unit. 2008. *Global Migration Barometer: Methodology Results and Findings.* Sponsored by Western Union. http://www.un.org/esa/population/meetings/ seventhcoord2008/GMB_ExecSumEIU.pdf (accessed February 2, 2012).

Emirbayer, M., and A. Mische. 1998. "What Is Agency?" *American Journal of Sociology* 103 (4): 962–1023.

Endicott, T. 2012. "Proportionality and Incommensurability." Oxford Legal Studies Research Paper No. 40/2012. http://ssrn.com/abstract=2086622 (accessed July 22, 2012).

Engblom, S. 2011. "Labour Migration, Trade in Services, Equal Treatment, and the Role of the EU." In *Moving beyond Demographics: Perspectives for a Common European Migration Policy*, ed. J. O. Karlsson and L. Pelling, 69–85. Stockholm: Global Utmaning.

Esipova, N., J. Ray, and R. Srinivasan. *2011. The World's Potential Migrants. GALLUP.* http://www.imi.ox.ac.uk/pdfs/the-worlds-potential-migrants (accessed April 22, 2012).

Esping-Anderson, G. 1990. *The Three Worlds of Welfare Capitalism.* Princeton, NJ: Princeton University Press.

———. 1999. *Social Foundations of Postindustrial Economies.* Oxford: Oxford University Press.

European Commission 2007a. *Attractive Conditions for the Admission and Residence of Highly Qualified Immigrants.* Press release. October 23. http://europa.eu/rapid/press ReleasesAction.do?reference=MEMO/07/423 (accessed December 23, 2011).

———. 2007b. *Simplified Admission Procedures and Common Set of Rights for Third-Country Workers.* October 23. 2007. http://europa.eu/rapid/press-release_MEMO-07 -422_en.htm (accessed December 23, 2011).

Expert Groups of Future Skills Needs. 2005. *Skills Needs in the Irish Economy: The Role of Migration.* Dublin: Forfas. http://www.forfas.ie/media/egfsn051027_role_of_migra tion.pdf (accessed December 23, 2011).

Faist, T. 2000. *The Volume and Dynamics of International Migration and Transnational Social Spaces.* Oxford: Oxford University Press.

Fargues, P. 2006. "International Migration in the Arab Region: Trends and Policies." Paper presented at the UN Expert Group Meeting on International Migration and Development in the Arab Region, Beirut, May 15–17.

Fitzgerald, D. 2006. "Inside the Sending State: The Politics of Mexican Emigration Control." *International Migration Review* 40 (2): 259–93.

———. 2009. *A Nation of Emigrants: How Mexico Manages Its Migration.* Berkeley: University of California Press.

Fix, M., and J. Passel. 2002. *The Scope and Impact of Welfare Reform's Immigrant Provisions.* Washington, DC: Urban Institute. http://www.urban.org/UploadedPDF/410412 _discussion02-03.pdf (accessed December 24, 2011).

Freedom House. 2012. *Freedom in the World, 2012: The Arab Uprisings and Their Global Repercussions.* Washington, DC: Freedom House.

Freeman, G. P. 1995. "Modes of Immigration Politics in Liberal Democratic States." *International Migration Review* 29 (3): 881–902.

———. 1998. "The Decline of Sovereignty? Politics and Immigration Restriction in Liberal States." In *Challenge to the Nation-State: Immigration in Western Europe and the United States*, ed. C. Joppke, 86–108. Oxford: Oxford University Press.

Freeman, R. B. 1999. "The Economics of Crime." In *Handbook of Labor Economics*, ed. O. Ashenfelter and D. Card, 3529–71. Amsterdam: Elsevier.

———. 2006. "People Flows in Globalization." *Journal of Economic Perspectives* 20 (2): 145–70.

Freeman, R. B., and R. H. Oostendorp. 2000. *Wages around the World: Pay across Occupations and Countries*. Cambridge, MA: National Bureau of Economic Research. http://www.nber.org/papers/w8058.pdf (accessed December 25, 2011).

Fudge, J., and F. MacPhail. 2009. "The Temporary Foreign Worker Program in Canada: Low-Skilled Workers as an Extreme Form of Flexible Labor." *Comparative Labor Law and Policy Journal* 31 (5): 5–45.

Gibson, J., and D. McKenzie. 2011a. *Australia's Pacific Seasonal Worker Pilot Scheme: Development Impacts in the First Two Years*. New Zealand: University of Waikato. ftp://mngt.waikato.ac.nz/RePEc/wai/econwp/1109.pdf (accessed December 25, 2011).

———. 2011b. "Eight Questions about Brain Drain." *Journal of Economic Perspectives* 25 (3): 107–28.

Givens, T., and A. Luedtke. 2004. "The Politics of European Union Immigration Policy: Institutions, Salience, and Harmonization." *Policy Studies Journal* 32 (1): 145–65.

Global Commission on International Migration. 2005. *Migration in an Interconnected World: New Directions for Action*. Geneva: Global Commission on International Migration.

Global Migration Group. 2008. *International Migration and Human Rights*. Geneva: Global Migration Group.

Goddard, V. 2000. *Gender, Agency, and Change: Anthropological Perspectives*. London: Routledge.

Godfrey, M. 2003. "Employment Dimensions of Decent Work: Trade-Offs and Complementarities." Discussion paper DP/148/2003, International Institute for Labor Studies. Geneva: ILO.

Goodhart, D. 2004. "Too Diverse?" *Prospect Magazine* (London) 95 (February).

Goodin, R. E. 1988. "What Is So Special about Our Fellow Countrymen?" *Ethics* 98 (4): 663–86.

Gran, B. K., and E. J. Clifford. 2000. "Rights and Ratios? Evaluating the Relationship between Social Rights and Immigration." *Journal of Ethnic Migration Studies* 26 (3): 417–47.

Grenier, P., and K. Wright. 2006. "Social Capital in Britain." *Policy Studies* 27 (1): 27–53.

Guchteneire, P. de, and A. Pécoud. 2009. "Introduction: The UN Convention on Migrant Workers' Rights." In *Migration and Human Rights: The United Nations Convention on Migrant Workers' Rights*, ed. P. de Guchteneire, A. Pécoud, and R. Cholewinski, 1–44. Cambridge: Cambridge University Press.

Guiraudon, V., and G. Lahav. 2000. "A Reappraisal of the State Sovereignty Debate." *Comparative Political Studies* 33 (2): 163–95.

Gutmann, A., ed. 2001. *Human Rights as Politics and Idolatry*. Princeton, NJ: Princeton University Press.

Hahamovitch, C. 2003. "Creating Perfect Immigrants: Guestworkers of the World in Historical Perspective." *Labor History* 44 (1): 69–94.

Hall, P. A. 1999. "Social Capital in Britain." *British Journal of Political Science* 29 (3): 417–61.

Hall, P. A., and D. Soskice. 2001. *Varieties of Capitalism*. Oxford: Oxford University Press.

Hall, P. A., and K. Thelen. 2009. "Institutional Change in Varieties of Capitalism." *Socio-Economic Review* 7:7–34.

Hamilton, B., and J. Whalley. 1984. "Efficiency and Distributional Implications of Global Restrictions on Labour Mobility: Calculations and Policy Implications." *Journal of Development Economics* 14 (1–2): 61–75.

Hammar, T. 1990. *Democracy and the Nation-State: Aliens, Denizens, and Citizens in a World of International Migration*. Aldershot, UK: Avebury.

Hanson, G. 2005. *Why Does Immigration Divide America? Public Finance and Political Opposition to Open Borders*. Washington, DC: Institute for International Economics.

Hanson, G., K. Scheve, and M. Slaughter. 2007. "Local Public Finance and Individual Preferences over Globalization Strategies." *Economics and Politics* 19 (2007): 1–33.

Hathaway, O. A. 2002. "Do Human Rights Treaties Make a Difference?" *Yale Law Journal* 111 (8): 1935–2042.

Hatton, T. 2004. "Seeking Asylum in Europe." *Economic Policy* 19 (38): 5–62.

Hausman, D. M., and M. S. McPherson. 1993. "Taking Ethics Seriously: Economics and Contemporary Moral Philosophy." *Journal of Economic Literature* 31 (2): 671–731.

Hawthorne, L. 2005. "Picking Winners: The Recent Transformation of Australia's Skilled Migration Policy." *International Migration Review* 39 (3): 663–96.

———. 2011. *Competing for Skills: Migration Policies and Trends in New Zealand and Australia*. Melbourne: Department of Immigration and Citizenship in Australia. http://www.dol.govt.nz/publications/research/competing-for-skills/report/full-report.pdf (accessed December 24, 2011).

Helton, A. C. 1991. "The New Convention from the Perspective of a Country of Employment: The US Case." *International Migration Review* 25 (4): 851–57.

Hennebry, J. L., and K. L. Preibisch. 2010. "A Model of Managed Migration? Re-Examining Best Practices in Canada's Seasonal Agricultural Worker Program." *International Migration* 50 (S1): e19–e39.

Henning, S. 2012. "Migration Levels and Trends: Global Assessment and Policy Implications." Department of Economic and Social Affairs. New York: United Nations. http://www.un.org/esa/population/meetings/tenthcoord2012/V.%20Sabine%20Henning%20-%20Migration%20trends.pdf (accessed April 5, 2012).

Hillman, F., and A. K. v. Koppenfels. 2009. "Migration and Human Rights in Germany." In *Migration and Human Rights: The United Nations Convention on Migrant Workers' Rights*, ed. P. de Guchteneire, A. Pécoud, and R. Cholewinski, 322–42. Cambridge: Cambridge University Press.

Hollifield, J. F. 2000. "The Politics of International Migration: How Can We "Bring the State Back In?" In *Migration Theory Talking across Disciplines*, ed. C. B. Brettell and J. F. Hollifield, 137–86. New York: Routledge.

———. 2004. "The Emerging Migration State." *International Migration Review* 38:885–912.

Hollifield, J. F., V. F. Hunt, and D. J. Tichenor. 2008. "The Liberal Paradox: Immigrants, Markets, and Rights in the United States." *SMU Law Review* 61 (1): 67–98.

Holmes, S., and C. R. Sunstein. 1999. *The Cost of Rights: Why Liberty Depends on Taxes*. New York: W. W. Norton and Company.

Holzmann, R., J. Koettl, and T. Chernetsky. 2005. "Portability Regimes of Pension and Healthcare Benefits for International Migrants: An Analysis of Issues and Good Practices." Paper prepared for the Global Commission on International Migration, Geneva, May 23. http://siteresources.worldbank.org/SOCIALPROTECTION/Resources/SP-Discussion-papers/Pensions-DP/0519.pdf (accessed February 9, 2012).

House of Commons International Development Committee. 2004. *Migration and Development: How to Make Migration Work for Poverty Reduction: Government Response to the Committee's Sixth Report of Session, 2003–04.* London: Stationery Office Limited.

Human Rights Watch. 2004. *Bad Dreams: Exploitation and Abuse of Migrant Workers in Saudi Arabia.* New York: Human Rights Watch.

Hune, S., and J. Niessen. 1994. "Ratifying the UN Migrant Workers Convention: Current Difficulties and Prospects." *Netherlands Quarterly of Human Rights* 12 (4): 393–404.

Huntington, S. P. 2004, *Who Are We: The Challenges to America's National Identity.* New York: Simon and Schuster.

Ignatieff, M. 2001a. "Human Rights as Politics." In *Human Rights as Politics and Idolatry,* ed. A. Gutmann, 3–52. Princeton, NJ: Princeton University Press.

———. 2001b. "Human Rights as Idolatry." In *Human Rights as Politics and Idolatry,* ed. A. Gutmann, 53–100. Princeton, NJ: Princeton University Press.

ILO (International Labor Organization). 1999. "Migrant Workers. Report III (Part 1B)." Paper presented at the eighty-seventh International Labor Conference, Geneva.

———. 2004. "Towards a Fair Deal for Migrant Workers in the Global Economy." Ninety-Second Session of the International Labor Conference, Geneva, June 1–7.

———. 2010. *International Labour Migration: A Rights-Based Approach.* Geneva: ILO.

International Steering Committee for the Campaign for Ratification of the Migrant Rights Convention. 2009. *Guide on Ratification: International Convention on the Protection of the Rights of All Migrant Workers and Members of Their Families.* Geneva.

IOM (International Organization for Migration). 2009. "The Human Rights of Migrants: IOM Policy and Activities." Geneva: IOM.

———. 2010. *Migration and the Economics Crisis in the European Union: Implications for Policy.* Geneva: IOM.

Jacobs, L., and D. King, eds. 2009. *The Unsustainable American State.* Oxford: Oxford University Press.

Jacobsen, D. 1996. *Rights across Borders: Immigration and the Decline of Citizenship.* Baltimore: Johns Hopkins University Press.

James, S. 2006. *Sweden: Lessons of the Vaxholm Builders' Dispute.* http://www.worldproutassembly.org/archives/2006/06/sweden_lessons.html (accessed December 25, 2011).

Jan, M. A. 2010. "Pakistan's National Emigration Policy: A Review. Islamabad: Sustainable Policy Development Institute. http://www.nccr-pakistan.org/publications_pdf/Migration/Jan_EmigrationPolicyReview.pdf (accessed August 31, 2012).

Joppke, C. 1998. "Why Liberal States Accept Unwanted Immigration." *World Politics* 50 (2): 266–93.

Jupp, J., J. P. Nieuwenhuysen, and E. Dawson. 2007. *Social Cohesion in Australia.* Cambridge: Cambridge University Press.

Kaczmarczyk, P., and M. Okólski. 2008. "Demographic and Labor-Market Impacts of Migration on Poland." *Oxford Review of Economic Policy* 24 (3): 600–625.

Khalaf, S., and S. Alkobaisi. 1999. "Migrant's Strategies of Coping and Patterns of Accommodation in the Oil-Rich Gulf Societies: Evidence from the UAE. *British Journal of Middle Eastern Studies* 26 (2): 271–98.

Kim, A. 2009. "Global Migration and South Korea: Foreign Workers, Foreign Brides, and the Making of a Multicultural Society." *Ethnic and Racial Studies* 32 (1): 70–92.

King, T. 1983. "Immigration from Developing Countries: Some Philosophical Issues." *Ethics* 93 (3): 525–36.

Klugman, J., and I. Pereira. 2009. *Assessment of National Migration Policies: An Emerging Picture on Admissions, Treatment, and Enforcement in Developing and Developed Countries.* Human development research paper 2009/48. New York: UNDP. http://hdr .undp.org/en/reports/global/hdr2009/papers/HDRP_2009_48_rev.pdf (accessed February 2, 2012).

Kolb, H. 2005. *The German Green Card.* Policy brief no. 3. Hamburg: Migration Research Group.

Kossoudji, S. A., and D. Cobb-Clark, D. 2002. "Coming Out of the Shadows: Learning about Legal Status and Wages from the Legalized Population." *Journal of Labor Economics* 20 (3): 598–628.

Landman, T. 2004. "Measuring Human Rights: Principle, Practice, and Policy." *Human Rights Quarterly* 26 (4): 906–31.

Langille, B. A. 2005. "Core Labour Rights: The True Story (Reply to Alston)." *European Journal of International Law* 16 (3): 409–37.

Lenard, P. T., and C. Straehle. 2011. "Temporary Labour Migration, Global Redistribution, and Democratic Justice." *Politics, Philosophy, and Economics* 10 (1): 1–25.

Letki, N. 2008. "Does Diversity Erode Social Cohesion? Social Capital and Race in British Neighbourhoods." *Political Studies* 56 (1): 99–126.

Lindstrom, N. 2010. "Service Liberalization in the Enlarged European Union: A Race to the Bottom or the Emergence of Transnational Conflict?" *Journal of Common Market Studies* 10 (5): 1307–27.

Lonnroth, J. 1991. "The International Convention of the Rights of All Migrant Workers and Members of Their Families in the Context of International Migration Policies: An Analysis of Ten Years of Negotiation." *International Migration Review* 25 (4): 710–36.

Lowell, L. 2005. *Policies and Regulations for Managing Skilled International Migration for Work.* New York: United Nations, Mortality and Migration Section of the Population Division/DESA.

Lucas, R. E. 1988. "On the Mechanics of Economic Development." *Journal of Monetary Economics* 22 (1): 3–42.

———. 2005. *International Migration and Economic Development: Lessons from Low-Income Countries.* Cheltenham, UK: Edward Elgar.

MAC (Migration Advisory Committee). 2008. *First Recommended Shortage Occupation Lists for the UK and Scotland.* London: Migration Advisory Committee.

———. 2009. *Analysis of the Points-Based System: Tier 2 and Dependents.* London: MAC.

———. 2010. *Limits on Migration.* London: MAC.

———. 2011. *Review of the Minimum Income Requirement for Sponsorship under the Family Migration Route.* London: MAC.

MacDermott, T., and B. Opeskin. 2010. "Regulating Pacific Seasonal Labour in Australia." *Pacific Affairs* 83 (2): 283–305.

Machin, S., and C. Meghir. 2004. "Crime and Economic Incentives." *Journal of Human Resources* 39 (4): 958–79.

Mares, P. 2011. "Temporary Migration and Its Implications for Australia." Canberra, September 23. http://www.aph.gov.au/senate/pubs/occa_lect/transcripts/230911/230911 .pdf (accessed December 24, 2011).

Marshall, T. M. 1950. *Citizenship and Social Class, and Other Essays.* Cambridge: Cambridge University Press.

Martin, P. 2003. "Managing Labor Migration: Temporary Worker Programs for the Twenty-First Century." Lecture at the ILO/International Institute for Labor Studies, Geneva, September.

Martin, P. 2006. "GATS, Migration, and Labor Standards." Geneva: ILO. http://www.ilo. org/public/english/bureau/inst/publications/discussion/dp16506.pdf (accessed December 25, 2011).

Martin, P., and M. Ruhs. 2011. "Labor Shortages and U.S. Immigration Reform: Promises and Perils of an Independent Commission." *International Migration Review* 45 (1): 174–87.

Martin, P., and M. S. Teitelbaum. 2001. "The Mirage of Mexican Guest Workers." *Foreign Affairs* 80 (6): 117–31.

Massey, D. 1987. "Do Undocumented Migrants Earn Lower Wages Than Legal Immigrants? New Evidence from Mexico." *International Migration Review* 21 (2): 236–74.

Maupain, F. 2005. "Revitalization Not Retreat: The Real Potential of the 1998 ILO Declaration for the Universal Protection of Workers' Rights." *European Journal of International Law* 16 (3): 439–65.

Mayer, R. 2005. "Guestworkers and Exploitation." *Review of Politics* 67:311–34.

McKenzie, D., and J. Gibson. 2010. *The Development Impact of a Best Practice Seasonal Worker Policy.* Washington, DC: World Bank. http://www-wds.worldbank.org/external/ default/WDSContentServer/WDSP/IB/2010/11/30/000158349_20101130131212/ Rendered/PDF/WPS5488.pdf (accessed December 25, 2011).

Michelotti, M., and C. Nyland. 2000. "The ILO, International Trade, and the 1998 Declaration on Fundamental Principles and Rights at Work." http://www.mngt.waikato.ac.nz/ departments/Strategy%20and%20Human%20Resource%20Management/Airaanz/ old/conferce/newscastle2000/Vol3/michelotti.pdf (accessed October 12, 2011)

Miller, D. 2008. "Immigrants, Nations, and Citizenship." *Journal of Political Philosophy* 16 (4): 371–90.

Ministry of Justice, Republic of Korea. 2008. *The First Basic Plan for Immigration Policy: 2008–2012.* Seoul: Ministry of Justice.

Ministry of Manpower, Singapore. 2011. *Employment of Foreign Manpower Act (Chapter 91A).* http://www.mom.gov.sg/Documents/services-forms/passes/WPSPassConditions .pdf (accessed August 31, 2012).

Mirilovic, N. 2010. "The Politics of Immigration: Dictatorship, Development, and Defense." *Comparative Politics* 42 (3): 273–92.

Mohapatra, S., D. Ratha, and A. Silwal. 2011. *Migration and Development Brief: Outlook for Remittance Flows, 2012–2014.* Washington, DC: World Bank. http://siteresources .worldbank.org/TOPICS/Resources/214970-1288877981391/MigrationandDevelop-mentBrief17.pdf (accessed August 31, 2012).

Morgenthau, H. 1951. *In Defense of the National Interest: A Critical Examination of American Foreign Policy.* New York: Knopf.

Münz, R. 2009. "Demographic Change, Labour Force Development, and Migration in Europe." Swedish EU Presidency Conference on Labour Migration and Its Development Potential in the Age of Mobility, Malmö, Sweden, October 15–16. http://www.se2009 .eu/polopoly_fs/1.16133!menu/standard/file/bakgrundsdokument1_090222_webb.pdf (accessed February 2, 2012).

Narayan, D., R. Patel, K. Schafft, A. Rademacher, and S. Koch-Schulte. 2000. *Voices of the Poor: Can Anyone Hear Us?* Oxford: Oxford University Press.

Ndiaye, B. 2011. "Addressing Irregular Migration through a Human Rights–Based Approach." Talk at the Global Forum on Migration and Development, Geneva, December 1.

Nozick, R. 1974. *Anarchy, State, and Utopia.* New York: Basic Books.

Nussbaum, M. 2000. *Women and Human Development: The Capabilities Approach.* New York: Cambridge University Press.

Nussbaum, M., et al. 1996. *For Love of Country: Debating the Limits of Patriotism*. Boston: Beacon Press.

Nye, J. 2002. "The American National Interest and Global Public Goods." *International Affairs* 78 (2): 233–44.

Obama, B. 2011. *Remarks by the President on Comprehensive Immigration Reform in El Paso, Texas*. May 10. http://www.whitehouse.gov/the-press-office/2011/05/10/remarks -president-comprehensive-immigration-reform-el-paso-texas (accessed December 24, 2011).

OECD (Organization for Economic Cooperation and Development). 2010. *International Migration Outlook 2010*. Paris: OECD.

———. 2011. *Recruiting Immigrant Workers: Sweden*. Paris: OECD.

Oger, H. 2009. "The French Political Refusal on Europe's Behalf." In *Migration and Human Rights: The United Nations Convention on Migrant Workers' Rights*, ed. P. de Guchteneire, A. Pécoud, and R. Cholewinski, 295–321. Cambridge: Cambridge University Press.

OHCHR (Office of the High Commissioner for Human Rights). 2009. *Migration and Development: A Human Rights Approach*. Geneva: OHCHR.

O'Neill, O. 2000. *Bounds of Justice*. Cambridge: Cambridge University Press.

———. 2002. "Global Justice: Whose Obligations?" Talk at the opening of the Center for the Study of Global Ethics, Birmingham, UK, May 23.

Orrenius, P., and Zavodny, M. 2011. "US Immigration Reform in a New Era of Globalization." http://dallasfed.org/research/events/2011/immigration_orrenius.pdf (accessed December 12, 2012).

Panizzon, M. 2010. *Trade and Labor Migration: GATS Mode 4 and Migration Agreements*. Geneva: Friedrich Ebert Stiftung. http://library.fes.de/pdf-files/iez/global/06955.pdf (accessed December 25, 2011).

Parusel, B., and J. Schneider. 2010. *Satisfying Labour Demand through Migration in Germany*. Nuremberg: Federal Office for Migration and Refugees, European Migration Network.

Passel, J., and D. Cohn. 2010. *US Unauthorized Immigration Flows Are Down Sharply since Mid-Decade*. Washington, DC: Pew Hispanic Center. http://www.pewhispanic.org/ files/reports/126.pdf (accessed December 25, 2011).

Pastor, M., and S. Alva. 2004. "Guest Workers and the New Transnationalism: Possibilities and Realities in an Age of Repression." *Social Justice* 31 (1–2): 92–112.

Pécoud, A., and P. de Guchteneire. 2006. "Migration, Human Rights, and the United Nations: An Investigation into the Low Ratification Record of the UN Migrant Workers Convention." *Windsor Yearbook of Access to Justice* 24 (2): 241–66.

Petersen, W. 1958. "A General Typology of Migration." *American Sociological Review* 23 (3): 256–66.

Pew Hispanic Center. 2009. "Mexican Immigrants in the United States, 2008." http://pew-research.org/pubs/1191/mexican-immigrants-in-america-largest-group (accessed March 15, 2012).

Piché, V., E. Depatie-Pelletier, and D. Epale. 2009. "Obstacles to Ratification of the ICRMW in Canada." In *Migration and Human Rights: The United Nations Convention on Migrant Workers' Rights*, ed. P. de Guchteneire, A. Pécoud, and R. Cholewinski, 193–218. Cambridge: Cambridge University Press.

Pierson, P., ed. 2001. *The New Politics of the Welfare State*. Oxford: Oxford University Press.

Piore, M. 1979. *Birds of Passage: Migrant Labor and Industrial Societies*. New York: Cambridge University Press.

Piper, N. 2009. "Obstacles to, and Opportunities for, Ratification of the ICRMW in Asia." In *Migration and Human Rights: The United Nations Convention on Migrant Workers' Rights*, ed. P. de Guchteneire, A. Pécoud, and R. Cholewinski, 171–92. Cambridge: Cambridge University Press.

Piper, N., and R. Iredale. 2003. "Identification of the Obstacles to the Signing and Ratification of the UN Convention on the Protection of the Rights of All Migrant Workers." Asia Pacific Perspective. Paris: International Migration and Multicultural Policies Section, UNESCO. http://unesdoc.unesco.org/images/0013/001395/139529e.pdf (accessed December 25, 2011).

POEA (Philippine Overseas Employment Administration). 2011a. *Governing Board Resolution No. 2, Series of 2011*. http://www.poea.gov.ph/gbr/2011/gb_2_2011.pdf (accessed August 31, 2012).

———. 2011b. *Governing Board Resolution No. 6, Series of 2011*. http://www.poea.gov.ph/gbr/2011/gb_6_2011.pdf (accessed August 31, 2012).

———. 2012a. *Governing Board Resolution No 07, Series of 2012*. http://www.poea.gov.ph/gbr/2012/gbr_7_2012.pdf (accessed August 31, 2012).

———. 2012b. *Governing Board Resolution No. 8, Series of 2012*. http://www.poea.gov.ph/gbr/2012/gbr_8_2012.pdf (accessed August 31, 2012).

Posner, R. 2002. *The Problematics of Moral and Legal Theory*. Cambridge, MA: Harvard University Press.

Preibisch, K. L. 2007. "Local Produce, Foreign Labour." *Rural Sociology* 72 (3): 418–49.

Preibisch, K. L., and L. Binford. 2007. "Interrogating Racialized Global Labour Supply." *Canadian Review of Sociology* 44 (1): 5–36.

Putnam, R. D. 2007. "E Pluribus Unum: Diversity and Community in the Twenty-First Century." *Scandinavian Political Studies* 30 (2): 137–74.

Rawls, J. 1985. "Justice as Fairness: Political Not Metaphysical." *Philosophy and Public Affairs* 14 (3): 223–51.

Reilly, A. 2011. "The Ethics of Seasonal Labour Migration." *Griffith Law Review* 20 (1): 127–52.

Reitz, J. 2004. "Canada: Immigration and Nation-Building in the Transition to a Knowledge Economy." In *Controlling Immigration: A Global Perspective*, ed. W. Cornelius, P. Martin, J. F. Hollifield, and T. Tsuda, 97–133. 2nd ed. Stanford, CA: Stanford University Press.

———. 2010. "Selecting Immigrants for the Short Term: Is It Smart in the Long Run? *Policy Options* 13 (7): 12–16.

Rivera-Batiz, F. L. 1999. "Undocumented Workers in the Labor Market: An Analysis of the Earnings of Legal and Illegal Mexican Immigrants in the United States." *Journal of Population Economics* 12 (1): 91–116.

Rodrik, D. 2002. *Feasible Globalizations*. Discussion paper no. 3524. London: Center for Economic Policy Research.

Romer, P. M. 1986. "Increasing Returns and Long-Run Growth." *Journal of Political Economy* 94 (5): 1002–37.

Ronnmar, M. 2010. "Laval Returns to Sweden: The Final Judgment of the Swedish Labour Court and Swedish Legislative Reforms." *Industrial Law Journal* 39 (3): 280–87.

Rosenblum, M. R. 2004. "Moving beyond the Policy of No Policy: Emigration from Mexico and Central America." *Latin American Politics and Society* 46 (4): 91–125.

Rowthorn, R. 2008. "The Fiscal Impact of Immigration on Advanced Economics." *Oxford Review of Economic Policy* 24 (3): 560–80.

Ruhs, M. 2008. "Economic Research and Labour Immigration Policy." *Oxford Review of Economic Policy* 24 (3): 404–42.

———. 2010a. "Migrant Rights, Immigration Policy, and Human Development." *Journal of Human Development and Capabilities* 11 (2): 259–79.

———. 2010b. "Numbers vs Rights in Low-Skilled Labour Immigration Policy? A Comment on Cummins and Rodriguez." *Journal of Human Development and Capabilities* 11 (2): 305–9.

———. 2011. *Openness, Skills, and Rights: An Empirical Analysis of Labour Immigration Programmes in 46 High- and Middle-Income Countries.* Center on Migration, Policy, and Society working paper no. WP-11-88. Oxford: Center on Migration, Policy, and Society, Oxford University.

———. 2012. "The Human Rights of Migrant Workers: Why Do So Few Countries Care?" *American Behavioural Scientist* 56 (9): 1277–93.

———. 2013. "Towards a Post-2015 Development Agenda: What Role for Migrant Rights and International Labour Migration?" Background paper prepared for the European Development Report 2013. Overseas Development Institute, European Center for Development Policy Management, and German Development Institute/Deutsches Institut für Entwicklungspolitik.

Ruhs, M., and B. Anderson. 2010a. "Semi-Compliance and Illegality in Migrant Labor Markets: An Analysis of Migrants, Employers, and the State in the UK." *Population, Space, and Place* 16 (3): 195–211.

———, eds. 2010b. *Who Needs Migrant Workers? Labour Shortages, Immigration, and Public Policy.* Oxford: Oxford University Press.

Ruhs, M., and H.-J. Chang. 2004. "The Ethics of Labor Immigration Policy." *International Organization* 58 (1): 69–102.

Ruhs, M., and P. Martin. 2008. "Numbers vs Rights: Trade-offs and Guest Worker Programs." *International Migration Review* 42 (1): 249–65.

Ryan, B. 2009. "Policy on the ICRMW in the United Kingdom." In *Migration and Human Rights: The United Nations Convention on Migrant Workers' Rights*, ed. P. de Guchteneire, A. Pécoud, and R. Cholewinski, 278–94. Cambridge: Cambridge University Press.

Sassen, S.. 1999. "Beyond Sovereignty: De Facto Transnationalism in Immigration Policy." *European Journal of Migration and Law* 1:177–98.

Saxenian, A. 1999. "Silicon Valley's New Immigrant Entrepreneurs." San Francisco: Public Policy Institute of California.

Scheffler, S., ed. 1988. *Consequentialism and Its Critics.* Oxford: Oxford University Press.

Schroder, M. 2009. "Integrating Welfare and Production Typologies: How Refinements of the Varieties of Capitalism Approach Call for a Combination of Welfare Typologies." *Journal of Social Policy* 38 (1): 19–43.

Sen, A. 1980. "'Equality of What?' Tanner Lectures on Human Values Delivered at Stanford University." In *1979 Tanner Lecture at Stanford*, ed. S. McMurrin, 195–220. Cambridge: Cambridge University Press.

———. 1999. *Development as Freedom.* Oxford: Oxford University Press.

———. 2005. "Human Rights and Capabilities." *Journal of Human Development* 6 (2): 151–66.

Shachar, A. 2006. "The Race for Talent: Highly Skilled Migrants and Competitive Immigration Regimes." *New York University Law Review* 81:101–58.

Shah, N. 2005. *Restrictive Labor Immigration Policies in the Oil-Rich Gulf: Implications for Sending Asian Countries.* IUSSP International Population Conference Tours, France, July.

Shue, H. 1988. "Mediating Duties." *Ethics* 98 (4): 687–704.

Sidgwick, H. 1908. *The Elements of Politics.* 3rd ed. London: Macmillan.

Singapore Government Press Center. 2010. *Deputy Prime Minister's (DPM's) Speech on Population at the Committee of Supply, 2010*. March.

Singapore Government Public Service Division. 2011. *Deputy Prime Minister's (DPM's) Speech on Population at the Committee of Supply 2011*. March.

Singstat. 2008. *Yearbook of Statistics 2008*. Singapore: Department of Statistics.

Stark, O. 1991. *The Migration of Labor*. Oxford: Basil Blackwell.

Soysal, Y. 1994. *Limits of Citizenship: Migrants and Post-National Membership in Western Europe*. Chicago: University of Chicago Press.

Spencer, S., and J. Pobjoy. 2011. *The Relationship between Immigration Status and Rights in the UK: Exploring the Rationale*. Oxford: Center on Migration, Policy, and Society.

Tamas, K., and R. Munz. 2006. *Labor Migrants Unbound? EU Enlargement, Transitional Measures, and Labor Market Effects*. Stockholm: Institute for Futures Studies.

Taran, P. 2000. "Human Rights of Migrants: Challenges of the New Decade." *International Migration* 38 (6): 7–52.

Taylor, J. E. 1992. "Earnings and Mobility of Legal and Illegal Immigrant Workers in Agriculture." *American Journal of Agricultural Economics* 74 (4): 889–96.

Thielemann, E. 2004. "Why Asylum Policy Harmonization Undermines Refugee Burden-Sharing." *European Journal of Migration and Law* 6 (1): 47–65.

Thomas, D. 2010. *Foreign Nationals Working Temporarily in Canada*. http://www.statcan.gc.ca/pub/11-008-x/2010002/article/11166-eng.htm#n23 (accessed December 24, 2011).

Tichenor, D. 2002. *Dividing Lines: The Politics of Immigration Control in America*. Princeton, NJ: Princeton University Press.

Tienda, M., and A. Singer. 1995. "Wage Mobility of Undocumented Workers in the United States." *International Migration Review* 29 (1): 112–38.

Timmer, A. S., and J. G. Williamson. 1996. *Racism, Xenophobia, or Markets? The Political Economy of Immigration Policy Prior to the Thirties*. Working paper series, vol. w5867. Cambridge, MA: National Bureau of Economic Research.

Togman, J. M. 2001. *The Rampart of Nations: Institutions and Immigration Policies in France and the United States*. Westport, CT: Praeger Publishers.

Transatlantic Trends. 2010. "Immigration: Key Findings." http://www.transatlantictrends.org (accessed March 16, 2012).

UK Home Office. 2005. *Controlling Our Borders: Making Migration Work for Britain*. London: Home Office.

———. 2006. *A Points-Based System: Making Migration Work for Britain*. London: Home Office.

———. 2011a. *Employment-Related Settlement, Tier 5, and Overseas Domestic Workers: A Consultation*. London: Home Office.

———. 2011b. *Family Migration: A Consultation*. London: Home Office.

Ullah, A. A. 2010. *Rationalizing Migration Decisions*. Surrey: Ashgate.

UN Department of Economic and Social Affairs, Population Division. 2006. "International Migration in the Arab Region." Paper prepared for the UN Expert Group Meeting on International Migration and Development in the Arab Region, Beirut, Lebanon, May 15–17.

———. 2011. *International Migration Report, 2009: A Global Assessment*. New York: United Nations. http://www.un.org/esa/population/publications/migration/World MigrationReport2009.pdf (accessed August 31, 2012).

UNDP (United Nations Development Program). 2000. *Human Rights and Human Development*. New York: UNDP.

——. 2009. *Overcoming Barriers: Human Mobility and Development*. Human Development Report. New York: UNDP.

——. 2010. "Origins of the Human Development Approach." http://hdr.undp.org/en/humandev/origins/ (accessed August 31, 2012).

United Nations. 2003. *Secretary-General, in International Migrants Day Message, Underlines Need to Maximize Benefits of Migration*. December 18. http://www.un.org/News/Press/docs/2003/sgsm9081.doc.htm (accessed August 31, 2012).

US Commission on Immigration Reform. 1995. *Legal Immigration, Setting Priorities*. http://www.utexas.edu/lbj/uscir/exesum95.html (accessed March 16, 2012).

US Department of State. 2011. *Nonimmigrant Visa Statistics*. http://travel.state.gov/visa/statistics/nivstats/nivstats_4582.html (accessed December 24, 2011).

Verma, V. 2007. *The Regulatory and Policy Framework of the Caribbean Seasonal Agricultural Workers Program*. Ottawa: North-South Institute. http://www.nsi-ins.ca/english/pdf/Regulatory_Policy_Verma.pdf (accessed December 25, 2011).

Vucetic, S. 2007. "Democracies and International Human Rights: Why Is There No Place for Migrant Workers?" *International Journal of Human Rights* 11 (4): 403–28.

Wadhwa, V., A. Saxenian, B. Rissing, and G. Gereffi. 2008, "Skilled Immigration and Economic Growth." *Applied Research in Economic Development* 5 (1): 6–13.

Waldinger, R., and M. Lichter. 2003. *How the Other Half Works*. Berkeley: University of California Press.

Waldrauch, H. 2001. *Die Integration von Einwanderern. Band 2: Ein Index der rechtlichen Diskriminierung*, vol. 9.2, *Wohlfahrtspolitik und Sozialforschung*, ed. Europäischen Zentrum Wien. Frankfurt: Campus Verlag.

Walzer, M. 1983. *Spheres of Justice*. New York: Basic Books.

Watts, J. 2002. *Immigration Policy and the Challenge of Globalization: Unions and Employers in Unlikely Alliance*. Ithaca, NY: Cornell University Press.

Wayland, S. 1997. "Immigration, Multiculturalism, and National Identity in Canada." *International Journal on Minority and Group Rights* 5 (33): 35–58.

Weiner, M. 1995. *The Global Migration Crisis*. Boulder, CO: HarperCollins.

Weissbrodt, D. 2008. *The Human Rights of Noncitizens*. Oxford: Oxford University Press.

Wexler, L. 2007. "The Non-Legal Role of International Human Rights Law in Addressing Immigration." *University of Chicago Legal Forum* 439:359–403.

Wickramasekara, P. 2008. "Globalization, International Labour Migration, and the Rights of Migrant Workers." *Third World Quarterly* 29 (7): 1247–64.

Wickramasekara, P. 2011. *Labour Migration in South Asia: A Review of Issues, Policies, and Practices*. Geneva: ILO. http://www.ilo.org/public/english/protection/migrant/download/imp/imp108.pdf (accessed December 28, 2011).

Winckler, O. 2010. "Labor Migration to the GCC States." In *Migration and the Gulf*, 9–12. Washington, DC: Middle East Institute.

Winters, A. 2004. "The Temporary Movement of Workers to Provide Services (GATS Mode 4)." Washington, DC: World Bank. http://siteresources.worldbank.org/INTRANETTRADE/Resources/WBI-Training/Winters_tmpmvt_sevicesproviders.pdf (accessed December 28, 2011).

Winters, A., T. Walmsley, Z. K. Wang, and R. Grynberg. 2003. "Liberalising Temporary Movement of Natural Persons: An Agenda for the Development Round." *World Economy* 26 (8): 1137–61.

Witte, J. M. 2008. *Realizing Core Labor Standards: The Potential and Limits of Voluntary Codes and Social Clauses*. Bonn: BMZ.

Woolfson, C., and J. Sommers. 2006. "Labour Mobility in Construction: European Implications of the Laval un Partneri Dispute with Swedish Labour." *European Journal of Industrial Relations* 12 (1): 49–68.

World Bank. 2005. *Global Economic Prospects, 2006*. Washington, DC: World Bank.

———. 2006. *At Home and Away: Expanding Job Opportunities for Pacific Islanders through Labour Mobility*. Washington, DC: World Bank.

———. 2008a. *Migration and Development Brief 5: Revisions to Remittance Trends, 2007*. Washington, DC: World Bank.

———. 2008b. *Migration and Remittance Factbook, 2008*. Washington, DC: World Bank.

———. 2011. *Migration and Remittance Factbook, 2011*. Washington, DC: World Bank.

———. 2012. *Country and Lending Groups*. Washington, DC: World Bank. http://data .worldbank.org/about/country-classifications/country-and-lending-groups (accessed February 4, 2012).

Yeoh, B. 2006. "Bifurcated Labour: The Unequal Incorporation of Transmigrants in Singapore." *Tijdschrift voor Economische en Sociale Geografie* 97 (1): 26–37.

Yoo, K-S. 2005. *Foreign Workers in the Republic of Korea*. Seoul: Korea Labor Institute.

Zolberg, A. 1999. "Matters of State: Theorizing Immigration Policy." In *The Handbook of International Migration: The American Experience*, ed. C. Hirschman, P. Kasinitz, and J. DeWind, 71–93. New York: Russell Sage Foundation.

———. 2007. "The Exit Revolution." In *Citizenship and Those Who Leave*, ed. N. Green and F. Weil, 33–62. Urbana: University of Illinois Press.

Index

A page number followed by f refers to a figure and a page number followed by t indicates a table.

CPSIA information can be obtained
at www.ICGtesting.com
Printed in the USA
LVOW10s2007090517

533933LV00002B/48/P